Building, Using, and Managing the Data Warehouse

THE DATA WAREHOUSING INSTITUTE SERIES
FROM PRENTICE HALL PTR

Planning and Designing the Data Warehouse

Building, Using, and Managing the Data Warehouse

BUILDING, USING, AND MANAGING THE DATA WAREHOUSE

Ramon C. Barquin
Herbert A. Edelstein

Editors

PRENTICE HALL PTR
UPPER SADDLE RIVER, NEW JERSEY 07458
http://www.prenhall.com

To join a Prentice Hall PTR Internet mailing list, point to:
http://www.prenhall.com/register

Library of Congress Cataloging-in-Publication Data

```
Building, using, and managing the data warehouse / Ramon C. Barquin,
  Herbert A. Edelstein
        p.    cm. -- (Data Warehousing Institute series from Prentice
  Hall PTR)
    Includes bibliographical references and index.
    ISBN 0-13-534355-0
    1. Database design.  2. Database management. I. Barquín, Ramón
  C., 1942-    . II. Edelstein, Herb.  III. Series.
  QA76.9.D26B87  1997
  005.74--dc21                                              96-53480
                                                               CIP
```

Acquisitions Editor: *Mark L. Taub*
Editorial/Production Supervision: *Dit Mosco*
Cover Art & Design Director: *Jerry Votta*
Cover Design: *Anthony Gemmellaro*
Marketing Manager: *Dan Rush*
Manufacturing Manager: *Alexis R. Heydt*

©1997 by Prentice Hall PTR
Prentice-Hall, Inc.
A Simon & Schuster Company
Upper Saddle River, New Jersey 07458

The publisher offers discounts on this book when ordered in bulk quantities. For more information, contact Corporate Sales Department, Prentice Hall PTR, One Lake Street, Upper Saddle River, NJ 07458. Phone: 800-382-3419; Fax: 201-236-7141; E-mail: corpsales@prenhall.com

Printed in the United States of America
10 9 8 7 6 5 4 3 2 1

ISBN 0-13-534355-0

Prentice-Hall International (UK) Limited, *London*
Prentice-Hall of Australia Pty. Limited, *Sydney*
Prentice-Hall Canada Inc., *Toronto*
Prentice-Hall Hispanoamericana, S.A., *Mexico*
Prentice-Hall of India Private Limited, *New Delhi*
Prentice-Hall of Japan, Inc., *Tokyo*
Simon & Schuster Asia Pte. Ltd., *Singapore*
Editora Prentice-Hall do Brasil, Ltda., *Rio de Janeiro*

CONTENTS

Series Foreword

Building, Using, and Managing the Data Warehouse is the second volume in the Prentice Hall series on data warehousing. In the first volume, *Planning and Designing the Data Warehouse*, we included what we would like to accomplish with this series of books, and it is worth repeating that **Series Foreword** here.

"Data warehousing is still very much an emerging technology. Some refer to it as an approach, a movement, or even a set of technologies. Whatever the result of this taxonomic exercise, it is obvious that there is a strong need for a clearer vision of what data warehousing, as a discipline, is and where it is going; more rigorous definitions of its various components; a common vocabulary for enhanced usage; a better understanding of the skills needed to properly undertake the different functions involved. Furthermore, how does data warehousing relate to other disciplines within information systems technology? Does it fit best within computer science, management information systems, information engineering, or some other such denomination? What business role does it play within an organization? What successful implementation strategies can be identified? In short, there are a significant number of questions that must, and will, be answered as data warehousing matures and blossoms.

Through this series we also expect to address some of the key technical problems that data warehousing practitioners are facing. Whether it be the issues related to data warehousing architecture, data warehouse database design, metadata repositories, data mining algorithms, or other specific topics, we will bring the top experts in the field to share with us their best knowledge and experience.

Like any other such endeavor, there are a substantial number of management considerations involved in data warehousing. From critical success factors to financial considerations, from cost accounting mechanisms to staffing issues, this collection will deal with them.

Ultimately, our goal is to present as complete a reference source as possible for individuals and organizations involved in planning, designing, building, managing, and using data warehouses. It is not a simple goal nor an easy challenge, but it is convergent with The Data Warehousing Institute's mission.

As President of The Data Warehousing Institute, I am in the fortunate position of being able to draw on the resources of the Institute to address the demands of being the editor for this Prentice Hall series on data warehousing. The Institute is committed to expanding the use of this technology and enhancing data warehousing professionalism. As such it runs a growing set of educational and technical programs which are groundbreaking in their quality and scope. In the process, the Institute has brought together within its "faculty" some of the top experts in the field and has identified the pioneering "case studies" where organizations have implemented successful data warehouses. In short, there is a very strong cross-fertilization between the Institute's activities and the issues we will be addressing in future volumes of this series.

We are convinced of the importance of data warehousing as an agent of change within the information systems industry, and we are pleased to be at the leading edge."

Ramon Barquin

Foreword

As does the first volume in the series, *Planning and Designing the Data Warehouse*, this book presents a collection of chapters written by pioneering data warehousing practitioners. These chapters will serve as a guide for the information systems manager or professional who is involved in building, using, and/or managing a data warehouse. While no single volume can deal with this topic exhaustively, we believe this set of essays by some of the most knowledgeable names in the industry will provide the practitioner with valuable insights into the process of building, using, and managing the data warehouse.The book is divided into four sections: **1: Introduction; 2: Building the Data Warehouse; 3: Designing the Data Warehouse**; and **4: Managing the Data Warehouse**.

In **Part 1**, the **Introduction**, IBM's George Zagelow's "Data Warehousing: Client/Server for the Rest of the Decade" analyzes the forces that are causing data warehousing to explode, and argues that this discipline will lead the charge in open systems well into the next century.

Anyone who has been involved with data warehousing knows that the toughest tasks are most often tied to the data extraction, cleaning, and transformation process. This is particularly true when dealing with multiple sources originally created with different Database Management Systems (DBMS). **Part 2, Building the Data Warehouse**, opens with "Migrating Data from Legacy Systems" in which Evolutionary Technology's Katherine Hammer, one of the leading experts in data migration, presents her views on the topic.

The need to be able to scale as you deal with ever larger databases and more complex problem domains is very real. In "Optimal Machine Architectures for Parallel Query Scalability," Mark Sweiger, from Sequent, tackles what is one of the more difficult but also most promising areas of data warehousing.

Data quality is such a critical aspect of data warehousing that we are including two chapters on the topic in this book. Originally undecided whether to include them in this section or the next, we concluded that data quality has to be factored in during the "building" phase and cannot be left behind until the "using" phase. Hence, "Building High Data Quality into Your Data Warehouse," by Vality Technology's George Burch, addresses this vital topic. It is followed by AMS's Dennis Berg and Christopher Heagele's "Improving Data Quality: A Management Perspective and Model," the closing chapter of **Part 2**.

Part 3, **Using the Data Warehouse**, opens with an essay by Katherine Glassey-Edholm of Brio Technology entitled "Bringing User Perspective to Data Warehousing," in which the author argues strongly for keeping the user foremost in our thinking as we launch data warehousing initiatives.

The use of objects, or object-oriented technology, in data warehousing is a strong and important leveraging thrust in the field. Oracle/Express Technology's David Menninger focuses his contribution to the topic in his intriguing chapter "Building Object-Oriented OLAP Applications: Not Just Any Object-Oriented Tool Will Do."

One of the highest payoff areas within the data warehousing domain lies in data mining and knowledge discovery. Some remarkable results are already attributed to this area of endeavor, and much potential is predicted, hence we are including two chapters on the topic. First, Paul Barth of Tessera Enterprise Systems, a true data mining pioneer, presents his experiences in "Mining for Profits in the Data Warehouse." Second, gurus Robert Small and Herb Edelstein, from Two Crows, address the issue of "Scalable Data Mining."

PRISM Solution's J. D. Welch, who is said to have built one of the very first architected data warehouses on record, has contributed "Updating the Data Warehouse." In this essay he addresses the tough topic of capturing changed data, reloads, and refreshes.

Part 4, **Managing the Data Warehouse**, includes four essays covering several broad areas of managerial interest. First, Boeing's Narsim Ganti presents a fascinating tour de force in his "Managing and Staffing the Data Warehouse" in which he addresses the key issues of personnel in the data warehousing environment.

On a related topic, Ramon Barquin, from Barquin and Associates, and founder of The Data Warehousing Institute, presents the Institute's official program to deal with education and training. Because of the diversity in both quantity and quality of instruction in the area, "An Education and Training Program for Data Warehousing" provides a welcome reference for enterprises involved in data warehousing initiatives who need to provide training in the field.

Closing the book is the chapter by NCR's Bernard Boar. A strategist by training, Bernie Boar has written extensively on the strategic implications of data warehousing. In "Understanding Data Warehousing: A Strategic Perspective," an adaptation of one of his earlier works, he dubs data warehousing as a "rising-tide strategy" and explains why it should be a key aspect of all corporate strategic thinking in the future.

Ramon Barquin and Herb Edelstein, editors

About the Data Warehousing Institute

The Data Warehousing Institute has two goals: (1) expanding effective use of data warehousing technology and (2) enhancing the careers of data warehousing managers and staff. It does this through sharing information about best practices and about lessons learned by data warehousing pioneers. It conducts courses, offers tips and techniques, provides references to outstanding speakers, consultants, and system integrators; and it conducts annual data warehousing user conferences where experienced data warehousing managers share the lessons they have learned about what works and what doesn't.

DATA WAREHOUSING USER CASE STUDIES

Organizations could avoid unnecessary delays and mistakes if they could find people who had already resolved the problems they are now facing. Our collection of user case studies helps Institute Associates by providing useful knowledge and a link to other users who may be willing to discuss their experiences. The case studies are a growing, living collection, constantly being augmented, edited, and pruned by each Special Interest Group (SIG).

SPECIAL INTEREST GROUPS

Institute Associates find significant value from communicating with other data warehousing practitioners who share their specific subset of issues, problems, tools, etc. The SIG groupings are organized by industry. At the 1995 Annual Conference, SIGs were launched in health care and manufacturing. The Institute is also launching SIGs in finance, government, telecommunications, wholesale/retail, and public utilities. Proposals for additional SIGs are expected.

DATA WAREHOUSING AWARDS

The "Best Data Warehousing Projects" awards help identify good models to follow.

DATA WAREHOUSING ELECTRONIC FORUM

Associates of The Data Warehousing Institute may gain access to Institute staff and other Associates through an electronic forum maintained in a widely accessible on-line service. Information about new announcements in data warehousing, new case studies, new consultants and system integrators added to the list, and "Best Data Warehousing Projects" can all be accessed through the forum. An up-to-date list of data warehousing conferences and resources is also maintained. In addition, the forum facilitates moderated broadcasts of messages from members to other members.

ANNUAL TRAINING CONFERENCE

Each year in January, teams of data warehousing practitioners come together to attend a dozen well-designed, in-depth half-day and full-day courses on key data warehousing methodologies and technologies. The courses are also offered in-house for requesting organizations. These courses are taught by a faculty whose members consistently win extraordinarily high ratings in conferences and seminars throughout the world.

REGIONAL AND INTERNATIONAL TRAINING PROGRAMS AND CONFERENCES

The Data Warehousing Institute conducts in-depth courses and conferences in many cities in the U.S. and around the world. These programs bring the top-rated speakers from the Annual Conference and the Annual Training Conference to people who were not able to attend. Many of the courses and conferences are hosted by a local company, government agency, or association. The host organization receives low-cost admission to the program. If you would like more information about hosting such a program, e-mail tdwi@aol.com, and indicate "co-hosted programs" in the subject line, or call the Institute at 301-229-1062.

THE DATA WAREHOUSING INSTITUTE ANNUAL CONFERENCE

Each summer, several hundred data warehousing managers and their staff meet to share experiences and to find practical solutions to the challenges they face. About half the delegates are experienced data warehousing practitioners; the other half are in the evaluation or pilot phase.

THE JOURNAL OF DATA WAREHOUSING

A quarterly technical journal of case studies and in-depth articles on data warehousing began February, 1996.

PARTICIPATING IN THE DATA WAREHOUSING INSTITUTE PROGRAM

The Data Warehousing Institute has an Associate's program currently numbering close to 500 participants. You can become an Associate by participating in an Annual Conference, a Training Seminar, or any other of the Institute's formal activities. Associates share a private electronic forum, receive a subscription to *The Journal of Data Warehousing*, and get reduced rates on Institute publications, conferences, and courses. When appropriate, Associates contribute case studies of their warehousing activities and the lessons they learned, help with special interest group activities, and share their knowledge at Institute workshops, conferences and in *The Journal of Data Warehousing*.

About the Authors

DR. RAMON C. BARQUIN

Dr. Barquin is the founder of The Data Warehousing Institute and current Chair of its Advisory Committee. He also heads Barquin and Associates, his own consulting firm. He specializes in developing information systems strategies, particularly data warehousing, for corporations. His presence in the information technology industry has spanned four decades and three continents. He had a long career with IBM covering both management and technical assignments, including overseas postings and responsibilities in Asia and Latin America. Afterwards he served as President of the Washington Consulting Group, where he had direct oversight for the performance of several major federal information systems contracts. An electrical engineer and mathematician by training, he holds a Ph.D. degree from MIT. The author of close to 100 technical and management publications, he has held faculty appointments at MIT, the Chinese University of Hong Kong, and the University of Maryland. An acknowledged expert in the field of data warehousing strategies, he has assisted AIG, CIGNA, Deloitte & Touche, Digital Equipment, EMC, IBM, ITT Hartford, Lockheed Martin, NASDAQ, NRTC, Occidental Petroleum, Shaw Industries, VMARK Software, the U.S. Departments of Defense and Health and Human Services, the FAA, the FBI, and other organizations looking for guidance with data warehousing initiatives. Dr. Barquin is also the editor for the Prentice Hall book series on data warehousing and co-editor of the series' inaugural volume: *Planning and Designing the Data Warehouse;* as well as co-editor of the November 11, 1996 **Fortune** *Special Supplement on Data Warehousing.*

DR. PAUL BARTH

Dr. Barth is Vice President, Technology, for Tessera Enterprise Systems, a database marketing company headquartered in Wakefield, MA. He is a recognized national expert in parallel processing technology and its application in large-scale databases. Prior to founding Tessera, Dr. Barth worked for Epsilon and for Thinking Machines Corporation. He is responsible for technology strategy and manages all software development activities. He holds a Master of Science degree from Yale University and a Doctorate in Computer Science from MIT.

DENNIS BERG

Dennis Berg is a Principal with American Management Systems, Inc. With 20 years experience in information technology consulting, Mr. Berg specializes in data resource and system life cycle management methods, quality improvement, and group decision-making and facilitation. He has consulted to several organizations in establishing corporate-wide data quality improvement initiatives. Mr. Berg possesses an MBA in Management Information and Control Systems from the Wharton School of Business, University of Pennsylvania, and a B.S. in Economics, also from the Wharton School.

BERNARD BOAR

Bernard Boar serves as an information technology strategist, architect, and consultant for NCR in Lincroft, NJ. He is the author of four books on the critical topic of I/T strategy and architecture. He has lectured and published extensively and is a member of both the Strategic Planning Society and the Strategic Management Society.

GEORGE BURCH

George Burch is the Chief Technology Officer, Vality Technology, and the principal architect of Vality's INTEGRITY Data Re-engineering System. He has been developing database information systems and tools used by Fortune 1000 companies for 25 years. His experience in finding and correcting data anomalies in large databases has been used to develop a tool set for building high-speed data re-engineering applications. These applications incorporate his pioneering data-stream technology, which he first developed through doctorate work at John Hopkins University. Mr. Burch has been a CEO or president of several start-up firms and has headed operating branches at major corporations.

HERBERT A. EDELSTEIN

Herb Edelstein is president of Two Crows, one of the top data mining firms in the country. He is an internationally recognized expert in data mining, database management systems, and electronic image management. As a principal and founder of Two Crows, Mr. Edelstein consults to both computer vendors and users, and teaches professional seminars on client-server computing, database management systems, data warehousing, and document management. He has been invited to chair and keynote numerous conferences on these topics. He is also a widely published author on imaging and database management topics, and was technical editor for the Codd and Date Relational Journal. Mr. Edelstein was Vice President of Marketing and Sales at Sybase. Previously, he was Vice President of Sales and Marketing for International Data Base Systems, Inc. Before joining IDBS, he was general manager of the Model 204 division of Computer Corporation of America. He joined CCA from American Management Systems.

DR. NARSIM GANTI

Dr. Ganti was the most highly rated user-speaker at The Data Warehousing Institute Annual Conference in 1995 and at the 1996 Training Conference in San Francisco. He has a rare skill in cutting to the essential elements of the data warehousing process, a process he has been managing at Boeing for nearly a decade. He is the Chief Process Architect at Boeing and recently deployed three data warehouses, involving internal and external data, for Boeing.

KATHERINE GLASSEY-EDHOLM

Katherine Glassey-Edholm is co-founder and Executive Vice President, Brio Technology. She is responsible for providing strategic product direction for the company. As co-founder of Brio, Ms. Glassey-Edholm has lead Brio's entry into the data warehouse market with her focus on creating decision support systems based on open client/server data warehouses that really work. Prior to joining Brio, she managed the Applications Development Group at Metaphor Computer Systems.

DR. KATHERINE HAMMER

Dr. Hammer is the co-founder and current president and CEO of Evolutionary Technologies, Inc. She is the creator and original design architect for EXTRACT™, the company's flagship product, which addresses the costly problem of complex data movement and management in heterogeneous computing environments. Prior to founding ETI, Dr. Hammer was with the Microelectronics and Computer Technology Corporation consortium (MCC) that developed the prototype for EXTRACT. In addition to experience in system programming at Texas Instruments, Dr. Hammer also taught college-level linguistics, including a stint as visiting scholar at the University of Texas at Austin. Dr. Hammer is the recipient of the 1993 Entrepreneur of the Year award and now serves on the Distinguished Panel of Judges for that award. She has been recognized in Who's Who of American Women and Who's Who in the World. In 1992 and 1995, Dr. Hammer participated in President Clinton's Economic Summit, and in 1992, she was chosen guest at Governor Ann Richards' High-Tech Executive Dinner. Evolutionary Technologies was selected as the Emerging Business of 1992 by the Austin Chamber of Commerce.

CHRISTOPHER HEAGELE

Christopher Heagele is a Business Analyst with American Management Systems, Inc., concentrating in the establishment of data quality improvement programs, data warehouse design and development, and business process and workflow design. He possesses a B.S. in Economics from the Wharton School of Business, University of Pennsylvania, and a B.S.E. in Mechanical Engineering and Applied Mechanics, School of Engineering and Applied Science, University of Pennsylvania.

DAVID MENNINGER

David Menninger is Director, Product Marketing, Express Technology, at Oracle OLAP Product Division, in Waltham, MA. Prior to its acquisition by Oracle, he was a Vice President for IRI, where he served as spokesman for their technology message. Previously, he was managing consultant at Softbridge's London office. He is also a contributing editor for *Data Based Advisor*. He holds a master's degree from Bentley College and bachelor's degree from The Wharton School.

DR. ROBERT SMALL

Robert Small is Vice President of Research at Two Crows Corporation. As a statistician with extensive experience in building and analyzing large databases, he has spent 13 years in the pharmaceutical industry. He directed the statistical and data management efforts for all international clinical pharmacology projects at Glaxo Wellcome. Previously, he was a faculty member in statistics at the University of Pennsylvania's Wharton School, and Director, Wharton Analysis Center. Dr. Small has a Ph.D. in Biomath (Statistics) from North Carolina State University, plus degrees in Mathematics and Physics.

MARK SWEIGER

Mark Sweiger has worked in data processing for 22 years in various technical, marketing, and managerial capacities. Currently, Mr. Sweiger is the Architecture Manager for Decision Support Systems at Sequent Computer Systems, Santa Clara, California. He is one of the original implementors of both relational database software (SQL) and database hardware machine architectures. He has championed the now ubiquitous RDBMS-software/symmetric-multiprocessor-(SMP)-hardware combinations that are the standard for both online transaction processing and data warehousing solutions. He has also done pioneering algorithmic work in OLTP and parallel query performance, and invented the first highly available UNIX cluster implementation (at Sequent). Mr. Sweiger has written dozens of articles for the trade press on various business, database, and machine architecture topics. In addition to the chapter in this book, he will have another chapter on NUMA machine architectures in an upcoming book entitled "Understanding Database Management Systems, Second Edition," to be published in the summer of 1997. As a result of his nomination, the R+V Insurance (Germany) Profit and Loss Data Warehouse (implemented on Sequent Computer Systems hardware) won first place in the Data Warehousing Institute's 1996 Best Practices Award competition in the OLAP category. Mr. Sweiger's current areas of interest include data mining and knowledge discovery tools for data warehouses, data warehouse management tools, data warehouse design and implementation methodologies, and methodologies for the assessment of the return-on-investment of data warehousing projects.

J.D. WELCH

Mr. Welch is currently the Senior Business Information Consultant for Prism Solutions. W.H. Inmon credits Mr. Welch with being one of the first to design, develop, and implement an architected data warehouse, and he managed the implementation of several data warehouse projects for the cellular telephone industry from 1984 through 1993.

GEORGE ZAGELOW

George Zagelow is the Program Manager for Data Warehousing Solutions for the IBM Software Solutions Division in Santa Teresa, California. He has responsibility for data warehousing across IBM including the breadth of IBM solutions. He has held a wide variety of software development and management positions both outside and inside IBM. His experience includes commercial applications, database management systems, open systems, client/server, and overall strategies for data management across IBM.

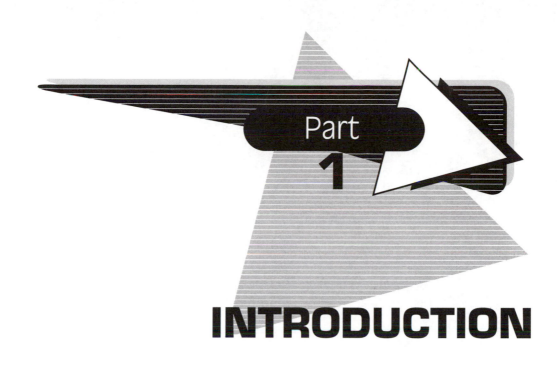

Part
1

INTRODUCTION

Chapter
1

Data Warehousing— Client/Server for the Rest of the Decade

George Zagelow

IBM

This chapter discusses current industry and technological forces that are driving the explosive interest in data warehousing. The topics covered include the following:

- Historical perspective—how we got here
- Operational data and its purity
- The requirement for better decision support
- Why not a single data store for both operational and informational use?
- The emergence of the data warehouse
- Data warehouse componentry
- Issues, challenges, and trends

HISTORICAL PERSPECTIVE—HOW WE GOT HERE

During the last three decades we have watched information technology make tremendous strides as we've moved to computerize every possible business process. In general, a combination of technological limitations and that of people-power has inhibited even faster progress. In addition, politics, competitive postures, and even perceptions, be they accurate or not, also played a significant role. But those things change over time, and so progress is made. It is amazing that no end to the application of computer technology is in sight. If anything, the curve is getting steeper, not flattening out. Because the spectrum of potential applications is so broad, every technological advance has the potential to change—drastically— the focal point for the next wave of computerization.

As a long-time database technologist, I find it is easiest to describe change from a data perspective. This will also be appropriate as an introduction to the challenges of data warehousing. By far the most prevalent application style was, and is, based on a file paradigm. The more complicated applications fueled development of technology for the factoring of database function out of the application. This took the form of hierarchical databases (such as IMS [Information Management System] and DL/I [Data Language/I]), network databases (such as IDMS [Integrated Data Management System]), as well as plenty of "homegrown" systems that used files but appeared to the application to have varying amounts of database function. These styles of physical organization were strongly biased toward *operational applications* because, at that time, computers were justified based on their performing basic business processes such as payroll or billing. Once a system was justified, anything else that could be computerized made the purchase that much more cost effective, so we proceeded to computerize all of the major business processes. Note that these applications tended to be treated as stand-alone efforts, developed over years, maybe by different sets of programmers, using whatever styles and technologies suited the whims of the development teams. Later, purchased applications took their place in the portfolio and added another dimension to the broad diversity of the application suite.

We had more than fifteen years of "legacy" before relational databases were developed. Already, pressure was mounting for better decision support. File, hierarchical, and to some extent network-based systems proved very difficult to query directly, so new tools started to appear. The first data warehouses were supported by products like FOCUS or RAMIS running on a VM mainframe. They were loaded and administered separately from the operational systems, much like warehouses of today. Then relational database and its Structured Query Language (SQL) appeared. Designed with an integrated query language, relational databases seemed ideally suited to help us finally reach "nirvana"—a single database store that would satisfy both the operational and query users using a single copy of the data. It is unfortunate that it hasn't quite worked out that way.

Operational Data and Its "Purity"

For purposes of this discussion, let's define *operational applications* as those applications performing the business processes described above, and *operational data* as the data accessed by those applications. In today's shops, we have what's left of a quarter-century of operational applications, most of whose operational data is stored in various file formats, IMS, CICS DL/I, CICS File Control, IDMS, Model 204, and so on, together with some relational data. Because of the differences in how these applications were developed/acquired, there is little consistency across them, and virtually no integration of them with each other. Further, the data itself can be in disastrous shape. There can be inconsistency in the meanings of data elements, such as multiple definitions of "customer" across applications. Even if there is agreement on what elements mean, the data may contain different representations, such as different spellings of the same name. It's little wonder that toward the end of the 1980s, large customers were approaching IBM with a sense of alarm: their systems were producing lots of reports, but the totals across systems were becoming almost impossible to reconcile. Their IT organizations were hard-pressed to help, as there were large backlogs of requests for new applications. From a sheer size perspective, the legacy was impossible to replace completely. And many shops had lost their entire skill base for individual applications.

THE THRUST TO DOWNSIZE

Against that backdrop, a major change in the IT model was also occurring. Pressure to control cost, as well as general frustration with IT's ability to satisfy application needs quickly, led many customers to try to downsize applications to non-mainframe platforms. This was primarily an operational systems idea: replace a production mainframe application with one running on a UNIX relational database, for example, and save significantly on the cost of the system. Instead of a reduction in the previously described legacy, most of it has remained with us. Certainly, less than 20 percent of the computerized data is in relational databases. So it's much more likely that the move to Client/Server produced more of a net addition to the legacy than replacing and simplifying our environments. Nevertheless, the investment made in C/S infrastructure over the last decade will prove invaluable as we turn our attention to the decision-support arena.

REQUIREMENT FOR BETTER DECISION SUPPORT

The prospects for decision support during the early 1980s were bleak indeed. Applications and data were inconsistent, and little was directly accessible. Some tools were available, but they were labor intensive from an IT administrative viewpoint. And the pressure was building rapidly. With the introduction of the PC and products like Lotus 1-2-3®, business users got a taste of the power and autonomy that PCs could offer. At first, access to corporate data meant taking the regular hard copy reports and literally rekeying into a spreadsheet. But that could not last, and from then on, the business user and central IT were on a collision course over access to the data. Not just access to hard copy reports, but transparent, automatic access to consistent, timely data, delivered to the tool of the user's choice on the platform of his/her choice.

A Single Database for Everyone?

Our initial thinking was that the introduction of relational databases would relieve the pressure for direct access to the data. And it did to some extent. QMF users have actively queried DB2 databases for more than a decade, with databases more than half a terabyte in size since the early 1990s. Still, relational technology answered only part of the original dream: to support both operational and decision-support users on the same copy of the data. At issue is the locking contention that surfaces when operational applications, which may be characterized by relatively short update transactions with real-time performance requirements, try to share data with the longer running scan-oriented queries. At worst, the workloads can paralyze each other, but with proper care, such sharing of data is feasible. But "proper care" generally implies controls on the types of queries allowed to run, which translates into a pre-canned query strategy that defeats the whole idea of ad hoc query. Also, as is usually the case, as the workloads grow, the ability to manage the situation erodes.

Workload contention is not the only reason to build a separate *informational* store. Because of the condition of the data (described above), significant cleansing and reconciliation may be necessary before it is usable by a business user. Second, the business user needs stable, point-in-time data for most decision-support applications. Because the operational systems may be updated continuously, a scheduling mechanism for controlling the application of update activity is usually required. And finally, the required data may be collected from a number of sources, with potentially massive summarization and/or aggregation required before it is usable.

While it may be possible to do all of this processing in real time, with the business user waiting for the result, the low-risk approach leads us to abandon the goal of a single data store and to favor separate systems, each optimized for its user group. A preprocessing stage is added to handle the cleansing, reconciliation, aggregation, and so on, necessary to prepare the *informational data* for direct use by the business user. Thus, the birth of the modern data warehouse.

THE EMERGENCE OF THE DATA WAREHOUSE

Once we commit ourselves to a separate data store for decision support, some very tough issues are, at least temporarily, behind us. (We get some new ones in their place, but we will save that discussion for later in the chapter.) First, what are the characteristics of the ideal warehouse store? It would have the information necessary to answer all of the "interesting" questions about all of the "interesting" subjects. The open-endedness of this requirement leads to our first challenge: How big should the warehouse be? Trying to find the answer to this question can literally paralyze users trying to get started in warehousing. Other potential characteristics could include providing the data in a form suitable for very quick multidimensional analysis, or providing a platform for the data discovery techniques we call data mining. Figure 1–1 shows the process for building such warehouse stores. The key groups of "customers" for this process are the various classes of end-user: business analysts, executive management, and so on. The goal is to deliver the data they need, when they need it, to their favorite tools, running on their favorite platforms. The data must be accurate, and the users must be autonomous to the extent possible. That implies the user must be able to deal directly with the data in the warehouse without asking for help. In addition, the users must be completely insulated from the information delivery processes. It's up to warehouse-providing vendors to deliver the tools and infrastructure to make this possible. The process requires that data be made available from any "interesting" data source, be it file or database, internal to the company or external. Prior to its use, data must be cleansed, reconciled, summarized, and/or aggregated, as the case may be. Because we are dealing with copies of data, we will need to understand the currency of the copies and the refresh strategies. And it must be automatable and repeatable. The pressure will be on the administrators to set up and maintain the operation of the warehouse delivery processes, as well as field questions that arise from the user community. Since administrators are far outnumbered by users in most installations, it's easy to see why automation and user autonomy are important. Central to the process is metadata. A thorough understanding of the "lineage" of each data element will be

Figure 1–1 Data-to-Information Process

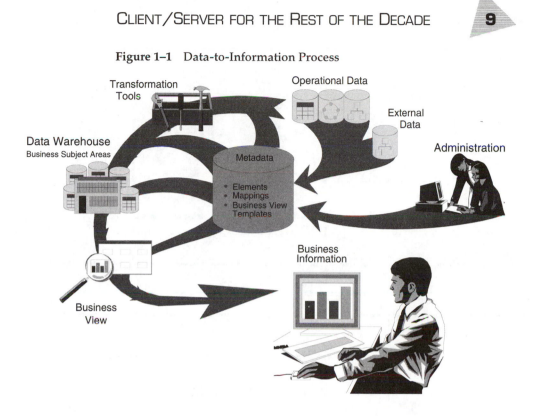

required for both the end-user, so he/she can understand what the data is, and the administrator, so he/she can set up the correct delivery process.

DATA WAREHOUSE COMPONENTRY

Figure 1–2 shows the kinds of function most customers will need to build warehouses. Let's spend some time discussing each of these areas. In the area of **data access**, the full functionality of client/server will be brought to bear, except that the target audience will be the decision-support user rather than the downsizing of production applications.

The "fire wall" between users and the warehouse will mainly be SQL in some form. The Open Database Connectivity (ODBC) form of callable SQL will be an important interface, as will various flavors of imbedded SQL. Other potential interfaces that could emerge as important would be the current proprietary interfaces supported by the OLAP (online analytical processing) vendors, and the standard being developed by the

Figure 1–2   Data Warehouse Components and Functions

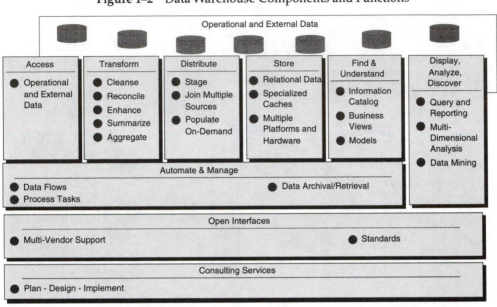

OLAP Council.[1] In terms of C/S protocols, the relational and middleware vendors all provide connectivity and, of course, the Internet will play a rapidly expanding role. The key requirement is connectivity to a large number of legacy sources. So, our work over the last decade on C/S will serve us very well. It should be noted, however, that decision support has a different data delivery model than the one C/S was developed for. C/S was developed to support real-time access. The applications may have stringent requirements for high performance when database calls are issued, because a user may be waiting for the completed transaction. The obvious examples are airline reservation systems and bank ATMs. By contrast, while decision-support users will still be accessing the warehouse in real time, the performance demands/expectations can be significantly lower, and the user is accessing a copy of the data. The key question becomes: How current must the copy be kept? The answer will be driven by the type of analysis the user intends to do, but nightly and weekly refreshes of the warehouse seem to be the standard. With this kind of synchronization requirement, warehousing becomes considerably easier to support, as access to legacy systems can be scheduled overnight or on weekends, with the processing being completed before the user needs to analyze the data. Since access, cleansing, aggregation, and reconciliation can be time-consuming operations, as can accessing the legacy systems themselves, having this processing window is a key advantage for the data warehousing process. This does point up one other consideration. As C/S was developed to support real-time access, use of the access functionality will change somewhat when it is used to populate the warehouse, in that it will be used in conjunction with some kind of scheduling mechanism in order to achieve the desired asynchronous replication capability.

In light of the earlier discussion of the state of the legacy data, **cleansing/transformation** probably represents the bulk of the work necessary to build the warehouse. So it is of extreme importance that this general area not be trivialized during the planning stage of warehouse development. This is one of the newer functional areas. Consequently, it is not as mature as, say, the C/S technology described above. Yet it is a rapidly evolving area in which several vendors offer unique functionality. In a more general vein, there is some capability to transform data as it's being moved through the use of SQL, generally in combination with data replication products. And there is our last resort, which is being widely applied due to lack of required tools: writing custom C or COBOL code to do the transformations. It is unfortunate that, with some of the older legacy systems, the business opportunity just may not be compelling enough to support development of the tools needed. So custom applications will be with us for the foreseeable future.

In the area of **aggregation**, most middleware comes with some kind of JOIN capability. (This is also a good place to note that products often don't align perfectly with the matrix in Figure 1-2. For example, a middleware product can provide C/S connectivity, JOIN capability, and data transformations through SQL.) The key technology to look for is a high-powered optimizer to improve the efficiency of the JOIN.

In the area of **replication**, most of the relational database vendors offer a replication suite. There are also several vendors who specialize in replication products. The main thrust here is to automate the movement of copies of legacy data into the data warehouse. And, since the data is presumably being copied from a production system, the idea is to move the data off that system as unobtrusively as possible. There are several differentiators in this segment. First is the number of legacy sources accessible (the more, the better). Note that much of this technology was developed for real-time access to a variety of storage styles. For transparency, some dialect of SQL is usually used to define the desired answer set. The marriage of SQL to some of the older legacy data, such as files or IMS, is not necessarily a marriage made in heaven. Usually there is no optimization whatsoever, and hence no ability to predict the performance characteristics of ad hoc queries. Also, the effect of allowing such ad hoc access could be disastrous to the performance of the production system (and is a driver to establishing the warehouse as a separate store, as we previously discussed). So, while tools have promised real-time access "transparently" across relational and non-relational data, the promise was a hollow one, particularly on the non-relational side. However, application of these tools in support of enabling of asynchronous copies for a data warehouse allows for a much safer scenario. The access can be precisely planned with some thought to optimizing the access and can be scheduled for "off peak" times. So, tools of questionable value in support of client/server real-time access will become much more viable in support of warehousing.

A second area of differentiation is the amount of data necessary to keep copies current. Ideally, both full and differential refresh of the copies should be supported. (Differential refresh sends only the data that has changed since the last refresh.) In general, there are two styles of differential refresh: log capture and triggers. Log capture is an application that watches the database log for change activity and traps that activity for sending to the copy site. It can be implemented almost invisibly, and it enjoys a sizable performance edge over relational triggers. Note that not all data sources will have logs to be captured or support for relational triggers, so full copies may be all that's available.

A third differentiator is the bias of the replication model. A point-in-time model will collect change activity for propagation at specified times, set by the user. This allows for very efficient batching of the update activity and is ideal for producing copies in support of time series analysis. The alternative is continuous propagation, where updates are broadcast as they happen. For decision-support usage, the point-in-time model is more applicable.

One more comment on replication. The general scenario for producing copies has three distinct parts: capture of the legacy data, transfer of the data to the warehouse, and application of the data to the warehouse store. Most vendors provide all three pieces using closed architectures. This is an area crying for some standardization, because no vendor provides all the access to all the interesting sources. Since the target warehouse is likely to be relational (see the next section), staging the captured legacy data in a relational table offers a point where tools from any vendor could access it. This is the approach we've taken with the IBM replication suite. We stage the full or differential copies in tables, and we publish the formats of those tables for potential integration with other replication suites. This approach also opens the replication data for additional cleansing or reconciliation.

For the **warehouse store**, the vast majority will be relational databases. The advantages are numerous: SQL was invented for direct query of data, most C/S connectivity is supplied by relational vendors, most replication has been designed with relational sources and targets, and most of the relational vendors are delivering parallel database solutions. There are important alternatives in this segment, however. The OLAP multidimensional engines offer unique performance characteristics across their problem domain. In addition, we may see traditional file stores as the only platform capable of supporting the performance requirements of some data mining operations. Differentiators for the relational engines will be overall scalability; availability across a broad spectrum of hardware platforms; "affinity" with legacy data platforms and stores; availability of extensions for Image, Text, etc., to support the next generation of applications; database management characteristics like availability, reliability, serviceability; and supporting tools.

In the area of **decision-support tools**, we see a definite progression. Warehousing generally starts with basic query as the ante to get in the game. There are several excellent and popular query/report writers in that segment. Then there are tools that support multidimensional analysis directly on relational, without the separate OLAP engine. And there are the new data discovery tools, which don't require an hypothesis at all. They run directly against the data and "mine" interesting relationships, sequences, and so on. Note that these tools are like tools in a toolbox—that is, they can be used in combination to produce the desired result. There is no single class of tools that satisfies the broad range of decision-support requirements.

There are several critical requirements in the area of **systems management**. "The warehouse" is likely to be a sizable distributed application with one or more relational and perhaps OLAP stores, replication componentry reaching into legacy systems across networks, and processes running on source and target systems to cleanse/aggregate/reconcile data. Consequently, all the tools for management of legacy and relational systems are applicable here. Also, tools for network management and client/server are applicable. Since the warehouse processes need to be periodically repeated, process management tools will be essential for automating the capture/cleanse/propagate/apply steps for each copy. And finally, as we can't realistically collect data indefinitely and store it online, tools for archiving and retrieving warehouse data are required. The requirement is for all this functionality to be able to manage multivendor solutions. To the extent functions are missing, the entire warehouse initiative is slowed or stopped. At a minimum, the ability to manage the solution can restrict the choices of componentry. Indeed, for larger warehouses, the management of the solution becomes a critical success factor.

Over the course of our discussion we have reviewed a large number of potential components and technologies that will play in the general data warehousing solution. Our first attempt to classify and position these elements was driven in the late 1980s/early 1990s by our larger customers, who, as described above, needed mechanisms to help reconcile their legacy systems. In 1993, IBM published a generic reference model for a data warehousing architecture.[2] It provides a framework for how to address warehousing, from a "top-down" perspective—that is, an enterprise-wide view of the problem. IBM has invested considerable resources not only to develop an overall architecture but to populate that architecture with a broad set of enablers that allow assembly of warehouses of virtually any size. This architecture remains valid today, and it contains much of the componentry reviewed in this chapter. It also has provisions for assembly of multivendor warehouses as the key interfaces, protocols, and standards are clearly defined. Practically speaking, such an architectural approach is an essential part of any warehouse design, particularly for the larger warehouses.

The area of **services** has proven to be much more important than we anticipated. We believed that delivery of the blueprint for warehousing together with the componentry for assembly would be sufficient to enable our customers to move gracefully into the warehousing arena. Such was not the case. Our recommendation of taking an enterprise view drives the implementation toward reconciliation of all the legacy systems prior to delivery of the warehouse itself. We'll discuss alternative approaches a little later, but suffice it to say, most customers find it difficult to assemble even data-mart-sized warehouses. Because they lack in-house skills, the existence of skills for hire becomes essential for their success.

ISSUES, CHALLENGES, AND TRENDS

This completes our brief overview of the componentry in Figure 1–2 . The remainder of this chapter will be devoted to a discussion of some of the issues, challenges, and trends that will face implementers of warehouses. We begin with a subject we were just discussing: **"top-down" versus "bottom-up" warehouse implementation**. As discussed previously, any attempt by a large organization to solve the legacy-incon-sistency problem will logically lead to a "top-down" warehouse design—one that encourages enterprise-wide modeling to drive the inconsistencies out of the source data

for the warehouse. This approach has proved to be too difficult for all but the most rugged of enterprises. And those with
the best chance of success have probably invested considerably in data and process modeling as their way of doing business. For many customers, development of an enterprise
model is so arduous and lengthy that it may never be completed. So what are the alternatives? A "bottom-up" approach
would be to build the enterprise-wide warehouse incremen-
tally: one datamart at a time. (For these purposes, let us define
datamart as a "small subject-oriented warehouse.") This
approach has the advantage that the inconsistencies that need
to be addressed are much narrower in scope (one subject), the
warehouse has smaller initial volumes to accommodate, and
the users quickly get experience so they can start tuning the
design (users often don't know what to ask for). The net result
is that the warehouse goes in much faster and the organization sees much quicker return on investment. Pragmatically,
the "bottom-up" approach is much more doable and has
become the predominate approach. But there is a key pitfall:
care must be taken to ensure that as datamart after datamart
goes in, the inconsistencies in the legacy that span datamarts
are driven out. Otherwise, the new warehouses will only per-
petuate the legacy problems. So the preferred approach will
be to evolve to the enterprise warehouse by implementing a
series of datamart-sized warehouses, and amortize the cost of
enterprise reconciliation across those datamart projects. Over
time, the union of the datamarts produces a logical enterprise
warehouse, one where company-wide questions can be asked
and answered. But the choice of whether the enterprise warehouse is actually populated as a separate store can be deferred
until the users require it for the performance they need (so
they won't have to JOIN the data across perhaps many datamarts), or until the operational characteristics of the loading
of the many datamarts forces one as a "buffer" between the
operational sources and the datamarts.

One area where implementers could really use some
help is with **improvements in tool integration**. This usually
comes down to a discussion of the administrative cost of
integrating tools from multiple vendors, where each tool has
its own different administrative interface and its own **meta-**

data. Pragmatically, the tool builders, wanting to deliver self-sufficient tools, will not ship their products without administration facilities. So the best bet for improvement comes in the sharing of metadata across tools so that common metadata need be entered only once. We can extrapolate the requirement to be some kind of common repository where all the tools from all the vendors would go to get the metadata (a familiar requirement that's been with us for a couple of decades). It's not likely we'll ever see such a repository for several reasons.

- New tools appear on the market so quickly that it would be impossible for a single vendor to supply the integration.

- Many of the tools and databases already exist, with their own metadata stores, and a major retrofit to use a common repository would be prohibitively expensive.

- Even if such a repository existed, presumably it would be owned by a single vendor. Vendors of other tools would be reluctant to depend heavily on it, so at best the integration would be optional.

Much more likely is a "federated" approach where the tools can share metadata with each other through some kind of interchange mechanism. The tool owners would be expected to import and export "interesting" metadata. For success, the expense for the tool to integrate needs to be very low. IBM offers this kind of approach across 20+ warehouse tools. And the Metadata Coalition,[3] a vendor-neutral organization that formed in 1995, has published a draft of an interchange mechanism along these same lines. Several other points should be noted. A metadata interchange strategy does not preclude an optional central repository of data collected from the tools. Then the individual tool repositories would function as "execution time" caches. The federated model would foster a peer-to-peer view of the repository that easily accommodates multiple repositories across multiple platforms. (The single repository model breaks when one tries to scale beyond one system. Solving this scaling problem leads back to the federated model we are discussing.) An interchange mechanism is a good start on this very difficult problem. But we will need a change propagation mechanism if we are to automate the synchronization of the federated metadata stores. With automatic synchronization facilities, a logical "common repository" could be configured in any size and topology.

While on the topic of metadata, data warehousing brings some unique challenges that we did not have with Computer Assisted Software Engineering (CASE), for example. First, we must understand that there exist both **technical and business metadata** supporting different classes of users. Technical metadata consists of descriptions of objects (tables, columns, etc.) in terminology familiar to programmers and database administrators. Business metadata describes warehouse objects in business terms (such as a report of yesterday's sales as of 3:05 A.M. today). Technical metadata is essential in automating the perhaps multiple transformations of the data on its journey from the operational systems to the warehouse. Business metadata is essential in making the analyst autonomous in his/her use of the warehouse. It should be noted that both technical and business users will need to understand the transformations that have affected the data: the business user, so that he/she can understand how the data was derived; the DBA, so that he/she can ensure that the correct data is getting to the warehouse. In general, it will fall on the DBAs and perhaps power business users to understand and bridge the technical and business metadata. This is an area where central IT can provide unique value, since the business user alone has no hope of understanding the existing legacy.

Another area that can inhibit the success of a warehouse initiative has to do with ownership of the warehouse: **IT or workgroup**. In many customer shops today, IT has lost much of the control it used to have in terms of funding projects. This is due to a combination of a general flattening of organizations, with a resulting empowerment of the workgroup, and an historical frustration with IT's ability to be sufficiently responsive to business requirements. For warehousing projects to have any hope of success, both groups must work together. The only hope for understanding and retrieving data from the legacy systems lies in IT. The only hope for delivering business value lies in the users. Our recommendation is that cross-discipline teams be charged with warehouse implementation.

One area of challenge will be the **size of the warehouses**. During a visit with a large retailer, I found that their estimated requirement was multiple datamarts (10 or so) of one terabyte each, and a global warehouse of 20 terabytes. The discussion was an interesting one, as IBM, as a warehouse user, has a similar range of requirements. The other aspect of this is growth, with many warehouses doubling in size every twelve to eighteen months. It's little wonder that each of the major relational vendors is embracing parallel technologies as a response to this growth. The challenge here will be the administration of these immense or soon-to-be-immense stores. To understand the feasibility of the desired warehouse, the best approach is to do as much modeling and prototyping as possible with a representative workload. From a technology perspective, look for differentiation in the areas of parallel SQL (the ability to divide a single SQL query across multiple processors), superior optimizer technology, massively parallel processors, parallel utility execution (loading, index creation, reorganization, etc.), and efficient integration with replication tools.

The next area for discussion is **online analytical processing**. The key issue is the long-term importance of the OLAP engines, given that there's not a lot of activity to parallel those engines, and the fact that all the relational engines are not only moving aggressively to solve the scaling issues but are also looking for optimizer improvements that make relational a more viable native store for direct multidimensional analysis. The most likely scenario is that the OLAP engines will continue to be a popular choice at the datamart level, fed from much larger relational stores. Because of the sheer performance of the OLAP engines, it's unlikely relational can totally displace them. But the vast majority of the warehouse data will be relational.

Another area that bears watching is the interrelationships between **Client/Server**, **Lotus Notes**, and **Internet** in support of both connected and mobile users. This is not a warehouse thought per se, but will certainly affect the direction warehouse technology will take. Over the last ten years, we have progressed to the point where we can talk about "classic" client/server. That is the SQL*Connect, the Open Client/Open Server, the DRDA, and so on. All have supported the peer-to-peer model of SQL distribution first proposed by the R* prototype, developed in the early/mid-1980s at the IBM San Jose (now Almaden) research facility. With the exception of Stored Procedure functionality, the trend has been to move more and more application function to the client, leaving data, print, and so on, as the server function. This movement was fueled by a perception that downsizing of applications to smaller machines would be cheaper, and that workers would be more productive. The machines *are* cheaper, but productivity has suffered as shops struggle to keep stable configurations on the desktop while keeping the technology current. With the rapid emergence of the Internet, there is a strong movement of functionality back toward servers. This trend allows for much easier configuration of the desktop: the minimal system would need only a web browser. The harder administration tasks become a server thought, across many fewer machines. There is also complete insensitivity of the end-user to the operating environment of the server systems, so organizations will have a much easier time configuring the services they need, across whatever platforms work best. This model is extremely compelling. So what will inhibit mass movement to the server-centric model? First, all the scalability issues previously discussed become of paramount importance. Also, the bandwidth of the network can become a serious inhibitor, as possible large amounts of data will flow. And third is the mobile computing model, where the user needs the capability to be productive even when disconnected. Those needs reinforce the "fat client" model.

So how does this fit with the decision-support world? For many users, using Internet and/or Intranets is ideal. As an example, consider one of the 80+ warehouses currently in operation within IBM—this one in support of the PC Company. The global warehouse is 200+ GB on DB2 for MVS, updated daily. Downstream are multiple datamarts on Arbor's Essbase and DB2 for OS/2, of 300 MB and 1 GB, respectively. The Essbase users are using Lotus 1-2-3®. The

DB2 users fall into a couple of classes. The large class uses the output from a couple of hundred pre-canned queries, which are left in bitmap form for either C/S or Intranet access. The smaller group generates ad hoc SQL to probe anomalies uncovered by the standard queries. For the majority of users, Intranet enablement is a powerful new access mechanism, with much lower cost HW / SW and virtually no administrative overhead.

Architecturally, the appearance of browsers as front ends to warehouses will force a significant change to the warehouse architecture. The user's applications move to the server, perhaps adding another tier to the server hierarchy, or perhaps sitting side-by-side with the warehouse. What was a client/server relationship across a LAN or WAN now could be local access or even more integrated, with the function becoming a stored procedure or user-defined function to the database. It's likely we'll see rapid evolution of this model and depending on performance and capacity of the networks and, servers, perhaps it will become the dominant model. Note that it's unlikely to displace the current "fat client" completely, because the mobile user will not easily give up the autonomy of having the function available on his/her notebook.

Lotus Notes users make up a sizable group that fits the profile of disconnected users. From a warehouse perspective, it certainly makes sense to allow Notes databases to feed warehouses, as well as to act as the warehouse store. So bridges to and from relational databases are already appearing in the marketplace. Whether the Notes environment plays a more central role in warehousing is yet to be determined.

The final discussion topic for this chapter has to do with **future warehouse applications**. There are several points to make here. First, we presumably have separated decision-support users from the operational applications, both to protect them from each other and to allow for custom-built warehouses optimized for decision support. Nevertheless, the effort we will expend to cleanse and reconcile the data in the warehouse will make it a desirable platform not only for decision support but for the next generation of operational applications. So the issues driving separation of classes of user could be right back with us. In a similar vein, there's not a lot of difference, from a componentry standpoint, between the building of warehouses and the reengineering of legacy applications. In fact, much of the warehouse activity within IBM is tightly aligned with reengineering. Reengineering of large application systems typically requires a staged approach, where both new and old systems are running side-by-side during the transition. In this model, the data flows are very similar to those of warehousing, with both activities relying heavily on client/server componentry. The primary difference is in the currency requirements of copied data. A typical reengineering would require a relational copy of the production legacy system, with near-real-time propagation of updates, while warehousing is much more point-in-time–oriented, maybe with nightly refreshes. But as decision-support users feel more and more competitive pressure to make quicker and quicker decisions, warehousing propagation delay time will be driven down, and this distinction between models will disappear.

Regardless of how the new applications are developed, these applications will be considerably different from the applications they replace. New enablers like image, text, voice, and video will spur development of applications utilizing these new functions, with a big increase in the growth of the data behind them. That, coupled with growth driven by collecting more historical and detail data, means the scalability of our solutions is in for a serious test.

CLOSING COMMENTS

As we have discussed, the challenges we face are many and significant. However, never have such a rich portfolio of products and services been available to tackle these challenges. Because so many organizations are actively pursuing warehousing, from a competitive standpoint warehousing has become mandatory. So it's of critical importance to move aggressively into the warehousing arena, but not recklessly. Each project should be chosen with care, especially the first one. It probably should be a datamart in support of a group of business users who are not only committed to the effort but who also have a good idea of what is needed to succeed. The idea is to start with one that really can't fail. With some experience and success, the evolution to larger warehouses will be considerably easier. And, yes, don't forget to reconcile the legacy as you go.

REFERENCES

1. The OLAP Council was established in January 1995 to serve as an industry guide and customer advocacy group for multidimensional database technology.
2. *Information Warehouse Architecture I*, SC26-3244, IBM Corporation; available through IBM branch offices.
3. The Metadata Coalition was established in October 1995 to seek quick agreement on and interchange mechanism for metadata.

Part 2

BUILDING THE DATA WAREHOUSE

Chapter
2

Migrating Data from Legacy Systems: Challenges and Solutions

Katherine Hammer

Evolutionary Technologies International

One of the biggest challenges facing any strategic IT project—whether implementing a new suite of applications, migrating to client/server architecture, or implementing a data warehouse—is the problem of retrieving the data stored in legacy systems and transforming it into a form suitable for the new environment. This problem is difficult for any number of reasons. Here are some of the most common.

- The same data is represented differently in different systems. For example, in one system salary may be represented as a monthly figure, and in another it is represented as a bimonthly figure; or in one system states may be represented by a two-digit numeric code, in another by a two-character code.

- The schema for a single database may not be consistent over time. Few DBAs have the luxury of rebuilding the historical database when changing the schema of a production database: there is simply not enough downtime. As a result, they must frequently take expedient shortcuts to incorporate the data required by changes in the application. For example, a particular value in some field may indicate that related data is stored in another table or file. Much of the problem is that the metadata describing these relationships is represented only implicitly in the application code.

- This type of schema modification has taken place regularly over a number of years, and no single person or set of people has the knowledge of all the historical changes.

- Data may simply be bad; for example, the same vendor may be represented multiple times within a single database by slightly different representations (such as DEC and Digital Equipment Corporation), or the value specified for some field may simply be invalid.

- The data values are not represented in a form that is meaningful to end-users. The designers of legacy systems were typically motivated to save disk space and CPU cycles. Consequently, there is heavy use of numeric codes and binary data. On the other hand, one of the strongest motivations for migrating to client/server architectures and particularly for implementing data warehouses is the availability of good end-user query tools. Yet no manager wants to see that 13,000 gallons of product 241 were shipped to customer 9812.

- Conversions and migrations in heterogeneous environments typically involve data from multiple incompatible database management systems (DBMS) and hardware platforms. Because most large companies have highly heterogeneous computing environments, IS personnel who may otherwise be relatively independent must cooperate closely to perform migrations successfully.

- The applications that run on legacy systems are frequently time-critical, and the efficiency of their successful execution directly affects the bottom line. Consequently, execution windows for data conversion programs must be coordinated carefully in order to provide the new application(s) with a consistent view of the data without impacting production systems.

As a result of the complexities introduced by these types of problems, most industry experts recommend an iterative, incremental methodology for strategic IT projects like those found in Rapid Application Development (RAD) and Joint Application Development (JAD).

THE NEED FOR AN ITERATIVE, INCREMENTAL METHODOLOGY

For many years IT organizations tried to use the same serial methodology for large migration problems that they used for relatively discrete projects, that is, analysis and design, followed by implementation and acceptance testing. Frequently, however, these efforts failed for some combination of the three following reasons.

- In a large organization, the complexity of the analysis and design can involve person-years of effort without any demonstrable results. In the highly political atmosphere of many large companies, this results in projects being canceled prior to any real effort at implementation.

- The sheer complexity of both the data analysis and the design of the target system has prevented effective progress.

- And perhaps most important, the rate of change in operational systems has outstripped the migration team's ability to keep current.

Industry analysts have maintained that large IT organizations spend 80 cents of every programming dollar on maintenance instead of on new development. As a result, it is extremely hard for a strategic migration effort to keep its design current with the latest versions of operational systems. Consequently, most authorities have begun recommending an iterative, incremental approach to designing and implementing new strategic applications, even though the new methodology adds another source of change to an already volatile implementation environment. By restricting efforts to those required to bring up and maintain a single subject warehouse, it is much easier to demonstrate value in a relatively short period of time and obtain management buy-in regarding the potential value of the approach. On the other hand, such an approach increases the likelihood that the target schema or interface programs will need to be modified.

IMPLICATIONS FOR METADATA AND THE DATA WAREHOUSE

There are actually three major sources of change that strategic IS initiatives must address. In addition to the changes to operational systems and those introduced by using an iterative, incremental methodology, IS initiatives must anticipate the challenges that result from changes in the business environment. The increased rate at which businesses merge or grow by acquisition, and restructure by divestiture or to accommodate changing industry regulations, affects strategic initiatives. The ability of the team responsible for the initiative to react cost effectively to these changes can ultimately determine its degree of success.

In fact, one could argue that the data warehouse can be used as a laboratory for determining the best way to combine tools and methodology to deal effectively with these different sources of change. The data warehouse—based on data drawn from operational systems—is built on shifting sands. If the warehouse team does not plan to deal effectively with these three sources of change, the warehouse could become the most costly of all applications to maintain.

The key to dealing with change cost effectively lies in metadata: capturing what is done at every stage of the project and how it relates to the metadata describing other systems, as well as being able to access this information to determine the impact of change. Aside from the challenges introduced by changes in business structure (such as mergers and acquisitions), two major sources of technical change affect the metadata used to implement a data warehouse: changes to operational schemas and changes to the meta-model used by the warehouse that occur because of the nature of an iterative, incremental methodology. For these reasons, two of the most important decisions a warehouse team can make are those regarding a versioning strategy and the design of a meta-model that minimizes the impact of change. The design of the meta-model will, in turn, depend upon the nature of the computing environment (how heterogeneous, how volatile the company's economic situation, etc.) and the team's choice of software tools.

ON THE LACK OF AN INTEGRATED DEVELOPMENT ENVIRONMENT

There is no single integrated set of tools that allows one to capture the whole process of design, data retrieval and transformation, and the relationship between source and target systems, much less the ability to deal with different versions of this information as one or more variables are changed. The good news is that most of the tools used to implement data warehouses are metadata-driven; the bad news is that they use different types of metadata and may or may not be able to exchange this metadata freely with the other tools an organization may want to deploy. Consequently, one of the best ways to discover the best combination of tools and methodology is to create sample change scenarios and design a meta-model that would allow the most efficient impact analysis and maintenance cycle, then use this meta-model and the steps required to perform the impact analysis and code modification to develop a requirements grid by which to evaluate the software tools one might wish to use.

FOUR DIMENSIONS OF METADATA

Listed above are three sources of change that the data warehouse team must anticipate—those arising from the normal regular changes to operational systems, those that result from using an iterative, incremental methodology, and those that result from external business drivers like acquisition. Figure 2–1 illustrates another way of looking at the sources of technical challenge with respect to the types of metadata required to minimize the impact of change. The need to adapt to

Figure 2–1   The Change Cycle

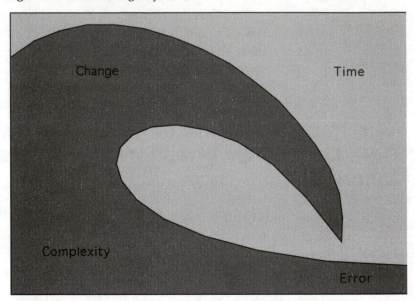

change, error, and complexity is regular over time and can be seen like waves on a beach. The types of activities required to deal with these problems remain constant but always different because—with the changes introduced over time—they have a different potential impact.

Metadata That Capture the Current Environment

The warehouse meta-model should maintain the following types of metadata:

- the record and data element definitions
- inter- and intra-database relationships. Inter-database relationships reflect the source-to-target mapping between operational systems and the attributes existing in the data warehouse and should include the ability to represent any business rules (that is, information regarding the test and transformation of one or more source data values to produce a new target data value).
- a definition of each interface program used to build or refresh the warehouse. The definition should include

    a. which inter-database joins it uses (that is, its inputs and outputs);

b. the timing and direction of the execution;

c. any execution parameters (for example, a refresh program that uses a time-date stamp contained within the database may need to be invoked with the time after which all updates should be retrieved);

d. dependencies on any other interface programs. For example, consider the case where a time-date stamp is supported in one of several operational source databases such that if one could retrieve the changed records from that database first, one could use the keys of the records retrieved to constrain the records accessed to obtain related data from other source databases. In this case, the dependence of these other interface programs on the successful completion of the first interface program should be recorded as part of the metadata describing the interface program;

e. the use or production of other ancillary databases. As indicated above, it is frequently necessary to transform data values in the process of migrating from legacy systems. Frequently, look-up tables or new-key/old-key correspondence tables are required to perform this data value test and transformation. To facilitate the maintenance of the warehouse, it is important that the definition of the interface program and the fact that it is dependent on this ancillary database be called out along with the location and nature of the ancillary database (for example, is it a file or a DB2 table?);

f. the name and location of the file that contains the source code for this data interface program; and

g. the tool and session name if this interface program was automatically generated.

Metadata Required to Reduce the Cost of Errors

In the process of data analysis and the testing of interface programs, errors in assumptions regarding data values will be discovered. The meta-model should allow the inclusion of the information discovered at the level of data element, record, database, and join (whether join is used to refer to a physical or to a logical relationship between records). This information includes but is not limited to

- legal ranges or values. This might include a list of legal values or a business rule (or expression) that describes the characteristics of a legal value, or even the name of a file or table that contains a look-up table. Note that the business rules may require referencing some other value within the entity. For example, if a record describing a job grade contained both a "minimum_salary" and a "maximum_salary" field, then the business rule describing the legal value might be that "maximum_salary" must be greater than the value that occurs for "minimum_salary" and vice versa.

- any exception logic that the data interface program should take if an illegal value is found.

Note that many of the errors encountered will involve implicit schema changes, where some flag (or date) in the record indicates to the applications accessing that database that they should interpret the data differently. Whether this information is recorded as attributes of objects in the current schema definition, or whether they should trigger a different version of the schema definition in the metadata, is probably a function of how different the two versions of the information stored in the schema are. For example, if after some point in time "M" and "F" are used for *male* and *female* instead of a previously used "1" and "2," then one could probably get by including all the values in the list of legal values. But, in the case that some value in a particular field means that widely different types of information are stored in the record, then a separate version of the metadata might be preferable.

Metadata That Can Reduce the Cost of Complexity

Other types of metadata may be needed to reduce the complexity of specifying, maintaining, and executing the data interface programs required to refresh the warehouse. For example, some production schemas are extremely complex, consisting of hundreds of pages of DDL (data definition language) or copybooks consisting of hundreds of thousands of lines. Likewise, the field names that occur in the actual schema definitions may be highly abstruse and not easily understood by the average warehouse administrator. Therefore, support for the definition of aliases for field names and the ability to define subschemas would be valuable extensions to the meta-model for reducing complexity.

Factoring in Time

Finally, given that the data interface programs used to refresh the warehouse must execute within particular timeframes, and that all of these relationships can change over time, the meta-model should accommodate two additional types of information:

- information about each database that can affect execution times, such as
  a. database size and volatility,
  b. the time window during which each database can be accessed, and
  c. the mechanism that should be used for changed data capture;
- versioning.

Choosing the appropriate versioning strategy can make a significant difference in reducing the costs incurred in iteration and maintenance. The easiest way to deal with different versions of metadata is to archive the entire meta-model whenever a change is made. However, such an approach does nothing to support impact analysis. Ideally, for each type of change that can be encountered in a particular environment, the versioning mechanism should support an efficient means of determining the impact of that change. There are two basic ways of providing this type of functionality.

1. Design the meta-model to anticipate change. For example, since one can anticipate that changes to operational schemas may result in changes to the mapping between source and target schemas, if one were designing a relational schema to represent the meta-model, it might be useful to break out both the

source elements and business rules in a separate table from the target value, as in

>   target-element-id
>   source-element-id
>   timedate-stamp

and

>   target-element-id
>   business-rule-description
>   business-rule (expression, code fragment, etc.)
>   timedate-stamp.

This type of structure would allow one to determine when and how the mapping had changed over operational schema changes. Of course, such an approach would require some programming to enforce the appropriate referential integrity across different types of updates.

2. Choose a tool or tools that provide sufficient versioning support to facilitate impact analysis.

A Sample Scenario

The following example illustrates how important the keeping of the appropriate types of metadata is for the effective use of an iterative, incremental methodology. Consider the case of a large manufacturer that has decided to implement a series of data warehouses to meet end-users' demand for data. The warehouse team decides that the best initial subject warehouse would focus on purchase orders. Their reasoning: because POs are generated per division, the organization might not be benefiting from the kind of quantity discounts it would receive if it were generating POs at the corporate level. But, because the company has grown by acquisition, this information is stored in different schemas on different DBMS products, and in a number of cases, these systems have used different key strategies for assigning vendor ID. In some cases, the tax ID was used, but in others, arbitrary numbers were assigned.

For the warehouse to serve its purpose, these differences in keys must be resolved so that Vendor X with ID 100 in one system is recognized as the same as Vendor X with ID 200 in another. (Note that this will require matching against the non-key information and that it may take some fuzzy matching on names and addresses to actually recognize that the two entries refer to the same vendor.) It will also be necessary to keep the old-key/new-key correspondences around in order to build the batch update programs that refresh the warehouse, as well as the original new-key creation logic in case new vendors are added to the operational systems.

Now imagine that the first warehouse has been implemented and received successfully, and the warehouse team decides that the second subject warehouse they want to build is one that reflects the cost of each of the products it manufactures. In this warehouse, they want the ID and name of any third-party component, its cost, and its vendor ID, where the vendor ID is the new vendor ID used to populate the first warehouse. To implement the initial load and batch update programs for this second warehouse most cost effectively, the team should be able to easily locate and incorporate the logic for generating and maintaining the new keys and the correspondence table. And because a significant amount of computing is required in the logic to check and create new keys, that computation would ideally take place only once and not in both sets of batch update programs. Moreover, not only would replicating the logic in both sets of programs be computationally inefficient, it would also increase the maintenance burden in the case that there were a need to change the logic at some later date. In short, the ideal way to proceed would be to replace each batch update program that updates the original warehouse with a single program that would retrieve the changed data required to update both warehouses in a single query.

The importance of this example is what it suggests about scheduling the design and development of subsequent warehouse applications. In the usual development scenario, the amount of time required to implement a new kind of application will be greater on the first project than on subsequent projects. For example, the first DB/2 application will take longer than a comparable second application. This assumption is based on the fact that a learning curve is associated with new environments, new user groups, etc. But in the case of using an iterative and incremental approach to data warehouse, one should not assume that subsequent warehouse applications can be developed more quickly or even <u>as</u> quickly as the initial subject warehouse. In fact, even this relatively simple example illustrates that without a methodology and careful control of the metadata, the complexity of augmenting and maintaining data warehouses for an enterprise could soon become as expensive as maintaining the current operational environments.

If, on the other hand, the metadata supported by tools and methodology chosen by the IT organization supports a quick change cycle, the warehouse designer should quickly be able to identify the location of the new-key creation logic and the ancillary old-key/new-key correspondence table, as well as the source-to-target mapping used to create/refresh the first subject warehouse.

THE IDEAL AND THE REAL

In the ideal world, all the above types of metadata would be provided by an integrated set of tools for automating the iterative and incremental design, implementation, and maintenance of the data warehouse. Moreover, because the same tools and methodology that could support the efficient evolution of the data warehouse address the same problems of maintaining any distributed, heterogeneous computing environment, such a tool-methodology configuration should be integral to any IT architecture moving forward.

It is unfortunate that no such integrated set of tools exists, although there are several classes of tools that handle different aspects of the process quite effectively. Figure 2–2 shows a tool landscape for the major classes of tools that can be used to automate the design, implementation, and maintenance of the data warehouse.

In general, there are seven classes of tools that address the data warehouse space problem.

- *CASE tools*, which assist in the creation of efficient RDBMS schemas for supporting particular applications, can also be used to generate certain applications which run against this RDBMS schema.

Figure 2–2   Warehouse Tools Landscape

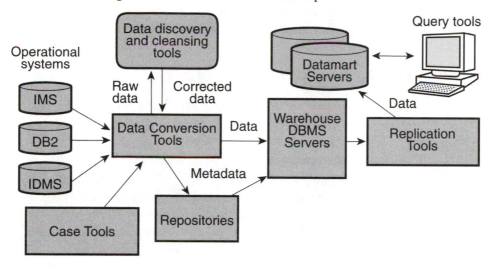

- *Data movement tools* automate the generation of programs to selectively retrieve and transform data from operational systems and populate the target data warehouse.

- *Data discovery/cleansing tools* compare the data values actually encountered in the operational systems and can, with instructions from the user, create corrected values. (Since these tools generally require flat file feeds rather than being able to access the native operational databases, they are shown as being fed and feeding the data movement tools.)

- *Repository tools,* whose goal is to be the centralized store and manager of the metadata describing all data processing within the IT organization, frequently provide a fairly rich source of versioning capabilities.

- *Warehouse database servers* consist either of a traditional RDBMS product or of a multidimensional DBMS product designed to support efficient processing of DSS queries.

- *Data replication servers* are used to trigger the distribution of subsets of warehouse information to datamarts. (These products are typically not capable of significant data transformation or reorganization and so are not placed as potential interfaces to the source operational systems.)

- *End-user query tools* provide the PC user with a user-friendly means of generating the desired queries/reports against the data warehouse or datamart.

Developing an Evaluation Grid

Given that there is no complete vendor solution, the best strategy for any organization seeking to use an iterative, incremental methodology for performing data migration from legacy systems would be to create a list of the types of change the organization is most likely to encounter (e.g., the introduction of changes to operational schemas, the introduction of new hardware and software systems, changes in the target schema, etc.) and determine the types of metadata required to respond to this change cost effectively. From this data one should be able to determine a set of requirements regarding

- the number of systems and tools that must be interfaced,
- the types of metadata required for the meta-model,
- the best versioning strategy for performing impact analysis, and
- the desired set of functionality for automating this process.

With this set of requirements in hand, it should be possible not only to evaluate the capabilities of the various tools that one might want to deploy but also to determine how and what kinds of metadata they need to exchange.

CONCLUSION

Because it is based on a volatile environment, the data warehouse is one of the most complex applications an organization can undertake. On the other hand, if an organization can determine the combination of tools and methodology that allows it to address this application, it will have solved one of its most pressing problems—how to reduce the cost of change in a distributed, heterogeneous computing environment.

Chapter 3

Optimal Machine Architectures for Parallel Query Scalability

Mark Sweiger

Sequent Computer Systems

INTRODUCTION

Parallel query database algorithms have become the basis of the creation, maintenance, and analysis of very large data warehouses. Examples of these algorithms include parallel full table scans, parallel sort, parallel hash join, parallel create index, and parallel database load, available on products such as Oracle, Informix, Red Brick, IBM DB-2 Parallel Edition, Tandem Non-Stop SQL, Teradata, and others. Parallel queries can be very complex, including repeated application of scans, joins, and sorts, with both the key attributes and key attribute data distribution varying widely from one operation to the next.

Because parallel query algorithms execute on common computer architectures, they operate on data that resides in one of four possible containers:

local memory
local disk
remote memory
remote disk

As long as data is only on local memory or local disk, data access times are uniform and, in general, parallel query algorithms scale well. Symmetric multiprocessors are examples of machines that have only local memory and local disk, with symmetric (uniform) access to these containers from all processors.

But when massively parallel, loosely coupled machine architectures, like the 2-D and 3-D meshes, the Y-Nets, the hypercubes, the crossbar switches, and other connection models, are involved, all four types of data containers, local and remote, are in use. If query data is on remote disk or remote memory, the machine architecture can grossly influence data access times, causing something called machine-architecture-induced data skew. This data skew can adversely effect parallel query performance, which assumes uniform access times. If access times are not uniform due to the way loosely coupled nodes are connected, machine-architecture-induced data skew can become so severe that the effect of parallelism is lost, effectively serializing the execution of otherwise parallel algorithms.

This essay will explain why uniform data access times and uniform data distributions are optimal for parallel query execution, what commercially available loosely coupled connection models exhibit machine-architecture-induced data skew and which do not, and why dynamic data redistribution statistically outweighs parallel query function-shipping as the principal method for overcoming machine-architecture-induced data skew in the loosely coupled hardware connection models.

WHY UNIFORM DATA ACCESS TIMES ARE OPTIMAL FOR PARALLEL QUERY EXECUTION

Data skew, no matter how it is caused, is the enemy of parallelism. Data skew is often thought to be a software or database-layout–induced problem, and while that certainly can be true, machine architecture can also cause data skew that no software or clever database administration technique can solve. We can see this by using a metaphor that compares parallel query execution to the parallelism found in the division of labor of industrial manufacturing.

Division of Labor and Skew

- Algorithmic parallelism is achieved using a paradigm similar to the division of labor.

- Each person (CPU) works on a separate set of material (data).

- The material (data) must be evenly distributed among the personnel (CPUs) or the effect of parallelism is lost.

In Figure 3–1, observe the increase in worker productivity after the material is redistributed uniformly among workers operating in parallel; the same amount of work gets done in three units of time instead of four.

Figure 3–1

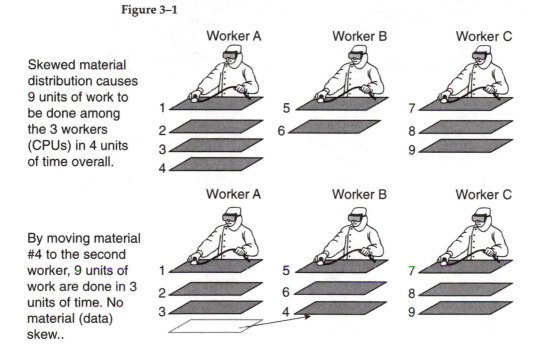

Skewed material distribution causes 9 units of work to be done among the 3 workers (CPUs) in 4 units of time overall.

By moving material #4 to the second worker, 9 units of work are done in 3 units of time. No material (data) skew..

Remote Material Location and Skew

Let's suppose that some material is located remotely from worker B. What is the effect on access times and the amount of work completed in parallel?

Figure 3–2

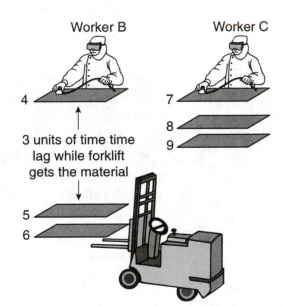

Even if material (data) is distributed, if some of it is farther away, it causes material (data) skew. If it takes 3 units of time to bring material to worker 2, then the total elapsed time would be 6 units of time to get 9 units of work accomplished.

Let's suppose that we redistribute material to maximize the productivity of all the workers.

Figure 3–3

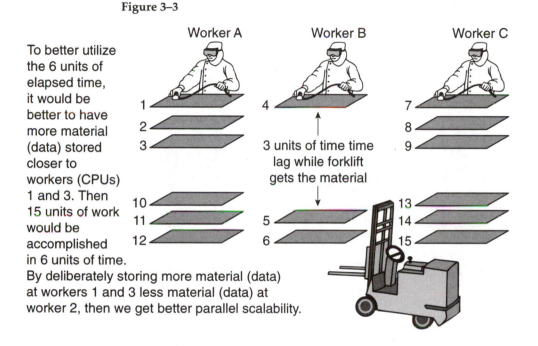

To better utilize the 6 units of elapsed time, it would be better to have more material (data) stored closer to workers (CPUs) 1 and 3. Then 15 units of work would be accomplished in 6 units of time.

By deliberately storing more material (data) at workers 1 and 3 less material (data) at worker 2, then we get better parallel scalability.

Uniform Distribution Prevents Data Skew

Although non-uniform material allocation gives better productivity despite the variable material access times, totally uniform material allocation and access times increase productivity further.

This metaphor of uniform material distribution and uniform worker access times to material is replayed identically in actual parallel query execution, where query data substitutes for the material and CPUs substitute for the workers. But first let's look at the relative differences between local and remote access times in computers vs. manufacturing, and let's define the different types of loosely coupled machine architectures available from various hardware vendors.

Figure 3–4

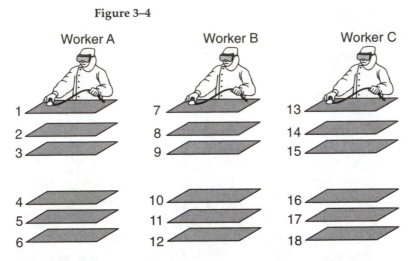

By uniformly distributing material among the workers, 18 units
of work are completed, 3 more than with non-uniform material allocation.

MACHINE ARCHITECTURE TAXONOMY

Access times in the industrial division of labor example are
significant, but those differences are increased by orders of
magnitude in computer systems. This means that getting uniform data access times and uniform data distribution is even
more important for optimal performance in parallel query execution than in the manufacturing division of labor example.

Figure 3–5

Local memory
is hundreds
to 1000's of
times faster than
these containers.

Container: local memory
Local memory access
a few microseconds

Container: Remote memory
100's of microseconds to 1's of milliseconds

Container: Local disk
1's to 10's of milliseconds

Container: Another node's disk
10's to 20's of milliseconds

Let's review some of the parallel machine architecture connection models and assess their ability to deliver uniform data access times.

Symmetric Multiprocessor (SMP)

Figure 3–6 The Symmetric Multiprocessor

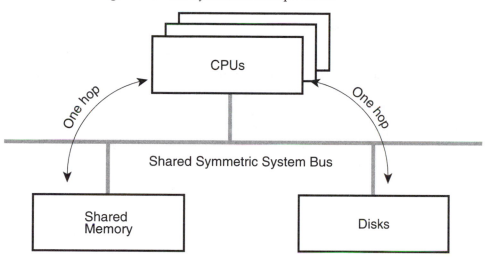

Symmetric multiprocessors, or SMPs, have always had uniform data access times, and this is one of the major reasons why SMPs have led in scalability, whether the workload was online transaction processing or parallel query decision support. Classical SMPs are characterized by a direct connection model where all components are equidistant and directly connected to one another and variation in data access times is a result of component speed and nothing else. Disks are the slowest of the components, but their slow access times can be mitigated by large memory buffers or optimal data layouts on the disk surfaces, such as striping for online transaction processing (OLTP) or partitioning for parallel full table scans.

A classical SMP is a tightly coupled connection model with all components connected to a single system bus. All inter-component data transfer must occur over this bus, and there are only two ways to make the bus faster: lower the latency through faster clock speeds, or increase bandwidth by widening the unit of data transfer via a wider bus. Most common is a combination of both techniques, resulting in the wide, very short busses of today's fastest SMP computers. These very short busses limit scalability because there is simply not enough room in their several-inches-long length to attach greater quantities of components, like CPUs, memory, or disk controllers.

Loosely Coupled Architectures

By loosely coupling components in a massively parallel fashion, the short bus scalability problem of SMPs would seem to be solved. Large massively parallel machines can have components that span cabinetry that continues for a hundred feet or more. It is unfortunate that, as shown in the division of labor example, the loose coupling can result in machine-architecture-induced data skew, and this data skew can kill scalability for all but the most contrived workloads. Furthermore, the way loosely coupled nodes are connected together, called the connection model, can greatly influence the amount of data skew, determining whether a particular MPP architecture does or does not scale well.

Let's review the possible loosely coupled connection models, starting with the most loosely coupled, least dense connection models, and moving toward the more dense connection models.

The Flat, Daisy-Chained Network of Computers

The least dense connection model is the flat, daisy-chained network of computers. This connection model is ubiquitous in both local and wide-area computer networks. Note that each node is connected to at most two of its neighbors. This means that the connection model has a connection density of two.

Figure 3–7   The Flat, Daisy-chained Network of Computers

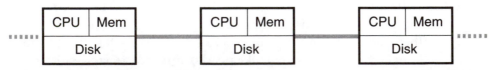

Many would view such a distributed collection of computers as not really massively parallel, but only a loosely related collection of machines that cannot be used to a solve a single problem in parallel. Nevertheless, parallel query software designers have written parallel software for flat connection models, notably Sybase's MPP product and, to some degree, Tandem's Non-stop SQL.

The 2-D Mesh

Probably the most widely implemented mainstream MPP connection model is the 2-dimensional mesh. The connection model looks like a lattice, and it has a connection density of 4, in that each node is attached to at most four of its neighbors, with a possible neighbor to the right, left, up, and down. Examples of such machines include Intel's former SPP machine, the Pyramid RM 1000, the Unisys OPUS, and others.

Figure 3–8 The 2-D Mesh

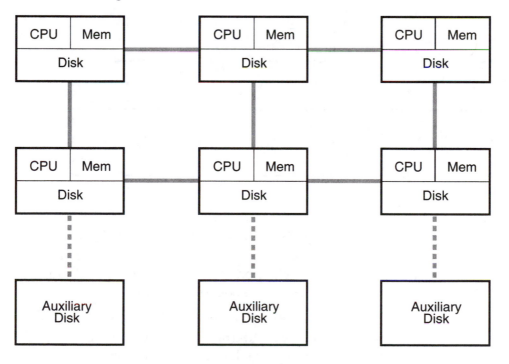

The Toroidal 2-D Mesh

A variation of the 2-D mesh is the 2-D toroidal mesh, which has the optimization of connecting the ends of the mesh so that it becomes possible to send messages from edge-node to edge-node in only one hop. This reduces internode message traffic and reduces the number of hops to get to distant nodes.

Figure 3–9 The 2-D Toroidal Mesh

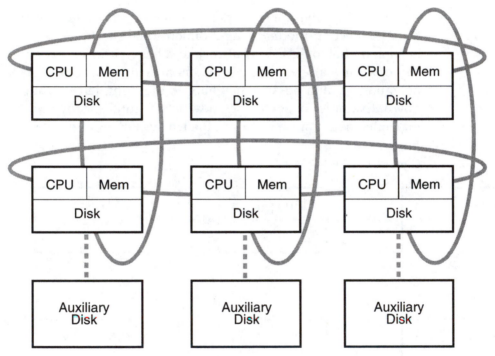

The 3-D Mesh

The next step up in connection density is the 3-D mesh. This mesh is a stack of 2-D meshes, and each node can have up to six possible neighbors, making this type of 3-dimensional lattice a connection model of density 6.

A variation of the 3-D mesh that is not shown here because it is too complex to draw is the toroidal 3-D mesh. In the toroidal 3-D mesh, the edge-nodes are connected in a similar toroidal fashion to the 2-D toroidal mesh, and this connection model has the same benefit of reducing internode

Figure 3–10   The 3-D Mesh

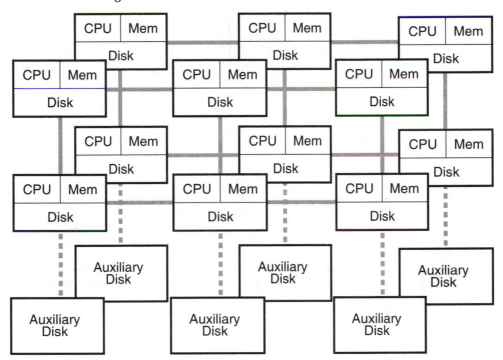

message traffic and message path length when compared to a simple, non-toroidal 3-D mesh.

The Teradata Y-Net

An interesting variation of the 2-D mesh is the old Teradata Y-net, which is a density 3 connection, that is, each node can have at most three neighbors. Unlike the mesh connection models, this is not a lattice-type, but is a tree, specifically a binary tree. Note how trees can be bisected into subtrees that do not interconnect by simply severing one connection; this is very different from any of the mesh lattices, which are more tightly connected. Y-nets are also interesting because they mimic an important database software data structure, the query parse tree, in hardware. Other than the neural network computers, this may be one of the only cases where a hardware machine connection model so closely maps a particular software architecture.

Figure 3–11 The Teradata Y-net

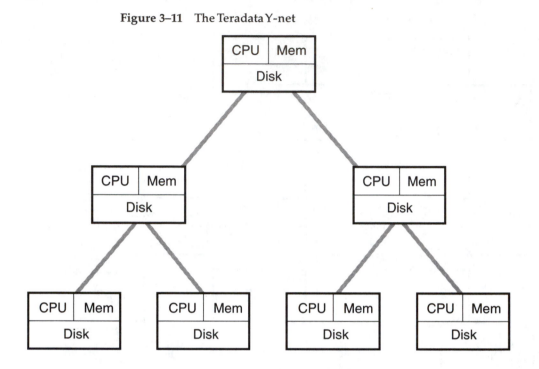

Hypercubes

Hypercubes are loosely coupled computers with varying connection densities. Classic hypercubes come in connection models whose density is a power of 2. For example, a degree 2 hypercube would contain 2^2, or 4, nodes, with each node having two neighbors. The farthest neighbor is no more than two hops away. In the degree 2 hypercube in Figure 3–12, solid dots represent the CPU, memory, and disk of each node.

A degree 3 hypercube would contain as many as 2^3, or 8, nodes, with each node having as many as three neighbors. The farthest neighbor is no more than three hops away.

Figure 3–13 shows a degree 4 hypercube having 2^4, or 16, nodes, each with four neighbors, and no neighbor more than four hops away. Notice the difference between the density 4 connection model of the hypercube and the flatter 4-way connection of a 2-D mesh (Figure 3–9). The hypercube is denser.

Note also that the farthest neighbor in a 2-D mesh is six hops away, two more than the degree 4 hypercube.

Figure 3–12 A Degree-2 Hypercube

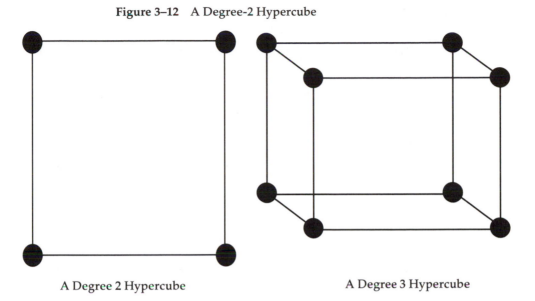

A Degree 2 Hypercube   A Degree 3 Hypercube

Figure 3–13 A Degree 4 Hypercube

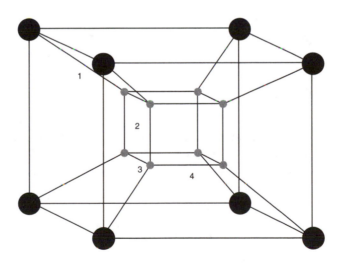

We cannot draw hypercubes of degree 5 or higher, but the formula still holds true. For example, a degree 10 hypercube would contain as many as 2^{10}, or 1,024, nodes, and each node would be no more than ten hops from its farthest neighbor. High-degree hypercubes are a much denser connection scheme than the 2-D and 3-D meshes.

Figure 3–14 2-D Mesh with the Same Number of Nodes as a Degree 4
Hypercube

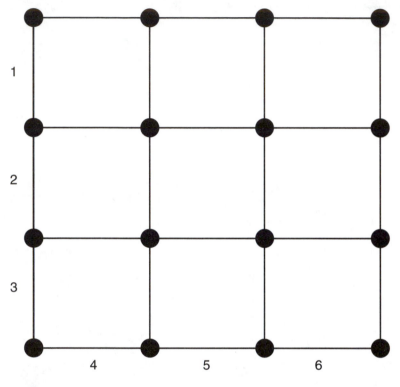

Crossbar Switch

The newest and best loosely coupled connection scheme
is the crossbar switch. Borrowed from telephony, this technology creates a direct, point-to-point connection between every
node, with only one hop through the switch to get from one
node to any other node. Unlike all of the previous connection
models, this one is symmetric, with all nodes connected
directly through the switch to all other nodes (see Figure 3–15).

Architectural Taxonomy Review

Here are the architectures we have discussed in a taxon-
omy of increasing connection density.

1. Flat, daisy-chained network of SMPs
   Example: NCR 3600

2. Y-Net
   Example: NCR/Teradata DBC 1012

Figure 3–15 A 4-Node Crossbar Switch

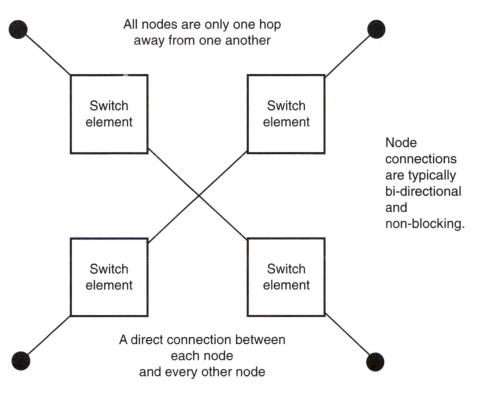

All nodes are only one hop
away from one another

Switch element

Switch element

Switch element

Switch element

Node connections are typically bi-directional and non-blocking.

A direct connection between
each node
and every other node

3. 2-D mesh
   Examples: Intel SPP/Unisys OPUS, SNI/Pyramid RM 1000

4. 3-D mesh

5. Hypercube
   Example: nCUBE

6. Symmetric crossbar switch (loosely coupled)
   Examples: Sequent SDI, Sequent NUMA-Q Clusters, IBM RS 6000 SP (SP-2), NCR WorldMark 5100M Bynet

7. Symmetric multiprocessor (tightly coupled)
   Examples: Sequent Symmetry 5000, SGI Challenge, HPT500, Sun SparcCenter 2000, Pyramid Nile, DEC Alpha 8400 and many others.

Architectures 1–5 are asymmetric connection models, meaning that some nodes are closer and some farther, from perspective of any specific node. Only the densest connection topologies, the tightly coupled symmetric multiprocessor, and the loosely coupled crossbar switch have symmetric connection models. Note that the less dense the connection model, the more asymmetric it becomes. For example, the probability that a node in a 2-D mesh is more than one hop away increases by a third when compared to a 3-D mesh. This is because nodes on a 3-D mesh have six near neighbors (reachable in one hop), while the less dense 2-D meshes have only four near neighbors for any particular node.

The asymmetric connection models of machine Architectures 1–5 cause machine-architecture-induced data skew, which prevents parallel query scalability. In the following section we illustrate this with an example of a parallel query executing on a 2-D mesh.

Parallel queries on Asymmetric Machine Architectures

Query Parse Trees

Even the simplest queries can be adversely affected by data skew caused by asymmetric connection models. Suppose we have the query

SELECT * FROM Table_a ORDER BY Column_2

This simple query can be parsed into the three-node query parse tree containing a parallel full table scan of Table_a that produces rows which are consumed by a parallel sort on column_2, and the resultant key-range sorted runs are concatenation-merged into the result. (See Figure 3–16.)

Executing a Parallel Full Table Scan with a Sort on a 2-D Mesh

A number of algorithms can be used to accomplish a parallel sort. One good method is to do dynamic data partitioning on the key values of each of the various steps of the query. Dynamic data partitioning assures that each step of the parallel query will get uniformly distributed data, ensuring that

Figure 3–16   Query Parse Tree Example

● Concatenation merge of sorted runs into result

● Parallel sort on Column _2 (ORDER BY)

●
Parallel full table scan of Table_a (SELECT*)

parallelism is maintained throughout the query's execution. In this example the full table scanners scan unordered data distributed uniformly over the disk drives and sample the scanned data for the sort key data distribution (Column_2). Based on the sampling, the sort processing is divided into key ranges that have approximately equal numbers of rows to be sorted. This algorithm allows the merge phase to be a simple concatenation of the key-range-sorted runs. Traditional merges of overlapping key-range runs are difficult to parallelize effectively because they naturally partition into a hierarchy, with less parallelism occurring as execution proceeds to the final merge.

Let's assume that this query will be executed with three parallel processes at each parallel phase of the query. Further, let's assume that we have only six processing elements (nodes) in our parallel query machine. That means there will be three full table scan (labeled FTS) processes, reading disks, feeding three sorter (labeled Sort) processes. Further, for the sake of ease of presentation, let's assume the 6-node asymmetric 2-D Mesh connection model shown below, although the following argument would be the same for any other asymmetric connection model. Also, assume the pictured disk configuration in Figure 3–17.

Note that we suffer from machine-induced data skew immediately.

- FTS(1) gets data from Disk(7) in three hops.
- FTS(2) gets data from Disk(9) in one hop.
- FTS(3) gets data from Disk(8) in three hops.

Figure 3–17

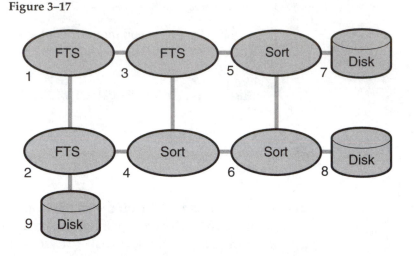

The full table scanner on node 2 (FTS(2)) will finish faster than either of the other scanners because the disk it is scanning is closer to it than with the other nodes.

A Manually Optimized Disk Layout for Parallel Scan Efficiency

Let's change the disk layout to give uniform disk data access times to the scanning processes (Figure 3–18).

Figure 3–18   A Manually Optimimized Disk Layout for Parallel Scan Efficiency

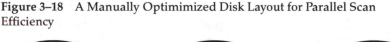

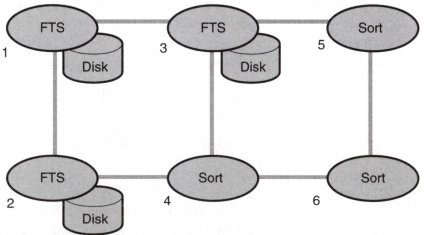

Disks are now local to the scanner process nodes, and we also suppose that the data is evenly distributed between the disks, with the same number of rows on each disk. Only a skilled DBA could accomplish this contrived data layout, but let's proceed with the query and see if this data layout eliminates machine-architecture-induced data skew for subsequent query steps.

In this algorithm, the FTS processes statistically sample the incoming data on sort key column_2 and partition the key range uniformly across the three sort processes. This means that each sort process will have a sub-key range containing approximately the same number of rows to sort. Further, let's suppose that the sampling detects only three key values beginning with A, B, and C, with equal numbers of each. This seems good, but let's look at the sort step more closely.

The Machine Architecture Is Causing the Data Skew

The data on the disks is uniformly distributed across the drives, but has no particular distribution with regard to sort key column_2. For example, there could be 50 names beginning with A on disk 1, 100 As on disk 2, and 10 As on disk 3. The only requirement of this algorithm is that each disk have the same number of rows, not that the sort key distribution of those rows be uniform across those disks. Let's suppose that the statistical partitioning of the sort sends sort key column_2 values beginning with "A" to sort process 5 (Sort(5)). Rows with column_2 value of "A" could come from any of the FTS processes. Sort(5)'s data access to the scanners is skewed as follows:

- Sort(5) receives data from FTS(1) in two hops (there are 50 As here).

- Sort(5) receives data from FTS(2) in three hops (there are 100 As here).

- Sort(5) receives data from FTS(3) in one hop (there are 10 As here).

This means that Sort(5) will consume data from FTS(3) faster than the other scanners, and if the other scanners have the majority of the data, as in this example, Sort(5)'s execution will be skewed by the longer access times to these more remote nodes that contain most of the data required by this sorting node. The situation is similar for the other sorter nodes.

While this example was for a 2-D mesh, the same machine-induced data skew problems occur for all asymmetric architectures, the toroidal 2-D meshes, 3-D meshes, the toroidal 3-D meshes, the hypercubes, the Y-nets, and the flat daisy-chained networks of computers. I hope it is becoming obvious that the only thing these asymmetric machine architectures can do well is full table scans, and even then will require special data layouts.

SMPs: No Machine-Architecture-Induced Data Skew

SMPs don't have machine-architecture-induced-data skew. If we take the previous example and map it to a shared-bus SMP architecture, the result is obviously symmetric (Figure 3–19). All the processes are within one hop of each other, one hop to the shared memory, and one hop to the disk drives. In memory, interprocess data transfer is simple memory references inside shared memory, which has at least 1000 times less latency than a single hop on a loosely coupled architecture.

Figure 3–19

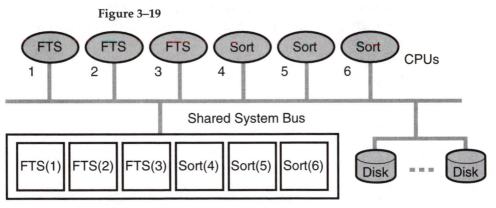

This means that SMPs redistribute data very nearly instantly, since latencies are so low. This very fast movement of data greatly enhances the performance of parallel query algorithms that require dynamic data redistribution, especially when compared to high-latency, loosely coupled machine architectures.

Crossbar Switch Connection Models Eliminate Data Skew

SMPs are great, but how do we get more scalability?

Suppose a query took 100 hours to run single-threaded. Suppose one wanted to reduce the query time to an hour. Then one would need a parallel system that had at least 100 CPUs, assuming perfect linear scalability. There are no 100-CPU SMP machines, and the prospect of such a machine is unlikely because of the short bus problem described earlier.

Loosely coupled architectures are required for this kind of massive parallelism, but as we have seen, the asymmetric connection models (Architectures 1–5) make them pointless for parallel query execution. Is there a better connection model for loosely coupled architectures, one that would prevent machine-architecture-induced data skew? The answer is the crossbar switch, the only symmetrically connected, loosely coupled machine architecture (see Figure 3–20).

Figure 3–20

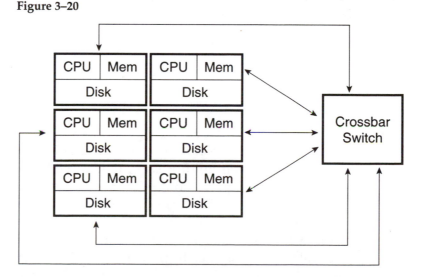

All nodes are directly connected to all other nodes via a crossbar switch. There is only one hop to and from any destination. The connection scheme can be made to be non-blocking with a sufficiently large switch, guaranteeing uniform data access times. An example of such a machine is the IBM RS6000 SP, also known as the SP-2. With the right software, database administration, and system management techniques, this type of machine architecture can scale.

Refinements to the Crossbar Switch Architecture

A refinement to the crossbar switch is to share the disk drives using the switch, thus combining the virtues of shared nothing and clustered architectures in one architecture. Databases can be more easily managed as a single shared entity, and shared disks can also be used to accomplish higher availability. Data access times are still uniform, as can be seen in Figure 3–21.

Figure 3–21

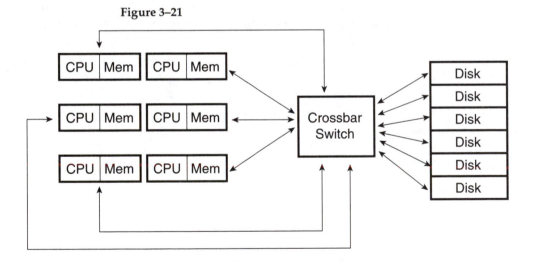

A final refinement of the crossbar switch design is to make the loosely coupled nodes symmetric multiprocessors, rather than small uniprocessor nodes (See Figure 3–22). The larger nodes require more point-to-point switch bandwidth, but operationally there can be fewer of them, since there are more CPUs in each node, and this is easier to manage at both the system and database levels. Intra-SMP parallel operations are also very fast, and the probability that an operation will be intra-node with a few SMP nodes is much higher than with hundreds of small uniprocessors.

Figure 3–22

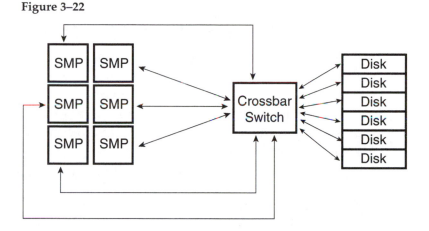

While some systems, such as NCR's Worldmark 5100 series and IBM's RS600 SP, support SMP nodes connected by a logical crossbar, only Sequent's Scalable Data Interconnect (SDI) clusters also support shared disks at this time and are thus topologically equivalent to this most optimal crossbar switch architecture.

FUNCTION SHIPPING, AN ALTERNATIVE TO DYNAMIC DATA REDISTRIBUTION

What Is Function Shipping?

The technique of moving data between nodes for uniform data distribution and the resultant maximum-degree parallel execution is called "dynamic data redistribution." While this technique is effective for enabling parallel query scalability on both SMPs and loosely coupled crossbars, it can consume vast amounts of connectivity bandwidth and be slowed by the latency of the connection. To avoid data redistribution, some software vendors, notably Informix and DB 2 Parallel Edition, offer parallel query solutions that can ship query operators to the data rather than data to the operators. This is called "function shipping." Function shipping is always a good idea if it does not reduce parallelism. Function shipping's benefit is proportional to the statistical probability that queries will not serialize with this technique.

Function Shipping and Serialization of Parallel Queries

As an example, suppose we have the telephone book in a database table with the names and telephone numbers stored in the name key ranges shown below. Further, suppose we execute the following query to produce a sorted list of names, similar to the same query we might execute to produce the actual telephone book:

SELECT * FROM TelephoneBook ORDER BY Name

On a 6-node 2-D mesh, the TelephoneBook table is distributed over key-range-partitioned disk storage shown in Figure 3–23. The query itself decomposes into three key-range partition scanners (PS) and three sorters (Sort) that consume the identical key ranges of the scanners. Note that this query algorithm and the data layout in key ranges are quite different from the dynamic data distribution example in this chapter, despite the fact that both strive to solve a similar problem.

Figure 3–23

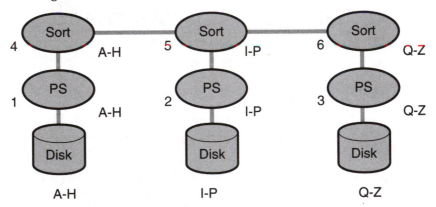

Since both the scanners and the sorters have the same key distribution, we can instead ship the sort functions to the scanning nodes, eliminating the overhead necessary to ship data to the sort nodes. This may improve performance if the bandwidth and latency required to ship the data from scanner nodes to sort nodes were a bottleneck. Notice that function shipping has caused half the machine to become unused, which further reduces potential query scalability.

Figure 3–24

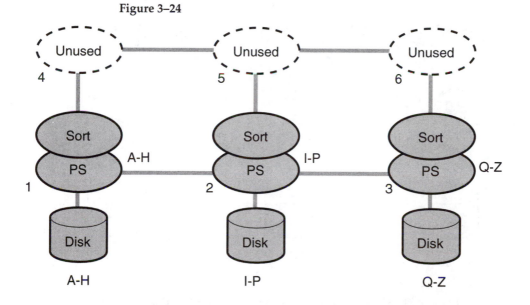

Each time a step of a parallel query executes, the next step consumes the results. It is hoped that the parallelism of the producer step is equivalent to the consumer step. The results of the prior producer step have a data distribution that may be uniform with respect to the next consumer step (ideal case shown in Figure 3–24), or the data of the consumer may be skewed on one or more nodes. If the data are skewed, it may seem optimal to ship the next step's function to the nodes that have the data and allow the query to complete there, rather than redistribute data among the nodes.

What if the data volume to be processed by the next operation (the consumer) is high and the data are sitting on only one or only a few of the available nodes? In that case, function shipping would cause the query to serialize its execution on a single node or a few nodes. (See Figure 3–25.)

Suppose we only want to sort the first key range of the telephone book, namely A–H. In that case, function shipping would cause all activity to occur on node 1, serializing the execution of the query.

Figure 3–25

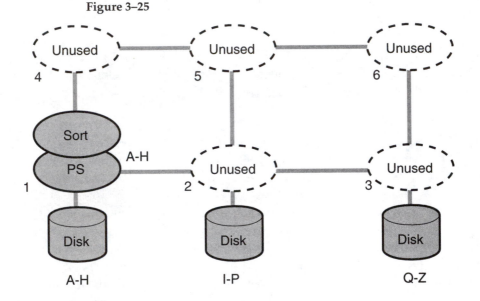

Dynamic Data Redistribution Is Statistically Required for Parallelism

Depending on the volume of data and its distribution, it may be more optimal to redistribute the data dynamically from the producer node to multiple consumers, rather than function ship, as shown in Figure 3–26.

If scanned data are redistributed to the other nodes by Dynamic RePartitioning Scanners (DRPS), then scanning and sorting can be done in parallel and possibly accomplished faster. In Figure 3–26, nodes 1, 2, and 3 share the disk drives that contain the A–H partition, making each DRPS scanner equidistant from the data. A true shared-nothing mesh would not have this disk connectivity model, but we show it as an example of what can be done.

Figure 3–26

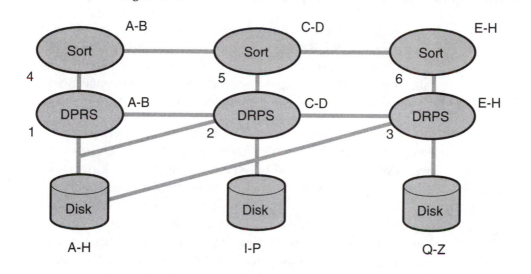

Function shipping works well where the parallel query producer processes have the same key data distribution as the parallel consumers, and the data is co-located on the same node, and the producer step is no more selective than the consumer step.

It is unfortunate that the statistical probability that a given DSS workload have the above producer/consumer data distribution is probably less than 1 percent. Some queries will be able to take advantage of function shipping some of the time, but there will always be a strong statistical probability that data redistribution will be required to sustain maximum parallelism.

The relative benefit of function shipping vs. data redistribution is related to the cost of moving data between nodes (the bandwidth between nodes and the latency) and the amount of data to be moved vs. processing the data upon the nodes on which it already resides.

If function shipping causes serial execution, then it is advantageous only on data sets that are very small. If the data set is large, and the internode bandwidth can overcome the serialization of function shipping, it is always better to redistribute data to prevent serialization.

Optimal Architectures for Dynamic Data Redistribution

In general, data redistribution is optimized by a symmetric connection model. The lowest-cost data redistribution architecture is the tightly coupled SMP. The cost of redistributing data in an SMP is usually a shared memory reference or, at worst, a memory copy, only microseconds at most.

The next-lowest-cost data redistribution machine architecture is the loosely coupled crossbar switch, which has uniform data access times between all nodes, making data redistribution as swift and uniform as possible between producers and consumers on different nodes. This is why crossbar switch architectures are used as the machine of choice, even by those database engines that have function shipping capability. Function shipping isn't bad; it should be used when appropriate. But it is simply no substitute for data redistribution, and this makes symmetric machine connection models even more necessary.

CONCLUSION

This chapter has presented a metaphor, based on human division of industrial labor, to show that uniform data distribution delivers the best parallel throughput. A review of the common machine architecture connection models has shown that the symmetric connection models are a necessary precondition for parallel query scalability, whether loosely or tightly coupled. The only scalable loosely coupled symmetric connection model, the crossbar switch, was identified. We have refined this architecture into a machine that has a few large SMP nodes and a single shared disk pool, and have shown that this is the most optimal loosely coupled design for parallel query execution. Finally, the essay has shown how function shipping can cause serialization of parallel queries, and the importance of data redistribution in maintaining parallelism.

Building High Data Quality Into Your Data Warehouse

George Burch

Vality Technology

THE DATA QUALITY PROBLEM AND ITS IMPORTANCE

Many IT organizations dramatically overestimate the quality of their data within aging operational systems. Similarly, they underrate the difficulty of transforming this legacy data into useful information that can effectively fuel their data warehouses, customer information systems, and client/server applications such as SAP R3. In moving legacy data to their new targets, data warehouse builders too often look only at superficial data definitions and fail to see serious legacy data contaminants lurking below field-description labels.

How will organizations ensure the credibility of their new information warehouses when the data that must feed these systems suffers from years of legacy evolution, disparate formats, "creative" data-entry practices, and spelling and keying anomalies? How will they build complex business relationships from legacy and external sources when the attributes that define business entities—customers, suppliers, products, and so on—are buried within free-form fields and hidden across multiple systems and millions of records?

Unless organizations investigate each and every instance at the data value level and then reengineer and consolidate the data prior to migration, they will naively flood their new databases with erroneous, inaccessible, and improperly integrated information. As a result, companies will be unable to attain an accurate, consolidated picture of their business entities across departments and business lines.

The challenge for each organization is to build complex business relationships from "pieces and parts" spread across disparate legacy sources (a) without the benefit of common keys to join related entities, and (b) with attributes that collectively define business entities lost within a murky sea of legacy data.

This essay will describe a four-phase methodology and the data-reengineering technology needed to transform legacy data into useful, accurate, integrated information. To attain the highest possible levels of data integrity within information systems critical to a business, we must first define "quality data."

High data quality enables an organization to improve decision-making and data-mining analysis, perform cross-product and cross-department marketing, enhance customer support and customer retention, develop streamlined corporate-wide purchasing strategies, and avoid the embarrassment and cost of blunders caused by bad data. For example, inaccurate data cause a bank to misspell customers' names, send foreclosure notices to customers with impeccable credit histories, and assess loan portfolios incorrectly.

A new information system will fail without investigation, standardization, and consolidation of data from disparate sources prior to migration, industry analysts warn. It is unfortunate that algorithmic, rule-based languages and data scrubbers are poorly suited for turning legacy data into useful information. These methods rely on rule-based dictionaries and look-up tables to find matches and to clean names and addresses. Yet programmers cannot possibly anticipate all conceivable variants in anomalies, line locations, data formats, and content. They cannot write rules for what they cannot see.

The traditional programming approach is to apply logic before looking at the data. This method might quickly bring data-quality levels to, say, 80 percent to 85 percent, but will be unable to raise quality beyond that, producing large exception reports that must be handled manually.

High data quality brings benefits to both business sponsors of essential information systems and to IT operations chartered to utilize data as a strategic asset. To show the greatest cost benefit of high data quality, we will examine four value propositions.

1. Data Quality Assures Previously Unavailable Competitive Advantage and Strategic Capability

- **Improved accuracy, timeliness, and confidence in decision making**

Simply stated, all the advantages of a data warehouse, decision-support system, and data-mining application could not be realized without high data quality. Attaining entity integrity is the only means for organizations to "see" across the corporate landscape. Through entity integrity, organizations can ensure the accuracy of complex business relationships built from the "pieces and parts" spread across their data. Entity integrity transforms imperfect and previously unaddressable (and, therefore, inaccessible) data into a consolidated view of customers, providers, products, and other business entities.

Through an unprecedented understanding of the business, entity integrity enhances data-mining results and decision-support capabilities. It ensures accurate responses to user queries and enables fast, accurate reporting across departments and business lines and lets users drill down and aggregate up to any level of detail. Gone are error-prone reports that were once manually compiled by "cutting and pasting" information from multiple disparate systems. And through consolidated views, entity integrity allows an organi-

zation to identify the multiple roles of its business partners. (For example, a manager may see that a customer who is late on his payments is also a key supplier.)

- **Improved customer service and retention**

    By painting a landscape view of a customer's complete portfolio of products and relationships, entity integrity enables an organization to enhance customer service. Service representatives no longer have to log onto multiple account-oriented systems to obtain information on a customer or prospect. They are better equipped to satisfy customer requests in less time. Better customer service translates into better customer retention.

    At a major New York bank, a service specialist talking on the phone with a client noticed he had only $35 in his savings/checking account. Before entity integrity, the service specialist would have been unaware that this same individual has $300,000 in mutual funds and is president of a large commercial depositor at the bank.

- **Unprecedented sales and marketing opportunities**

    By building consolidated views of business entities, entity integrity enables, for the first time, cross-product and cross-department selling, and identifies members of the same household for highly targeted marketing initiatives.

- **Support for business reengineering initiatives**

    Entity integrity supports business reorganizations by enabling an organization to restructure systems physically in support of a more efficient organizational alignment. It accomplishes this by transforming data within "fractured," department-oriented legacy systems into an accurate and streamlined view of the business.

2. High Data Quality Improves Productivity

- **Enables smart corporate-wide purchasing strategies**

    By attaining a global view of purchasing practices across departments, entity integrity reduces purchasing expenditures by allowing an organization to evaluate purchasing trends and needs; and to develop buying strategies that utilize economies of scale and timely purchasing.

- **Streamlines work processes**

Worker productivity and business-process efficiency are increased by entity integrity's transforming "fractured" data collection into a smooth work flow.

Mid-level managers at a major phone company once had to compile reports by pulling data into spreadsheets from multiple systems. The systems stored data on the same business entities in different formats and anomalies, which were difficult to consolidate. In addition to time wasted, reports were of highly questionable accuracy. Now high data quality delivers standard formats as well as unique entity identifiers for all customers, providers, products, etc., within a single information system, which dramatically enhances reporting procedures.

3. High Data Quality Reduces Costs

- **Reduces physical inventory by identifying anomalies and redundancies within manufacturing parts, pharmaceutical prescription drugs, and so on.**

BASF Corporation reduced its inventory by 27 percent after it uncovered anomalies for the same chemical compounds.

- **Simplifies database management and reduces storage requirements for information systems**

By establishing entity integrity, manufacturer J.M. Huber Corporation has realized a 36 percent reduction in the number of customer records and a 37 percent reduction in the number of customer address records, including bill-to and ship-to locations. J.M. Huber's centralized information system feeds operational systems for all five of its business units.

- **Reduces mailing and production costs**

Commercial Union estimates it saves $203,000 annually in postage alone.

Data quality after using a conventional data scrubber	93.1 percent
Data quality after applying data reengineering	98.8 percent
Quality improvement	5.7 percent

Data quality in this instance was the ability to locate and eliminate duplicate records of customers once hidden behind anomalies and multiple account numbers for the same entity. A 5.7 percent improvement was realized by eliminating 53,000 duplicate records. Assuming $.32 postage to mail a statement, Commercial Union estimates it saves $16,960 per mailing in postage, a yearly savings of $203,520 assuming monthly mailings. A sizable savings will also be achieved from reduced production and materials costs.

- **Reduces clerical staff**

Attaining high data quality dramatically reduces the clerical staff needed to review exception reports manually.

- **Spares costly redesigns of data models**

High data quality provides integrity not only in data values but in metadata as well. High data quality brings to the surface critical information once buried in legacy data, information that is essential for building and validating an accurate data model. Newly surfaced information—unavailable from existing meta sources—spares costly redesigns by discovering physical planning information and unforeseen, undocumented business practices up front.

4. The Absence of High Data Quality Precludes Effective Use of New Systems

Enterprise information systems being built today depend on data extracted from multiple, aging legacy systems. Mapping legacy records directly into new deliverables will subject critical information systems to data contaminants that destroy the value and integrity of the data. Millions of legacy records—lacking domain and entity integrity—will impair corporate decision making and cause loss of marketing opportunities, customers, and money. Industry examples are numerous.

- A data error within a bank allowed 300 credit-worthy customers to receive mortgage default notices. When one of the borrowers told a bank collector that his mortgage had already been paid, the disbelieving collector said impatiently: "I've been hearing that all week."

- A marketing organization sent multiple direct-response pieces to the same individual (through the failure to attain entity integrity). A 6 percent redundancy in each mailing cost the company hundreds of thousands of dollars over the course of a year.

- A managed-care agency could not relate prescription drug usage with patients and prescribing doctors. The agency's on-line analytical processing application (i.e., data mining) failed to locate trends or circumstances that would have significantly improved efficiency and inventory and opened new selling opportunities.

- The lack of a customer information system with a consolidated view wastes thousands of hours of time when managers must painstakingly compile reports by pulling data from disparate sources. The dubious accuracy of these reports allows top management to make faulty and costly decisions.

- A music producer could not pay royalties to deserving artists because songs distributed internationally lost their unique identifier through song-title translation and the foreign country's own numbering scheme.

- A manufacturer had one division that bought from and sold to ten different locations of another division within the same company. Each location had a different customer number to represent that division, and each used completely different vendor numbers. A study performed prior to the acquisition of Integrity, a data cleansing program, indicated that these and other inefficiencies were costing the company several hundred thousand dollars annually.

5. High Data Quality Avoids the Compounding Effect of Data Contamination

The difference in data accuracy from, say, 95 percent to 98 percent may be significant, due to the compounded effect of data contamination. Since data anomalies, by nature, tend to cluster around the biggest customers, even a small percentage of legacy data contamination compounds to invalidate information. By Pareto's law, 80 percent of queries will access data relating to 20 percent of a company's customers—exactly where the data contaminants reside. Without high data quality, new information systems produce erroneous responses to queries about a company's largest, most important customers.

WHAT IS HIGH QUALITY DATA?

The definition of data quality depends on how the data are to be used. Despite alleged deficiencies, data that reside today in legacy environments may work fine for running operations: invoices go out, employees and suppliers get paid. In defense of database administrators, operational data was never structured to power enterprise information engines. Only when data migrate to a warehouse environment from disparate operational systems do contaminants surface to infect target databases. For example, two operational systems use different data structures. The data values within those structures could be in perfect compliance. Yet merging internal and external data sources creates format discrepancies and introduces duplicate business entities lacking common keys (through anomalies and multiple account numbers for the same customer, supplier, etc.).

A field within an operational system might contain multiple entities, attributes and relationship identifiers (e.g., DBA, c/o, custodian for) that stretch well beyond the metadata field description of "Name." For example, the values "Donald J McCarthy Revocable Trust U/A DTD 3/3/89 Donald McCarthy & John McCarthy Trustees 237 Pembroke" violate a business rule by containing more information than just the name, values "Donald J McCarthy." Nevertheless, this violation will not preclude Don from receiving his monthly statement.

Only when the business opts to build a consolidated customer statement, showing all accounts held by an individual, do data problems arise. Now that same individual may be entered under many different account numbers on many different systems, each with a different spelling variation: Donald McCarthy, DJ McCarthy, Don MacCarthy. How will the business locate and physically or logically consolidate each instance of the individual to build a consolidated view?

Unlike operational applications, decision support/data warehouse/data mining systems require a high level of "purity" within the data. Some of the most important characteristics of good data include the following:

1. The data must have **addressability**. For example, a legacy field containing DR LAWRENCE E MATHEWS, III, BENEFICIARY FOR CINDY H. MATHEWS must be parsed into separate "elements" to provide the system with access to a first name, middle initial, last name, prefix identifier, relationship identifier, etc. First, addressability to each element will enable an effective mapping to relational tables. Second, addressability will simplify, if not enable, standardization of information from multiple sources. Third, individual elements serve as attributes needed to match related entities in the absence of common keys.

2. The data must have **domain integrity**. In other words, data values must fall with defined ranges. For example, a medical record reporting that Ralph Dunne had a hysterectomy lacks domain integrity.

3. The data must be **accurate**. The license plate VFZ-402 may have domain integrity, but it may be the wrong license plate for a particular car.

4. The data must be properly integrated to attain **entity integrity**. Only one unique set of attributes can exist to identify a business entity, such as a customer or product. If 27 different values exist within your data for the supplier Randall-Myers Chemical Company and you are able to identify only 26 of those 27 instances, entity integrity does not exist. Queries seeking total business with that supplier will be wrong.

5. The data must **adhere to business rules**. Vality Technology once performed a data investigation of a phone field for a large phone company, revealing nearly 100 different "patterns" of phone numbers when only one pattern was acceptable—555-555-5555. Under another data investigation, Vality uncovered thousands of individuals with the same social security number. The data-entry clerk, in order to comply with a business rule, filled in her own social security number when she lacked a number for an individual. A low-level data investigation is the only means to check for business-rule compliance.

6. The data must **satisfy business needs**. A low-level data investigation of existing values in operational systems may reveal obscure and undocumented business practices, data types, and other metadata needed to build and validate an effective data model that accurately and adequately reflects the way a company does business. For example, a data investigation might uncover credit information hidden in a name or comment field, suggesting that the data modeler design a system that can more appropriately capture the information.

7. The data must have **integrity**. The data cannot be accidentally destroyed or altered. Updates cannot be lost due to conflicts among concurrent users. Much of the responsibility for data integrity falls on the DBMS. Robust update, backup, and recovery procedures are needed.

8. The data must be **consistent**. Standardized codes, formats, abbreviations, and so on simplify data integration and facilitate the use of data across systems, departments, business lines, and business partners.

9. Data **redundancy** must be <u>intentional</u>. In most data warehouse implementations, data are at least partially redundant with operational data. For certain performance reasons, and in some distributed environments, an organization may correctly choose to maintain data in more than one place and in more than one form.

10. The data must be **complete**. For example, all dependents and dependent birth dates should be listed on customer records within a householding application.

11. The data must have correct **cardinality**. Complex relationships between entities must correctly define one-to-one, one-to-many, and many-to-one links. For example, "one" owner exists for "one" financial account, but "many" participants exist on one account—owners, trustees, custodians, beneficiaries, etc.

DATA REENGINEERING: A FOUR-PHASE PROCESS TO ATTAIN HIGH DATA QUALITY

A more effective approach must make no assumptions about what might lie in your data. The required methodology must infer instructions on how to process each record from the record itself. In place of the traditional logic-first approach, data reengineering uses a data-first approach, relying not on rule-based programming and look-up tables, but on parsing, lexical analysis, pattern investigation, and data typing. While look-up tables might be used to supplement this technique, a low-level data investigation is the only means to attain quality levels above those reachable by conventional data scrubbers.

Data reengineering provides a four-step process to transform data effectively from any number of legacy files and external sources. Unlike conventional data-cleaning methods, data reengineering offers the flexibility to adapt to an organization's unique data requirements and business rules, which vary not only from industry to industry but from business to business within an industry. These steps are *Data investigation, Data standardization, Data integration,* and *Data survivorship and formatting.*

Data Investigation

The data investigation phase gives IT organizations a sound understanding of their information. It provides 100 percent visibility into the state of their data, revealing data values that stray from their metadata field descriptions and exposing

Figure 4–1 A Four-Phase Data-reengineering Process transforms legacy data, saddled by account orientations, into consolidated business views across departments, product lines, and business units.

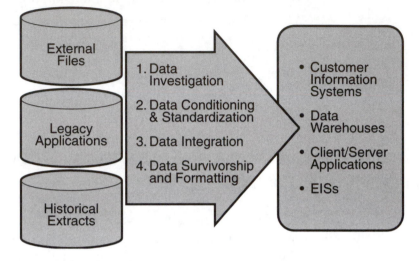

"creative" data-entry clerks who find clever ways to circumvent business rules. Results of this data audit help IT staff avoid costly time delays by identifying and correcting data problems *before* they have an opportunity to corrupt the new system. The data investigation lets IT groups plan for what would otherwise be unexpected data values and exceptions.

The steps involved in the data investigation are:

- **Parsing**—decomposing multi-valued fields into individual pieces.

- **Lexical analysis**—determining the "meaning" and business significance of individual pieces.

- **Pattern investigation**—developing maps of field content and structure that provide 100 percent visibility into the state of your data.

- **Data typing**—assigning a user-defined data type for each and every element within each field of every record. (Strong data typing will be a prominent feature of SQL3. For example, an address field once defined as "street" might now contain individual table slots for number, street name, suffix, directional, etc.)

An advantage of the data investigative approach over conventional pre-built data scrubbers is flexibility to evaluate all the data. Conventional data-cleaning applications have restricted parsing and look-up tables to work on only well-understood field types such as personal names and domestic addresses. Through pattern processing, any field type from product codes to phone numbers, code numbers, part descriptions, textual comments, and foreign-address formats can be examined.

Through lexical analysis and pattern processing, the investigation phase actually completes the bulk of the re-engineering effort. In the process of conducting the analysis, you physically manipulate the data—selecting, "patternizing," parsing, "typing," and arranging the information for formatting.

Beyond data fix-up, a data investigation will uncover essential business information needed to plan and validate the data model. This business metadata—such as obscure and undocumented business practices, unusual data types, and physical planning information—is missing from existing meta sources such as data dictionaries, copybooks, and meta movement products. For its ability to mine important metadata needed to accurately model how one does business, data reengineering must be applied at the very outset of the data warehouse project.

Data Standardization

Understanding one's data dramatically simplifies the effort of **standardizing and conditioning** information extracted from multiple operational systems. Once all data patterns and "permutations" are charted, conversion routines can transform the information to the desired standard (for example, converting "Mass." to "MA" and "c/o" to "care of").

Data Integration

Once data have been "typed" and standardized, the **integration** phase identifies and consolidates related records lacking common keys through statistical matching techniques. Matching builds complex relationships from data buried in legacy files. In the absence of common keys, each record's data types can serve as "surrogate" keys for matching. Through rapid analysis of user-defined match sets, related customers, suppliers, locations, and products once hidden across multiple systems and external files can be located.

Effective statistical matching techniques ideally should provide these features:

- Flexible construction of search keys to optimize machine resources.

- Flexible definition of match fields to increase data points for statistical analysis.

- Variable weights and penalties for each data point to take into account an organization's business rules and produce scores relative to probability (such as "register a high score if street address matches exactly").

Benefits of statistical matching include:

- matching for an organization's own data and business rules,

- matching with statistical certainty, and

- attaining critical entity integrity.

Data Survivorship and Formatting

Data survivorship assures that the best data available survive for loading into the target source. Users should be able to assign any number of parameters to determine survivorship, such as date of information, source of information, and format. For example, survivorship based on format might vote between three addresses found for a given customer (Two Heartswell Lane, Two Hartswell Lane, and Two Hartswill Lane), opting to send the most prevalent spelling format forward.

But what if users resist having the data changed to some "central" standard? Through foreign keys, synonym tables, and cross-record linkages, IT organizations can preserve the original legacy values, yet still produce accurate answers to queries that require a consolidated view. Users may not under-stand that in a relational system, you can relate many records to represent complex relationships without destroying, elimi-nating, or changing any of the original data values. You do not need to "dedupe," or standardize, "DEC," "Digital," and "Digitl (sic) Equipment" into one surviving record. You can give users an accurate consolidated view simply by linking the records after their relationships have been determined.

Data reengineering completely decomposes and rebuilds free-form legacy data into clean tables (or other output) defined by an organization. It complements the data-extract process by feeding data movement tools clean, consolidated, accurate information.

There are some instances when data reengineering can-not solve data-quality problems. For example, values may be missing within a social security field, or a gender field may contain nonsense information. Nevertheless, data reengineer-ing can pinpoint missing and "noisy" values and tag records for manual, human intervention.

Improving Data Quality: A Management Perspective and Model

Dennis Berg and Christopher Heagele

American Management Systems, Inc.

INTRODUCTION AND CONTEXT

The dissemination of data, and its use in making business decisions, will likely increase dramatically with its migration to a data warehouse. For many organizations, data quality is a concern that exists in the background as more pressing matters take priority. Yet the introduction of a data warehouse makes more data readily available to more individuals, with the result that data plays a more prominent role in key business decisions. Consequently, the introduction of a data warehouse will likely increase the priority of data quality as the risk and cost of inadequate quality become more visible and more real.

As the saying goes, "garbage in, garbage out." Is all our data "garbage"? Hardly. Yet, enough of our data may be dirty such that, when combined with otherwise clean data, the collection of data as a whole is tainted and perhaps highly suspect. The garbage analogy is apt due to several important similarities to poor data quality. Both can accumulate at a very rapid rate. Cleanup of both is messy and distasteful. And institutionalizing the activities, or "practices," to prevent further accumulation requires substantial behavioral changes. Of course, the result of creating a clean environment can be rewarding and profitable. From the data warehouse perspective, if any significant portion of the data contained in a warehouse is viewed as garbage, the warehouse will fall far short of expectations and may not survive. To data warehouse users, their perception of data quality represents their reality and will influence their support more than specific data quality measurements.

This chapter focuses on how to deal effectively with the messiness of managing data quality improvement. Data quality has been compared to "that crazy relative who is locked up in the basement. We all know who is there, and one day we need to deal with this problem. But nobody dares get very close to it, and we try not to talk about it much." Sound familiar? Much of the messiness results from resistance to dealing with the root causes of the problem—some institutional, and some at the individual, or personal, level.

Our intent is to shed light on the challenges of improving data quality, and to provide a framework for addressing them. We take a managerial rather than a technical view. A growing body of literature covers how to manage data as a resource, and techniques and tools for doing so have come a long way. With regard to data quality, effective labor-saving tools emerged over the past several years for measuring data quality, detecting likely erroneous or "dirty" data, and for cleaning up dirty data by automating the tedious task of determining the correct value for suspect data. Yet many of the management issues do not appear to be widely recognized and planned for by those undertaking to improve data quality.

The two key challenges are how to gain a sufficiently high level of support and interest to start effective data quality improvement efforts and how to sustain that interest and support over time. These challenges exist at senior management levels as well as at middle management and lower levels. Surmounting these challenges seems to us more immediate and important than the more technical issues concerning the selection of improvement techniques and supporting toolsets. Failure to resolve the management challenges will make data quality improvement efforts difficult to focus and will make it hard to sustain the interest and energy levels needed to continue them. We believe resolution can be accomplished best by understanding and concentrating on the following topics.

- The inherent resistance to data quality improvement

- Recognizing the true importance and value of data quality to an organization

- A framework to organize and focus data quality improvement efforts

- Data quality improvement lessons learned by other organizations

Some of what we have to say about these topics will seem new, while other points have been made many times and may appear to be simple common sense. So keep in mind that knowledge and common sense have impact only if they are translated into concrete, repeated practices.

Reasons for the Resistance to Data Quality Improvement

Many organizations show little enthusiasm for data quality improvement, compared to other initiatives. Relatively few individuals in any organization are willing to invest their time and energy to assume the leadership of data quality improvement efforts. Few managers actively seek to have data quality added to their official responsibilities in an organization. These observations apply both to correcting existing dirty data and to establishing practices to avoid the creation of dirty data. It is fortunate that a decreasing number of organizations continue to view the Information Systems Department as having lead responsibility for data quality. More organizations are recognizing that improving data quality is best accomplished as a business responsibility, assigned to those sectors who possess the knowledge and control the resources involved in generating and collecting business data, and in cleaning up existing data. Despite this shift, many common impediments and disincentives remain. The following problems often hamper efforts to clean up existing dirty data.

- Many organizations who have not invested in automated data quality diagnostic or cleanup tools tend to develop in-house diagnostic reports and tools that have limited capabilities and flexibility. Automated tools help identify suspected dirty data and can suggest the appropriate replacement data values. Manual efforts to examine data and note problems are tedious and laborious. Sustaining the motivation of individuals involved in these efforts is demanding and frustrating.

- Important documentation needed to research and resolve dirty data is difficult to locate and access, and may even be nonexistent.

- The immediate personal satisfaction gained from resolving or correcting dirty data is fairly low for most individuals, few of whom enjoy performing this type of work.

- Many individuals who are asked to pay more attention to data quality have significant other competing responsibilities of a higher priority. Data quality is seldom an explicit prominent responsibility in the job description of those who collect or generate business data.

- The scale of the problem seems insurmountable. Further, identifying and disclosing data quality problems seems as scary as Pandora's box and best left untouched lest careers be damaged.

- Few significant rewards exist for data quality improvement accomplishments, per se. Some organizations have created systems for measuring data quality improvement and providing rewards for notable accomplishments, but the majority have not. Data quality improvement has not been the ticket to higher pay or career advancement.

Establishing new processes for preventing dirty data brings its own set of challenges.

- Changing work processes and procedures can require substantial retraining of many employees and a substantial investment of resources and time. Changing processes that collect data from outside sources (such as customers, suppliers, and other organizational entities within the same company) face similar challenges.

- Changing work procedures to emphasize data quality may require (or may be perceived to require) a diversion of time and resources that could otherwise speed workflow, improve customer service, or provide other more immediately visible, tangible benefits. Of course, improved data quality can contribute to achieving these benefits also.

- Different organizations may have different definitions and work practices for the same data. Gaining consensus across organizational lines on data definitions, required edit checks, how to handle missing data, etc., is extremely challenging when organizations have different perspectives and incentives.

- Quantifying the value of improved data quality is difficult and usually speculative. Few organizations have measured the cost of specific instances of dirty data. As a result, budget requests to improve data quality (on its own merit) meet with skepticism, and have difficulty competing with requests for other activities and projects.

THE IMPORTANCE OF DATA QUALITY TO AN ORGANIZATION

Data quality is important whether it is maintained in a single information system or is retained as well in a warehouse, yet obtaining resources and management attention to improve data quality has proven difficult. What seems to underlie this difficulty is an accurate appreciation for *how* important data quality is to an organization as well as precisely what is meant by the term "data *quality*." We define data quality as a state, or condition, that can be measured. This state represents the ability of data, and information derived by calculation, to meet requirements related to business objectives, and meet them in an efficient manner. We do not advocate viewing data quality in terms of "zero defect" or perfect data. We have observed that attaining very high levels of data quality does indeed have a cost, and can take considerable time when addressing more than several data elements. The costs can grow astronomically when seeking perfection of historical data (the inclusion of which is vital to the success of a warehouse) as well as current data. In today's business climate, few if any organizations can afford to seek perfection. We advocate a balanced, risk-based approach that defines data quality needs and investments in improvements, based on perceived business impacts and risks.

A key element in determining the importance of data quality is the expected usage of the data, and the business risks and opportunities associated with those uses. The importance of data quality will vary for different data, and will vary for different usage of the same data. Full consideration of the expected usage is vital and can be performed best by those who actually use the data or are designing new business processes and practices that will reshape data usage.

The importance of data quality can be assessed by asking the following questions and applying these questions to specific data (i.e., specific data elements or small data sets consisting of several related elements). These questions can apply to the organization as a whole, to a specific division, or to lower-level business entities. It helps to have many people, including senior managers, ask and answer these questions for the same data since the very process of considering these questions helps build data quality awareness and support for data quality improvement.

- What decisions do we make that rely significantly on this data?

- What are the impacts of these decisions in terms of
  lost revenue?
  increased costs?
  delays in responding to changing business conditions?
  regulatory and legal exposure and risk?

relations with customers, suppliers, and other external parties?

public embarrassment and corporate standing?

- What are the opportunities and payoffs to improve our understanding of the marketplace and our competitors?

A balancing question is also important:

- To what extent can we mitigate the impact of a bad decision and afford to invest fewer resources in prevention?

Clearly, to answer all these questions for a large number of data elements or data sets would be a major investment. As we discuss in the next section, it is important to target and limit the scope of the data that serve as the initial focus for data quality. We also advise that most organizations plan to expand this scope gradually over time, reflecting business needs and priorities.

A RECOMMENDED FRAMEWORK FOR GUIDING DATA QUALITY IMPROVEMENT

Many choices and decisions are involved in structuring efforts to improve data quality, including which data to start with and selecting the appropriate standards of data quality. The framework presented here will help to guide organizations in starting data quality improvement initiatives and in refining and tuning them over time. The key elements of this framework are a Data Quality Action Plan (DQAP) and the process used to develop the plan. This highly collaborative process involves a potentially large number of individuals who understand your business and your data in the context of their respective organizational units, objectives, and work processes. The use of trained facilitators to support this process is highly recommended. Although this process could be followed with a few individuals representing only one or two functional areas of your business, the greatest benefits and sustained support result from the broadest-based efforts.

The process consists of twelve steps.

1. **Determine the initial critical business functions to be considered**. Whether focusing on the data to be retained in a warehouse or in a single more narrowly focused system, the number of data elements to be considered needs to be narrowed down to those that are most important from a business perspective. Not all data elements are critical. First identify those business functions that relate to the population to be considered, then designate those functions that are most critical to the business. We strongly suggest the results of this step be formally approved by senior management. (Note that other functions that use the same data will be reintroduced later in the process.)

2. **Identify criteria for selecting critical data elements**. The selected critical functions will likely use a broader scope of data than can be reasonably tackled at one time. In this step, using the selected critical functions as a guide, establish the basis for selecting the most critical data elements (CDEs). These CDEs will be the first specific focus of the data quality improvement efforts. Additional less-critical data may be added to the data quality improvement initiatives in the future once the quality standards for critical data have been attained.

   The basis for selecting CDEs is the identification of specific business conditions for which data that is not accurate, timely, complete, or consistent will harm the business. These conditions might, for example,
   – halt business processing or cause unacceptable delays.
   – result in a substantial misapplication of resources.
   – create a significant legal risk to the business.
   The criteria identified should be specific to the selected business functions and should be approved by senior management. It is important to gain senior management approval at every step because these approvals help build the case, and "stage set" senior management, for the eventual substantial resource request.

3. **Designate the critical data elements.** This step applies the designated business conditions to the previously identified set of data for critical functions. For each data element (or set of related elements), ask whether

any of the business conditions applies. At this stage, the applicability of one or more conditions designates data as critical. Some data not designated critical will be dropped from further consideration in the initial data quality improvement planning. Other data will be critical in the context of one condition only, while other data will be critical for multiple conditions. This information may be used later to pare down the number of data elements under consideration if a large number are found to be dirty. Again, senior management should review and approve the designated CDEs. This activity may also result in some iterative tuning of the business scenarios, and their reapplication to the data being considered, to provide a greater comfort level with the "official" set of CDEs. Note that this tuning is performed to assure that the results best reflect the business, not to tune the results to avoid controversial data and other sensitive areas.

4. **Identify known data quality concerns for the critical data elements, and their causes.** In this step, identify the CDEs which are perceived to have a problem. This determination is made based on the experience of the group of people who regularly use the data. A simple three-tier ranking is useful for this determination. For each data element, ask the following questions, considering the dimensions of accuracy, completeness, timeliness, and consistency.

   – Do you rely on this data consistently without question, and without problems?
   – Do you occasionally question the quality of the data, and find problems upon further examination?
   – Do you generally exercise extreme caution in using this data or consider the data suspect based on a known pattern of problems?

   This is the step that reintroduces other business functions beyond those used to select the initial set of CDEs. Data deficiencies that impact any significant business use should be considered important.

   CDEs that fall into the second or third ranking are considered dirty data. Start with the dirtiest dozen data elements (or data sets) for further work and address others later.

5. **Determine the quality standards to be applied to each critical data element.** For each dirty CDE, this step establishes the quality standard to be met for the dirty quality attribute (i.e., completeness, accuracy, timeliness, consistency). Each standard generally consists of two parts, a definition and a tolerance level. The definition clearly depicts the business conditions that meet the attribute (for example, for timeliness, the data be available to users within one business day of the event that created the data). The tolerance level defines the frequency with which the defined quality condition needs to be met (such as 95% of occurrences within one day, 100% within three business days). Note that standards for attributes perceived to be "clean" are not defined.

6. **Design a measurement method for each standard.** Data quality levels need to be measured to determine starting quality levels and degree of improvement. This step creates the process that will be used to measure attainment of each designated quality standard for each element. Emphasis should be placed on designing measurement methods that provide valid results, yet are relatively simple and inexpensive to perform. Unless a measurement can be fully automated, use sampling-based measurement methods rather than performing 100 percent measurement.

7. **Identify and implement quick-hit data quality improvement initiatives.** The analyses performed in the preceding steps frequently uncover dirty data problems for which the cause and the solution are readily apparent. For these situations, especially if the solution is not controversial or particularly expensive, take immediate remedial action in parallel with the succeeding steps of the process. For example, minor software changes or revisions to a data capture form might prevent a specific problem from recurring.

8. **Implement measurement methods to obtain a data quality baseline.** The previously defined measurement methods are put in place to begin the capturing of objective quality data. These first measurements provide the starting point for determining whether data quality improvement activities are effective. They

also confirm whether perceptions of quality problems for perceived dirty data are indeed real. Repeat measurements over time to track improvements and determine when data quality standards are met.

9. **Assess measurements, data quality concerns, and their causes.** After the initial measurements, confirm specific problems found and determine their causes. These causes may be attributable to random error and mistakes, but more often are attributable to other non-random factors. These include:

   – clarity and understanding of data definitions
   – business forms, procedures, and workflow
   – employee training on job responsibilities and tasks that impact data quality
   – automated processing capacity limitations and delay
   – misdesigned software
   – error correction procedures

   This step is frequently very challenging, requiring careful analysis and selection of the appropriate technique to distinguish problem symptoms from the underlying causes of a recurring symptom.

10. **Plan and implement additional improvement initiatives.** As a natural outcome, plan and implement activities and initiatives to respond to the identified problems and their causes. These activities may be fairly simple in nature, or may require major redesign or rethinking of existing business processes. Participation and active support of the appropriate management levels are very important for this step.

11. **Continue to measure quality levels and tune initiatives.** Effective data quality improvement initiatives will yield clear improvements and also identify opportunities to tune individual improvement activities to increase their effectiveness and efficiency. This step also identifies when further measurement of previously dirty data is no longer needed. Discontinue measurement in those cases where ongoing measurement consumes significant resources and the most recent measurements show a trend of consistently meeting the established quality standards.

12. **Expand process to include additional data elements.** The data quality improvement initiative started on a relatively small, focused scale to ensure early success and build support. In this step, once the initial efforts have been stabilized, the initiative can be expanded to include additional known dirty or questionable data from Step 4. The entire process may also be repeated to focus on the next priority level of business function, those initially considered not critical in Step 1, or on functions that are newly considered critical by senior management.

SOME LESSONS LEARNED

Experience is a great teacher—sometimes painfully so. We share below the most significant lessons we and our clients have learned in establishing data quality improvement initiatives for formal data warehouses and other systems that involved substantial consolidation and sharing of data.

Link data quality improvement to specific business objectives, processes, and results. Funding for data quality on its own merit is a hard sell. Requests for funding of data quality initiatives are best received when structured as integral to another business initiative that it supports and that will have a clear, justifiable payoff.

Utilize senior management to drive improvement initiatives. Given the typical levels of resistance, senior management support must be active and highly visible. The form of active support can vary from organization to organization. What is important is that data quality improvement and its business impact be viewed as a true agenda item of senior management and not simply as an idea that has been sold by middle management with passive senior management support and reluctance to deal with the tough issues.

Balance the long-term vision with achievable short-term objectives. Setting data quality goals and estimating business benefits resulting from their attainment can result in some fairly lofty targets and expectations. While appropriately high goals are desirable as a vision, shorter-term objectives should be both ambitious and reasonably achievable within at most one year. Remember, results are being measured, and retaining credibility is vital to sustaining support and momentum.

Tackle the easiest problems offering the highest payoffs first. Most improvement initiatives identify many opportunities for improvement. To gain early success and expand interest in and support for the program, tackle the high-payoff easy opportunities first.

Coordinate data quality efforts across business functions for the same data. In general, setting data quality standards should reflect the most stringent requirement looking across functions that use the same data. Focusing on only the predominant users and overlooking an important business use of data risks the design of an improvement that will not meet critical need. While in some cases it may not be cost-effective to meet the most stringent need, this need should at least be recognized and considered.

Do not create blanket quality standards. Each data element has different uses and different impacts on your business. Establishing one standard for all data may appear simple to administer but will result in standards that are inappropriately high for some data and too low for other data.

Create plans that are achievable within the likely available resources. Two elements of data quality improvement are measurement of quality levels and the adoption of new practices to improve quality. Both of these activities, especially measurement, can be very expensive. Creating initial improvement plans needs to consider the limitations of staffing and other resources that, as a practical matter, can be allocated within the organization to data quality activities. Additional resources will be more easily obtained after concrete results are demonstrated.

Actively involve business staff at multiple levels. Data users and providers exist at many levels in an organization. Including all levels in data quality improvement planning and execution helps all individuals better understand and appreciate the interdependencies between organizations and individuals.

Use proven methods and tools. Your organization's data quality problems have been resolved successfully in the past, perhaps by a particular unit within your own organization. Start by using proven analysis techniques and automated tools. Until your improvement efforts have built up a strong track record, avoid new leading edge (sometimes called "bleeding edge") techniques and tools.

Bring in and leverage outside expertise. Determining appropriate data quality standards, designing quality measurement systems, and determining the best approach to resolving a particular data quality problem can introduce conflicts and tradeoffs that are new to the organization. Using outside experts to address these and other stressful areas can expedite your efforts, minimize conflicts, and create more quickly an understanding of the complexities of improving data quality and a greater confidence in dealing with them.

Expect traditional business policies and practices to be a major contributing factor to data quality problems. Many of the policies and practices that guide data collection and generation focused on specific business scenarios and data usage that preceded more widespread sharing of data. Expanded data sharing will require a new look at the rules and standards for collecting and generating data to enable support of a broader set of uses.

Provide early orientation and training to those involved in a data quality improvement initiative. Thinking about and discussing data quality in detail will be new for many individuals involved in your data quality improvement efforts. For many this will be very awkward initially, and for some it will be intimidating and threatening. The analysis of data quality problems and their causes may appear to affix blame for problems and mete out punishment, and in some cases jeopardize job security. Early orientation and training will help assure that all participants can bring a healthy perspective to their roles.

Establish a safe environment for the discovery of problems and their causes. Assessing data quality can reveal much that appears to be wrong with an organization in the design of its business practices and in their execution. For many individuals, this is personally threatening and discourages their effective, full participation. In some cases, individuals will attempt to focus the assessment away from known problem areas.

Senior management must provide assurances that data quality improvement is intended as a non-personal focus, and act consistent with this message.

Establish a core team or support group. As data quality improvement activities expand throughout an organization, new individuals will become involved and encounter situations and issues discovered earlier by others. Creating a centralized core team helps leverage the benefits of earlier efforts. At a minimum, the core team can act as a clearinghouse of information within the organization. In a more active role, the core team may consist of individuals who were key contributors to earlier efforts and whose time is made available to consult with and guide the efforts of individuals who are new to data quality improvement.

Establish qualitative and quantitative reporting of program results. Reporting data quality improvement results through quantitative measurement provides an objective measure of progress. However, much of the work performed to improve quality precedes the ongoing measurement of quality and observation of tangible improvements. To help sustain interest and momentum, and communicate progress in the early phases of a data quality improvement initiative, reporting of results to business managers should include qualitatively oriented information such as the creation of new data quality standards and the design and adoption of new business practices that are oriented to improving data quality.

Provide incentives and recognition that go beyond the usual. Data quality can be viewed as a game that offers opportunities for internal competition. Providing acknowledgment to teams that have made significant data quality improvements has proven to be a strong motivator. Effective recognition has included adding an awards ceremony at internal staff meetings, publicizing accomplishments in company and departmental newsletters, and granting cash awards for improvements that contributed significantly to company profitability.

Yes, data quality improvement can be an arduous, messy effort. But when the challenges are anticipated and understood, the effort can be well-focused, successful, and satisfying.

Part
3

USING THE DATA
WAREHOUSE

Chapter 6

Bringing User Perspective to Data Warehouses: Twenty-one Points of Consideration

Katherine Glassey-Edholm

Brio Technology

It is now commonly accepted that we build data warehouses because we want users to make better decisions—we want them to gain insight into their corporate data. In a fundamental sense we want them to do things they've never been able to do before. With that perspective in mind, considering the needs of the end-user only during the selection of data retrieval technologies seems short-sighted. Rather, it is our contention that the user's perspective must be embedded throughout the entire process of building a data warehouse, from design to deployment. This chapter suggests some concepts and principles of bringing the user perspective to data warehousing projects. Its purpose is to suggest some specific ideas that might help data warehouse projects be more successful. The essay is organized into four basic principles, eleven questions, and six lessons.

The experience and anecdotes quoted here are drawn from a number of customers who have been doing data warehousing under a variety of names, some since the early '80s.

In aggregate, this represents fifteen years worth of experience on nearly 100 projects whose objectives were to empower end-users to do their own data access and analysis using dedicated databases.

FOUR PRINCIPLES

Four principles are the starting points of this essay and should be the starting point of any project.

Principle #1: Design the warehouse to fit the philosophy of the organization.

All organizations have IT objectives and philosophies that will be more or less conducive to data warehousing. One of the facts that warehouse evangelists can forget is that the warehouse must fit the "style" of the company that is to use it. Designing a leading edge solution and using new technology on the "bleeding edge" may not be a good fit with a company that is technology risk-averse. Building a system that relies upon end-users doing all of their own report-generation may not go over well in an environment that is not committed to end-user empowerment, or that is culturally bound to fixed-format paper reports.

Before beginning any warehouse project, it is important to know what goal is expected. Be aware that not everyone associated with the project has the same objectives. To further complicate matters, not all achievements will be expressed in revenues or cost savings; some objectives may be expressed as reducing backlog, or improving user motivation, or making better decisions. One project literally was started because there was an extra database server around and some energetic IT staff figured they might as well use it for something. So they threw data into it and said, "Ok, now we have a warehouse." It grew and evolved into a vibrant system. Another project came into being to meet the demands of the CFO who said, "We are an n billion-dollar-a-year technology company, and I'm sick and tired of meetings where three different people have three different numbers, and they are all somewhat right; I want one number." More frequently, IT organizations are stretched to such limits that they are eager to adopt new technology and systems architectures that will enable them to be more responsive and pro-active.

Principle #2: Know your users.

The second important principle is to know your users and their business. The data warehouse project leader is obligated to remember that the system is successful only if it is used. The whole purpose is to allow people to get to data and get to work. If the project leader doesn't know the users—what they want to do and how they think about their business—it is close to impossible to succeed. It is essential that IT professionals on the data warehouse project break the IT knowledge barrier. This means more than reading report requests and writing reports. The first job is to try to understand the nature and context of the business and what the users wonder about.

Principle #3: Pick the right tools.

One of the basic challenges of data warehouse projects is to pick the right products. Now that we are in a client/server environment it seems as though the number of choices to make is becoming exponential, not linear, with the complexity of our systems. Each choice takes time, and we never have enough time to review everything completely. If we did, we would be out of date before the evaluation was complete anyway. So the question is, "Where do you spend the time?"

The database server is crucial—if your server can't handle the demands of your users for at least the next 18 months, you may have trouble.

The next most important decision concerns the tools used by end-users. If there is one mistake commonly made, it is to leave the decision about end-user tools either too late, or to believe that it is essentially unimportant. Too many companies have deployed software to end-users simply because it was free, came bundled with system X, or was recommended by a vendor. Cost *is* usually a factor, and compatibility with other components is essential, but the most important factor in the selection of end-user tools is how well the product meets the needs of YOUR end-users.

Principle #4: Close the loop.

Finally, you must manage the deployment and close the loop. You will not be finished simply because there is some data in the warehouse and you have middleware and connectivity. Think of all you don't know at that point. Who are your users? What do they do? How are they going to use it? How are they going to learn it? How will you monitor what they're doing with it? How can you know if it works? Part of successful deployment of a great data warehouse is for you to create the feedback cycle that will provide the information and the opportunity for you to make your warehouse even better in the future.

Eleven Questions

The following questions should be asked and answered before beginning a warehouse project or in its very early stages.

Question #1. What type of organization do you have?

- What are your organization's data access preferences, and how do you assess them?

- Do you have to control access to data tightly?

- Are your end-users empowered and encouraged to ask questions?

- Is your company generally slow or quick to change?

- Is it possible for you to effect change in existing production systems?

- Are you an early adopter of technology or a late adopter of technology?

The decisions for the warehouse should reflect the answers to these questions. If the company seems prepared to support the paradigm shift that is required to make optimal use of a data warehouse, then dive right in.

Question #2. Who should be on your team?

A warehouse project is not a one-person task; it requires a team effort. The ideal team should have representatives from each of these five categories:

Database designers. Good physical database design is essential because it has more impact on the performance of the system (from the users' perspective) than anything else, even the database server itself. The ideal database designer needs to know more than just Code and Date. You need database designers who understand both business people and analysts—people who can think about the business and present the business of the organization in the data structures of the warehouse. Database designers frequently become metadata managers, so they must be able to communicate in both technical and business terms.

Data archaeologists. The data archaeologists are the people who know the legacy systems inside and out. In many projects, up to 60 percent of the total team effort is spent locating, scrubbing, reconciling, rationalizing, and figuring out what the data means before it reaches the warehouse. You simply can't get the data out of legacy systems unless you have data archaeologists who know what's in the old systems, unless you're willing to invest staggering amounts of time to uncover the past. Leaving those people off your team and assuming that they will answer the questions you need when you ask them is inviting delays and increased costs.

Systems programmers. Transformation programmers are needed to ensure that the data from the legacy systems moves cleanly and repetitively into your warehouse. Even commercial tools need programmers to manage them, so don't skimp on this resource.

Users and trainers. Deployment should be considered from the beginning. As soon as you can, invite on the team the people who are actually going to be the evangelists of the solution into the user community. Invite your training organization as well. If you do, you establish a strong connection to the user community. You will also have quick access to current business knowledge to balance the technical expertise of the rest of the team

Question #3. How large should the warehouse project be, and where should we start?

Another critical question concerns project size and entry point. The answer is to pick the right set of users. Many of the most quickly successful projects started by focusing on the needs of a user community that shared a common profile. Size alone is not an important determiner of success. Even though small is beautiful, many big projects are hugely successful if they meet the needs of a common profile group of users.

What do you look at to determine that profile? Most important is the data those users work with. Common data is essential. The second characteristic concerns the type of work being done. Telesales staff and market researchers are unlikely to be satisfied with identical data warehouse solutions. If all of the people who are going to use your systems are operating at about the same level, if they work with the same kind of data, if they do the same kind of work, it's going to be much easier to build a system that actually meets their needs when you're done.

Question #4. Who visits the warehouse? Who are the users?

Understanding users is crucial to meeting their needs. Users can be categorized into four groups.

Report viewers tend to work with the world through structured reports.

Data tourists want guidance as they tour their data but can sometimes take the initiative to go off the beaten path and investigate things on their own.

Information surfers want to look at any data, anywhere, anytime with instant response. Typically they are frustrated by the limitations of most current systems and frequently have learned SQL, SAS, and Focus on their own in order to do the analysis they need.

System planners are also users of the data warehouse. They visit the warehouse every day—testing, validating, tuning, and observing its behavior.

Report viewers typically look for answers in the same location on the same report on a predictable schedule. They couldn't care less about what tool is used to produce the report, and they might even prefer to look at the report on paper. Report viewers typically have no tolerance for a system that requires them to remember how to do something. They may work with the system only once a week or once a month, and so their systems must prompt them through even the simplest processes. The good news about meeting the needs of report viewers is that they are not instant-response-demanders. They know they are going to get the report eventually, whether it shows up at 9:02 or 3:02. In access-tool terminology, report viewers need EIS solutions, or standard reports.

Contrast that with the needs of the data tourist. A tourist visiting a new city starts with a guidebook that points out the highlights, points of interest, and where to eat. The guide shows where to get started. A *data* tourist wants the same kind of assistance. They want recommendations as to interesting places to go. They want a system that can collect and cluster data together so that it makes sense. Data tourists typically prefer a structured report to start with, but that report has to have some variability. They have to be able to set their own variables so that they can look at Milan one day and Rome the next.

While they use standard reports with variables, data tourists also need to customize their own reports and save a record of the paths they took through their data. Finally, tourists are somewhat less tolerant of delays than are viewers, so they expect good response during a single session. Data tourists need a stable Managed Query Environment (MQE) that allows interactive analysis and variable, customizable reports.

The information surfers are the most demanding but, fortunately, the smallest percentage of the average population. They constitute at most 10 percent of the typical user community. Surfers want the ability to ask any question of any data at any time with instantaneous response. Surfers are rarely satisfied by existing reporting systems because they are always asking questions that you never expected. Surfers need true interactive multidimensional analysis and will be frustrated by the restrictions of a tightly controlled Managed Query Environment.

The system planners, who interact with the data every single day as they work through the development cycle, need to work with a system as it's in progress. Data-access tools with thick, static semantic layers are unsuitable for the planner. Thus, planners often avoid all end-user tools and become distanced from the user's experience.

Planners, who are ultimately responsible for support of the final system, look at tools in terms of their support burden. Key for the planner is central deployment for minimal maintenance. In addition, planners must select products that allow for changes to the database, or its metadata, that are not destructive of user's work.

The requirements placed on desktop tools by each of these groups is quite different and can be characterized by the following chart. The features that are essential for one group are for other groups completely useless, which makes it quite a challenge to find a single solution that is acceptable across the board.

Figure 6–1   Need for Features by User Groups

	EIS/Fixed Format Reports	Managed Data View	Variable Queries and Reports	Ad Hoc, Interactive Analysis	Live View of Data Structure
Report viewers	Essential	Essential	Basic	Low	None
Data tourists	Basic	Essential	Essential	Low	None
Information surfers	Optional	Low	Basic	Essential	Essential
System planners	None	None	None	Basic	Essential

Question #5. Why is a data warehouse project like an iceberg?

Answer: Because so much is hidden beneath the surface. The IS view sees all the difficult and essential tasks that lie below the surface of the project: SQL optimization, data modeling, legacy extracts and data integrity, schema design, indexes, and load performance. From the users' perspective the only thing visible is the proverbial "tip of the iceberg." Users see only the schema you provide through either a semantic layer or the physical tables, and they see the tools you provide for query, report, and analysis. They also see how quickly the system responds to their requests. Two critical pieces of advice fall from this simple observation.

a. Don't spend all of your time in that 90 percent below the water that no user is ever going to see. We say that the last 10 percent is bigger than the first 90 percent. The sad truth is that if you neglect the 10 percent above the water and make bad decisions about tools and design, no one will know how excellent the rest of the project may be. No users will see your beautiful clean data if you've hidden it away behind an impenetrable schema, or if the tools you provide are difficult to use or are unsuitable to the users' tasks.

b. The other corollary is that you've got to begin your project with the end in mind. Remember that you are building the warehouse for the end-users. Throughout the project, keep in mind that the mission of the warehouse project is to allow end-users to access data on their own.

Let's look at a real-life example, a medium-sized insurance company. Prior to the start of the data warehouse project, the IS organization inferred the needs of end-users from the reports they requested. The IS organization knew the reports were usually big and complicated, produced many pages of tightly formatted results, and frequently were difficult to write. IS assumed that big, complicated reports were what users wanted. So when they began the warehouse project they started out by trying to replicate the longest and most complicated user-requested reports as "standard reports." They built hundreds of reports, wrote governors, and built indexes to maximize the performance of those reports. They also gave users an ad hoc query tool which, they thought, would be used at most 5 to 10 percent of the time.

Care to guess how many of those reports are in use today? About a dozen. What they find today is a lot of little, quick queries hitting the database. A typical query might scan 50,000 rows and return four rows of aggregated results—one row for each quarter. The query returns so little data because that is the answer to a single question. A follow-on question is typically to discover details behind one of those rows. That second query will scan perhaps 10,000 rows and return 100 rows.

What the IS organization discovered was that users didn't really want a multipage report with M x N x O dimensions and subtotals every which way. Users actually prefer to work sequentially with small collections of data that result from "small questions." Before the warehouse, IS had not known those kinds of reports were even desired because they were never requested.

The lesson to be learned from that story is that data warehousing is a new paradigm. It is efficient for users to work in their natural trial-and-error fashion when they have easy-to-use desktop tools and a reasonably responsive database system. Don't expect the behaviors of today to apply in the new environment. Don't rely upon past experiences with OLTP systems to predict user needs in the warehouse. And don't apply old-style OLTP technologies to warehouse problems.

Question #6. What kind of a database should you build?

Which database designs work better than others? To answer this question it is easier to warn against what does not work than dictate what does.

- If you simply move your transaction system into a separate database and call it a warehouse, it will not work. Users will not be happy with it. 3rd normal form does not produce designs that respond quickly to typical queries that may require 5 or 15 joins.

- Do not hide normalized database designs under thick semantic layers; performance will suffer, as will maintainability.

- Don't skimp on disk space or indexes.

Question #7. Does the database make sense for the user?

The most important principle to keep in mind when you're designing your database is to remember who it's for: it's for your users. Build the warehouse using business terms for field/table names if you can. You don't have to call it QXR1; you can call it "Weekly_Sales." That's your choice—it's your database. In your metadata layer you can record the fact that it came from QRX1 and it's a weekly aggregate of the field that's called QXR1 in the accounting system. But in your warehouse, if it's Weekly Sales, call it that.

Question #8. Can you use a star schema?

Another principle that is easy to implement is to employ a "star schema" design (some people call this "tall table" design). Tall tables mean there are many fields in a table rather than many tables. Essentially, you construct a star schema by denormalizing as much as possible until you combine all attributes of similar objects in single tables.

Two benefits compel a star schema. The first is query performance. Servers simply do better with fewer joins. The second reason is that users understand their business in those kinds of terms. The average end-user doesn't know that in a completely normalized database, an address might be stored in several tables, one for each component of an address, city, state, country, etc. Such a structure allows dB designers to enforce integrity on input, but the price is that you'll have to join five tables together just to get a single address record back. The average user doesn't have a clue that that's what the physical databases look like. They expect to see an address record together, so build the table in the warehouse that looks just that way. Remember, you do not have to enforce update data integrity in a data warehouse. Data integrity is enforced at load time, so it doesn't matter how redundant the data is in the warehouse.

Question #9. What about aggregates?

Another question concerns aggregates. Where do they go? Do you need them at all? Too bad there isn't a single right answer to these questions.

At least one customer has done it both ways and presents an interesting case study. When this entertainment industry organization first built a warehouse, they wrestled with this question: to pre-aggregate or not? They decided to build aggregates and store them in separate tables. Users were taught which tables to use for which types of queries.

Two years later, there is not a pre-computed aggregate in the database. They determined that the basic performance of their database, an intelligently denormalized schema managed by a popular RDBMS running on a UNIX box, was good enough that their users could compute all aggregates on the fly. Ad hoc aggregates were feasible because the query tool was easy, and the server was fast enough. An additional benefit of eliminating the aggregate tables was that it reduced the work required of IT: they were spared the task of maintaining those separate tables, of building them, and of recomputing and reloading data.

Question #10. How do you choose user tools?

Simple: put yourselves in the users' shoes. If you can't, get users to work with the tools you recommend, then allow them to pick. Remember that the last 10 percent is 90 percent of the perceived value of the project. The users are interacting with your database through the medium of the query tool you provide. Much of their sense of the warehouse will be set by these products. It is important, therefore, to find the tools they can work with.

We tend to distinguish query tools from a lot of other kinds of data-access products because we think of query tools as versatile objects that can be adapted to many purposes. The idea is that a tool can be used by many people of many different levels of expertise to accomplish very different results. Anyone can use it, and anyone can accomplish different results with it.

You can, of course, fill in your tool kit with specialized tools that meet specialized needs. But you should start with the basics and pick at least one product that will fill the basic needs of each type of user. The process most companies use is to transform each type of users' needs into the features that a query tool would need to provide to be satisfactory. Any product that does all the essentials is probably a good bet to take into a live trial.

Figure 6-1 (repeated below) summarizes the requirements on data retrieval tools placed by each category of user.

	EIS/Fixed Format Reports	Managed Data View	Variable Queries and Reports	Ad Hoc, Interactive Analysis	Live View of Data Structure
Report viewers	Essential	Essential	Basic	Low	None
Data tourists	Basic	Essential	Essential	Low	None
Information surfers	Optional	Low	Basic	Essential	Essential
System planners	None	None	None	Basic	Essential

Report viewers need push-button front-end functionality that produces standard-format output. Viewers need EIS systems that allow them to open a spreadsheet, open a mail document, open a word processor, and push a button that says "Give me my report." These days, you can demand EIS systems that integrate with standard desktop products and are easy to build and require no special maintenance, set up, or administration.

The tool for a data tourist is the classic managed query tool that offers protected, pre-defined views of the database, pre-built reports, and variable, prompted constraints. And of course you need an attractive, easy to use, point, and click GUI. We've observed that data tourists need to be nudged into doing some analysis on the data. It's really comfortable to push the button, get the report, hand it to your boss, and not think about it too much. But the better MQE products contain simple analysis tools in addition to report-writers.

Information surfers are the hardest to satisfy because they want "more, now." They want to discover things in the data that no one has ever seen before. Typically, they will not be content with pre-built models of the data, so MQEs can be frustrating to surfers. They aren't content with only "abstractions" of tables. They aren't satisfied with only pre-built reports. They're going to want to combine elements that have never been combined before. They are not going to want to traverse a hierarchy that has been preset by someone else because they are looking for relationships that no one has anticipated. So the key requirements on tools for surfers are that they are completely open-ended, provide a direct connection to the database, and have multidimensional capabilities.

The information planner needs a tool that provides a direct view of the physical tables and offers control over the modeled layer. With a live view you can actually define tables, load data, and look at the results immediately. You don't have to define additional layers. Planners want to support query tools that have centralized, repository-based administration. And if you can find one of those that also provides automatic version control and protection for the user community against the changes you're making, you will have a good solution. Auditing capabilities are also a key requirement so that IT planners can monitor the usage of the system and improve its performance, or educate its users through time.

Question #11. What are the best query tools?

Today, the best query tools are all-in-one solutions. They can provide a starting point for your tourists, be integrated into desktop systems for your report viewers, and include multidimensional analysis so your surfers can go beyond reporting.

In addition, some query tools can run in heterogeneous platform environments. Some of them will work identically on desktop platforms, Windows, Macintosh, and UNIX. Some of them will have a centralized repository architecture and will minimize your dependence upon proprietary metadata.

LESSONS LEARNED

Lesson #1: Clean and structure your data on the way in; don't wallpaper over bad database designs with thick semantic layers.

Once you place data in the warehouse, it stays there and is highly visible. Make sure the data goes in the right way and you won't have to clean it as it goes out to each user's desktop. If the data design doesn't make sense to the users, it shouldn't be in the warehouse. Clean it up when it goes in and get the design right in the first place. Remove the inconsistencies, cleanse it, and purify it. For example, make sure that if you have a field called "gender," it contains "**M**s" and "**F**s." And make sure that every table in which you have a field called "gender" always contains **M**s and **F**s. Don't let one of them contain zeros and ones and the other, M & F.

Lesson #2: Use the power of the desktop.

If you use the right architecture, your system will work better. The best architecture is one that leverages the tremendous computing power in the CPUs on those desktop machines. We suggest that you consider doing multidimensional analysis not at the server, but at the desktop. We find that servers sometimes become overloaded, that no matter how fancy your symmetric multiprocessor is, you still have to share that processor among multiple users. What you have in your database server is lots and lots of storage space, lots and lots of disk, but not as much memory. On your desktops you typically have lots of available memory to play with. So we suggest that you consider doing the multidimensional analysis on those small chunks of data at the desktop and let the server do the sorting and selecting and aggregating.

Lesson #3: You're the boss, so write your own rules.

One of the joys of data warehouses is that there are no rules. You have a blank slate on which to create. There are no legacy users to preserve, no 20-year-old systems to support. You are not obligated to anyone. The only rule is to do what works. It's just you, your users, a bunch of data, a server, and some tools. Imagine the possibilities.

By all means, use a star schema for your data—performance and usability will improve if you do. If you are in a relational environment, do your best to leverage the search, retrieval, join, and aggregation capabilities of that engine. But don't be afraid to break the old OLTP rules of 3rd or 5th normal form. Those rules are not what make a database. It is such a common mistake, and so easy to avoid, to believe that you should follow the old rules, even when in a data warehouse. Don't. Design the data schema that makes sense to your users.

Lesson #4: Small is beautiful.

Let's admit it—data warehousing is still a new idea. There are few books to read and no methodologies to purchase, so you will not get everything right the first time. The only way to learn is by trial and error. And logic suggests it's a lot better to experiment and learn on small systems, with not too much data and not too many users, than it is to build your first system with terabytes on the server and thousands of clients.

Some very smart people get hooked on the vision of the great integrated corporate warehouse in the sky, in which all data is clean, related to every other element, perfectly up to date, and responds in seconds to any request. I have bad news if that is what you have promised your management. It won't happen. If you want to get there, you have to do it in small, incremental steps. You build that universal data warehouse one datamart at a time.

Most successful data warehouses started with a small group of users who agreed on fundamentals and who needed a manageable amount of data from a limited number of sources. Small projects succeed when large ones fail because small projects can cycle more quickly. They have less inertia so it is easier to move them in the right direction. Small projects also produce results more quickly. It simply takes less time for everything: less time to locate data, transform it, load it, build indexes; less time to train users and tune performance. A good rule of thumb is to design your warehouse projects to have finished the first cycle within 12 months.

Lesson #5: Anticipate change.

It is an interesting characteristic of the data warehouse that it is never done. Now this may offer lifetime employment for the members of the team, but it also makes it difficult to know when to show it off to management and when to schedule team vacations. Try to avoid speaking of "when the warehouse is done." It will never be done, and that is as it should be. It will always be under construction. Plan to live in a construction zone. It's like living in Manhattan. The streets are never done—as soon as they fix the water pipes, they dig in the same place to upgrade the phones. In the warehouse, as soon as you have one data set complete and one group of users up to speed, another group of users will ask you to load their data too, and the process starts all over again.

In the data warehouse, you should assume lots of variability and pick tools and technologies that are very modular and use open standards as much as possible. With regard to user tools, tools that require little to no maintenance and that can self-adjust to changes in data schemas or metadata will make your job much, much easier.

Lesson #6: Unlock the creativity in your users.

Satisfying the needs of the end-users is key to the success of your project. But you must do more than just give them great tools and clean data. You must also inspire them to be creative. Part of the paradigm shift that has happened in the data warehouse is that you may have to teach your users how to take full advantage of the new environment. You have to take the initiative and show users that it is okay to ask "why?" Users need your help to understand that there are no "stupid" questions of a data warehouse. You must teach your users to be creative, to satisfy their natural curiosity. For people who are accustomed to production reports that come in stacks of paper on the desk, it's going to take a new mindset. It's your responsibility, and that of the entire warehouse team, to help your users move smoothly into the new paradigm. Choosing tools that are well-designed, easy to use, and a little bit fun will make your job easier and your project more successful. If you do all this—if you design it well, fill it with clean, well-organized data, teach users how to use it—your users will come to the warehouse and they will stay.

Building Object-Oriented OLAP Applications: Not Just Any Object-Oriented Tool Will Do

David Menninger

Oracle/Express Technology

Object-oriented tools are becoming more prevalent and more complex. Although the advantages of using objects in application design are numerous, using generic object tools for specialized analysis applications can lead to lengthy development cycles and frustrated end-users. This essay will explore the evolving object-oriented tools specifically designed for Online Analytical Processing (OLAP). Basic object-oriented concepts and vocabulary are introduced, as well as how these are applied to OLAP. Examples, using Oracle's Express Objects, are provided to reinforce the concepts, which can sometimes be rather abstract.

When building or using objects for OLAP applications, there are several key considerations:

- Breadth and depth of component functionality

- Applicability of components to OLAP-type operations

- Leveraging components across all classes of users

Object-oriented OLAP application development environments must include a wide array of extensible objects, including small discreet components as well as larger OLAP-specific components that can be shared by end-users and application developers.

What Is Object-Oriented Technology?

Technology can be described as "object-oriented" if it supports the concepts of *encapsulation*, *inheritance*, and *polymorphism*.

Encapsulation

In abstract terms, encapsulation is the combining of characteristics and behavior into a single entity. In programming terms, it is the combination of data and code in a single unit of work often called an "object." All access to the data within an object is via interfaces incorporated into the object. At first, this concept appears similar to structured programming, but as the name implies, structured programming deals only with organizing code into reusable modules. The interprocess communication facilities for sharing data in a structured programming environment basically amount to shared data pools. There is no mechanism to prevent one process from corrupting the data of another process.[1] Encapsulating the data with interfaces to "sanctioned" data manipulation routines reduces the chance of data corruption, that is, bugs.

Think about a car as an object. A car has many components, but they are all combined into an automobile, and we interface with the automobile as an entity. We don't pour fuel into the engine to make the car run. We put fuel into the gas tank, and the gas tank has connections to the engine. We put

---

[1] This is not to say that you cannot create erroneous data values. However, you cannot inadvertently write blocks of memory that are not associated with the object.

Figure 7–1 Encapsulation vs. Structured Programming

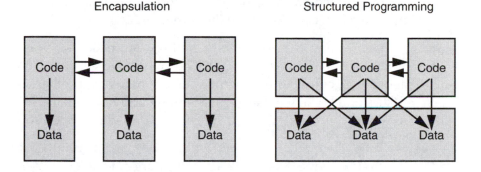

the car in gear, step on the accelerator, and the car moves. When we buy an automobile we don't go to the showroom and select engine rods, pistons, chrome, glass, tires, and material to fashion into upholstery. If this were the case, we could very easily connect them in the wrong way or leave out a component. Our lives are made much simpler because the manufacturers have *encapsulated* the components into an automobile.

Inheritance

Inheritance is cloning one entity from another. Cloning means that the characteristics and the behavior that were encapsulated in one object are duplicated in another that then has the same characteristics and the same behavior. Why do we want two of the same thing? The answer is that they are not going to stay the same. (See the next section on polymorphism.) Why not maintain two copies of the code and the extra memory needed to store and process the second copy? When one object inherits its definition from another object, it maintains a reference (that is, a pointer) back to the original set of information. Literally the *same* characteristics and the *same* behavior exist, not a *copy*.

The relationships between these inherited objects are typically referred to as ancestors and descendants. More specifically, the immediate ancestor is referred to as the parent, and the immediate descendent is referred to as a child. Siblings are all objects that share the same parent.

Continuing the automobile analogy, suppose you want to buy a BMW 325 or Saab 900. You may have an option to choose a specific color or engine size, but many of the characteristics and behaviors (such as its styling and how it handles) are already defined and are inherited from the model you select.

In the three examples of inheritance in Figure 7–2, Button2 is derived from Button1 and Button3 is derived from Button2. In the first case, only the text of Buttons 2 & 3 and their positions have been changed. All other characteristics have been inherited from their respective parents. In the second case, the font for Button2 was changed to italic and Button3 inherited the change. In the third case, the font for Button1 was changed from bold to regular and the change was inherited by Buttons 2 & 3 without overriding the italic property of Button2.

Figure 7–2

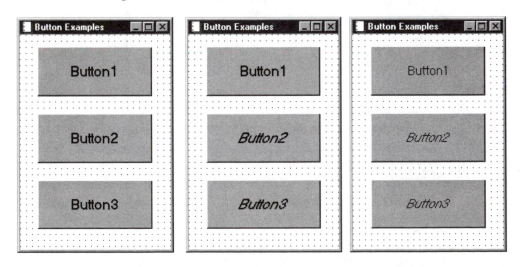

Polymorphism

Polymorphism is the ability of different objects[2] to behave differently in response to the same messages or events. Typically, polymorphism implies that the code inherited by an object can be altered or replaced. For example, a table and a graph may both be objects for viewing data, yet the print routine for the table may be completely different from the print routine for the graph.

Loosely interpreted, polymorphism could also describe *any* differences between the ancestor and its descendants. For example, certain characteristics of the descendant may be overridden in order to alter its appearance. Additional characteristics may be added to a descendant to support functionality found in the descendant, but not in the ancestor.

Back to the automobile manufacturers. Suppose they offer anti-lock brakes as an option. The behavior of the models with anti-lock brakes will be different than those without. In both cases, however, the way the brakes are applied is via the brake pedal. In addition, the different brake mechanisms have no effect on the way the car accelerates, or on its cornering ability.

Referring to the button example, suppose you wished to associate a message box with the click event of each of the three buttons. By adding the following code to Button1, all three buttons will display the "Hello World" message as shown in Figure 7–3 when they are clicked.

```
Sub AfterClick ()
Msgbox "Hello World"
End Sub
```

Figure 7–4 shows inheritance as above. However, if you want Button2 to behave differently from Button1, you could

---

[2] Typically an ancestor and one or more of its descendants, or several descendants that all share the same ancestor from which the behavior is inherited.

Figure 7–3

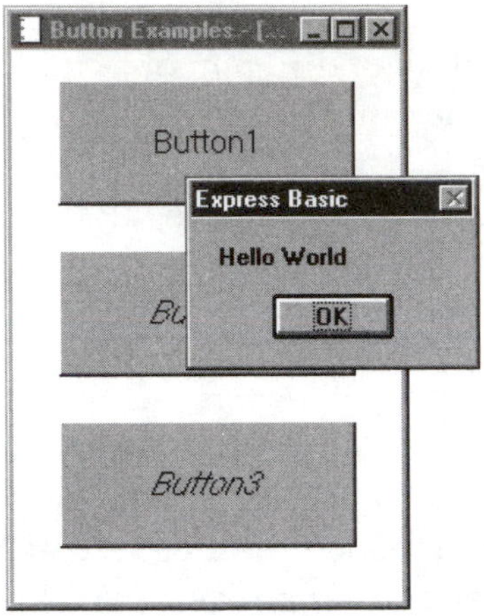

Figure 7–4

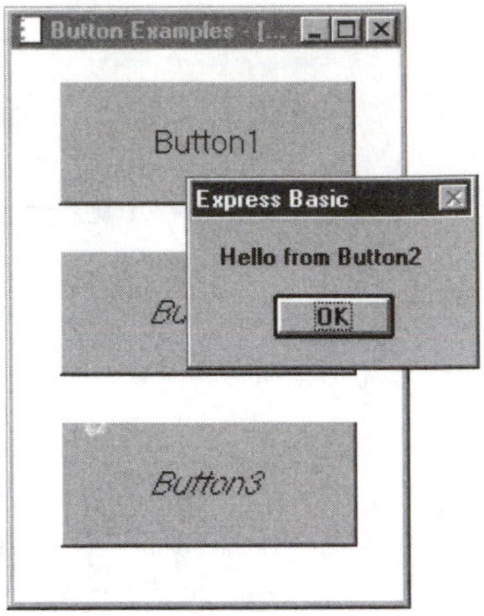

associate a different set of code with the click event of Button2.

```
Sub AfterClick ()
MsgBox "Hello from " & me.text
End Sub
```

With this change, Button2 and Button3 demonstrate polymorphism. Although they are derived from Button1, they exhibit different behavior from their ancestor. Button2 and Button3 will now display a message box with a string expression constructed using the text from the button itself.

The Value of Object-Oriented Technology

Frequently when you are constructing applications, you need to use many things over and over again. The key benefit of object orientation is reusability. Imagine the scenario where you need to prepare a series of financial analyses for numerous geographic regions. Due to local tax regulations, the financial analyses will vary slightly from region to region. Object-oriented technology allows you to reuse the bulk of the analyses from one region to the next. Then, as the basic financial analysis process changes, you will need to make only one set of changes: some for the end of each month, some for the end of each quarter, and some for the end of each year. The changes will ripple through to all those places where it should.

It's really polymorphism in conjunction with inheritance that creates the high degree of reusability and the corresponding increases in developer productivity that are associated with object-oriented programming. It is not the purpose of this essay to justify the value of object-oriented technology—that could be the subject of many papers unto itself. Nevertheless, it should be obvious from this brief discussion that object-oriented technology holds the potential for significant productivity gains.

WHAT IS OLAP?

OLAP is an acronym for OnLine Analytical Processing. The phrase was coined by Dr. E.F. Codd, of relational database fame, in 1993. Online Analytical Processing (OLAP) contrasts with Online Transaction Processing (OLTP). The latter deals with recording data of various activities, while the former deals with interactively analyzing the data that has been recorded or projecting future data. A multidimensional conceptual view is one of the chief tenets of OLAP. (It is assumed the reader already has some knowledge of the subject.)

Functionality

The multidimensional model associated with OLAP allows the user to freely associate different dimensions or keys with rows, columns, or pages of the display. Rotating the display (that is, changing its orientation) and drilling down to successive levels of detail are the most common and most basic functions associated with OLAP. Users can frequently analyze their data more efficiently if they can choose an orientation that highlights anomalies or trends in the data. But OLAP is much more than rotating or drilling down. It is the ability to create and examine calculated data interactively on large volumes of data. It is the ability to determine comparative or relative differences, such as percent of total or variance from budget. It is the ability to perform exception and trend analysis on calculated data, such as determining which products sold in the Benelux region have show an increase of more than 10 percentage points in the twelve-month moving average of sales. And ultimately it is the ability to perform advanced analytical functions, such as forecasting, modeling, regression analysis, and solving simultaneous equations.

Application Domains

These types of analytical functions tend to appear most often in several broad categories of applications, including:

Executive Information Systems (EIS)	Planning and Forecasting Systems	Sales and Marketing	Financial Applications
Key performance indicator tracking	Production forecasting	Sales tracking	Budgeting
Exception reporting	Capacity planning	Promotion analysis	Variance analysis
Competitive analysis	Resource allocations	Product profitability	Financial modeling
	Investments/ acquisitions	Distribution analysis	Cash management
		Customer profiling	

OBJECT ORIENTATION APPLIED TO OLAP

Development Alternatives

Obviously there are a number of alternatives on the market for developing object-oriented applications, ranging from C++ to client/server development environments to OLAP-specific development environments. While C++ offers object-oriented features and enormous flexibility for *systems* programmers, it is hardly a tool for widespread use among *application* developers. Client/server development environments, such as PowerObjects, Developer/2000, Visual Basic, and PowerBuilder, offer rapid application development and various degrees of object orientation. However, these tools are designed for record-oriented systems, and they offer little or no support for multidimensional data. The other alternative is an application development environment designed specifically for building OLAP applications.

Boulders vs. Pebbles

How do you, as a developer or designer of systems, know what constitutes an object within your particular application domain? Using object-oriented approaches is an exercise in abstraction—trying to create a self-contained entity that performs all the functions that might ever be asked of it. For some, this exercise can prove to be frustrating. Peter Coad offers some practical advice on identifying objects, their properties, and their behaviors:

> I'm a _____ . I know my own _____ and I can _____ myself.[3]

For example, take the case of a window.

> I'm a *window*. I know my *position*. I know my *size*.
> I can *open* myself. I can *close* myself.

These are some of the properties and behaviors associated with window objects. Obviously this is a very elemental object, at least with respect to analytical applications. We could have much more complicated objects, such as a sales analysis.

> I am a *sales analysis*, I know my own *pipeline*, I know my own *close ratio*, and I can *forecast* myself. I can *report* myself by region, or by product. I can *forecast* myself optimistically or pessimistically.

Many object-oriented environments offer numerous small discrete objects (or *pebbles*) and expect the developer to create the more complicated objects (or *boulders*) themselves. For example, most object-oriented environments will offer edit boxes, combo boxes, list boxes, push buttons, ratio buttons, check boxes, group boxes, and other standard types of windows controls as base classes or starting points from which the developers can create larger, more application-specific objects. Several environments such as PowerObjects, Visual Basic, PowerBuilder, and Delphi have incorporated larger objects for accessing record-oriented relational data, and these products

---

[3] As quoted in *Client/Server Today,* March 1995.

have enjoyed a wide degree of success. These larger objects allow developers to more rapidly create highly functional applications. The developer focuses their time and attention on providing a specific business solution rather than on figuring out how to populate the grid control with data from the data source.

In reality, the developer needs both types of objects: *boulders* with large amounts of predefined functionality as well as the *pebbles* for fine-grain control. In fact, *boulders* are often "compound" objects: the combination of several other objects into a single larger object. Reflecting further on the success of the client/server object-oriented tools, it is clear that data-aware *boulders* provide some of the highest value to application developers.

OLAP-Specific Objects

Data-aware, multidimensional controls

What distinguishes an OLAP-specific object-oriented environment from other types of object-oriented environments are its data-aware, multidimensional controls. A data-aware, multidimensional control encapsulates knowledge of its data source as well as ways to display and manipulate data in a multidimensional fashion. For example, the most common data-aware, multidimensional control is a table or grid that allows drill down and rotation. Could you create one of these yourself? Of course, but is that the best use of your organization's resources?

The multidimensional display in Figure 7–5 allows the user to drill down or up for different levels of detail. The orientation of the display can also be "rotated" (i.e., interchange the products with the geographic regions) for a different perspective of the data. It also allows the user to select different data to display, set selection criteria, format the display, print all or a portion of the table, and so on. The developer does not have to write any code to utilize any of these features.

Other types of data-aware display mechanisms are graphs, maps, and other data visualization mechanisms. In general these objects need a variety of properties and meth-

Figure 7–5

Untitled1							_ □ X

Time (5) May96 ▼ Product (4) Total Prod ▼

Geog. Area (9) Channel (3) Measure (2)

May96 Total Prod	TotChannel		Direct		Catalog	
	Margin	Average Price	Margin	Average Price	Margin	Average Price
− World	420,215	45.12	313,620	45.12	106,595	45.12
+ Americas	129,306	44.94	96,646	44.94	32,660	44.94
+ Australia	111,369	42.16	83,192	42.16	28,177	42.16
− Europe	145,561	45.67	108,413	45.67	37,148	45.67
+ France	34,897	53.73	25,984	53.73	8,913	53.73
+ OtherEur	44,701	50.46	33,282	50.46	11,419	50.46
+ Germany	23,494	35.91	17,560	35.91	5,934	35.91
+ UK	42,470	42.50	31,587	42.50	10,883	42.50
+ Asia	33,978	55.81	25,369	55.81	8,609	55.81

ods to form a complete unit of work: formatting information, data sources, orientation, how much data to fetch, ability to update the source data, and so on. But regardless of how much design and development effort goes into creating these objects, an organization's specific applications or business practices may require some extensions or modifications. Since the objects' properties and methods are accessible, their appearance and behavior can be altered or combined to create even larger objects. For example, you may wish to alter the behavior of the right mouse button. In the standard object, this provides access to some of the data selection and formatting options. In your organization, you may choose to have right mouse button mean "drill down" from the current location. You could derive your own table object from the standard table and implement this type of behavior. Then, throughout your applications you would use the modified version of the table. Yet you still have access to all the other features, including the data-specific features that have been built into the object.

Another frequent activity in OLAP applications involves the manipulation of hierarchical lists of dimension values. Dimension lists are used for selecting which data to include in a screen, for navigating through information on the screen, for indicating how to aggregate data, and so on. Again, you could create them on your own from a smaller object, but in an OLAP-specific environment, they should be one of the standard features.

OLAP applications by their nature involve frequent and iterative data selection processes. These processes are associated with the data display mechanisms, but they can also be used independently of the displays. Consequently, robust selection mechanisms and data-mining tools are critical elements of an OLAP development environment. The selection techniques include character string matches, ranges of values, hierarchy levels, branches of a hierarchy, and top/bottom searches. In addition, the conjunction between criteria should be flexible to allow successively restrictive results (intersection), additive results (union), and complements or inversion of the result set with the excluded set. These selection methods are available in whole or in part. And the result of the selection process is an object as well. This object can be used to link several displays together, by sharing all or a portion of the selection object. The iterative nature of the selection process also dictates that as selection criteria are entered, individual actions can be trapped for synchronization with other portions of the application. For example, if the data selection process narrows the result set to Western European operations, you may wish to remove any references on the screen to products that are not offered for sale in Western Europe.

Data-aware multidimensional controls also allow for on-screen manipulation of the result set. For instance, the data displayed in a table can be aggregated to a higher level of summarization using a number of built-in aggregate functions. The aggregation is performed, and the display is updated automatically.

Other OLAP objects

Other types of objects that are not necessarily data-aware are important to OLAP applications as well. For instance, briefing books are a common metaphor for delivering sets of analyses, reports, or graphs to other users. It provides a logical context for a series of related screens along with built-in navigation mechanisms for moving through the screens. In Figure 7–6, the several screens are linked together in a briefing and can be accessed via the VCR-style buttons or via the drop-down list box.

Figure 7–6

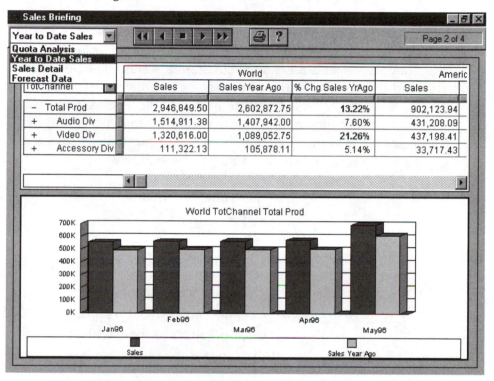

Leveraging Objects Across User Communities

By its very nature, OLAP application development involves several classes of users. The primary categorization is between end-users and developers. Since OLAP applications are designed to support decisions-making processes, the user community often includes high-level decision makers or others who focus more on business than on technology.

If you accept as a premise that the key benefit of object-oriented technology is reusability, then it makes sense to try to leverage the objects across the widest spectrum of users as possible. To understand the points of possible leverage, it is important to understand the classes of users and the tasks they perform (at least in the context of OLAP applications).

End-user tasks

The term "end-user" encompasses a broad range. It is more accurate to think of the continuum of users ranging from casual end-user to power-user to professional developer. It is no longer clear where one ends and the other begins. Casual end-users are usually readers or inquirers of information. They may spend much of their time in electronic mail. They read and review reports and briefings that have been prepared for them by others. They might run some applications that support specific business processes. In response to any of these actions, it may prompt them to ask some questions or research a particular issue that has caught their attention.

Casual User	"Hang out" in e-mail Read reports & briefings Run pre-built applications Ask questions about the data
Power User	Ad hoc data analysis Create/distribute reports & briefings
Professional Developer	Develop applications for end-users Develop objects to share with other developers Create multidimensional model

The power-users may perform all these same functions, but they are much more likely to write information for themselves and others to consume. They often develop ad hoc analyses, and they create reports of their findings to distribute to others in the organization.

Professional developer tasks

The professional developer, who may be part of a centralized information systems function or who may be part of a departmental information systems function, develops for both of the audiences above. Traditional turn-key applications are developed and delivered to end-user communities. A turn-key OLAP application might be a production forecasting system that takes feeds from the production line, the inventory system, and the purchase order system. These types of applications take advantage of the computational capabilities of OLAP servers as well as the multidimensional displays that allow production managers to review the forecast results.

Another scenario involves the professional developer who provides templates to a power-user, who in turn uses the templates to deliver a report or briefing to an end-user. For example, the power-user may need to prepare a sales-forecasting system, but he would like to impose some rigid controls on the sales-forecasting process. He wants to carefully control the parameters used in the forecast by creating a series of dialog boxes with validation of the parameters against pre-established criteria. The professional developer can develop the dialog boxes and deliver them to the power-user to use in conjunction with the analyses in the sales forecast reports and briefings.

In addition, in larger organizations the professional developers also develop for their colleagues. Development activities may be split among different team members any number of ways. Frequently, a core team is established to identify and create common objects that would be useful across all types of applications. These common objects might be standard report-and-display templates or common algorithms, or they may encapsulate third party routines that the organization has licensed.

To achieve maximum effectiveness from an object environment, it must recognize the various audiences that it can benefit. A common object model across these user groups and a mechanism for distributing the objects among the users will allow the benefits of object orientation to permeate the organization. Objects must be sharable in both directions: from end-user to developers and vice versa.

CONCLUSION

Object-oriented technology can deliver valuable benefits to an organization. The reusability associated with objects can increase the productivity of developers and shorten application development cycles. However, the concepts can be abstract. Therefore it is important to provide the organization not only with small discrete objects but with larger robust objects. These objects will provide immediate productivity for users who do not wish to construct their own objects, and they will provide context for those who wish to leverage the objects for more specific application to a particular functional requirement.

OLAP applications are different by nature than relational systems. They require unique types of objects—including multidimensional, data-aware controls—as well as an environment to share the objects across a broad range of users.

Chapter 8

Mining for Profits in the Data Warehouse

Paul S. Barth

Tessera Enterprise Systems

Chris had been thinking for several weeks of canceling his Gold Card. He had just paid off his balance. He was disenchanted with the card's annual fee and was considering switching to a lower-interest competitor. That evening, Chris received a letter from the card issuer's bank telling him that his annual fee had been waived for the next year and awarding him a $50 credit for being a "valued customer." Pleased with this turn of events, Chris held onto his card and made several purchases over the next year that resulted in several hundred dollars in interest fees for the credit card issuer.

The scenario above is an example of how corporations are leveraging the vast knowledge stored in large-scale data warehouses. In this and many other cases, businesses are combining advanced statistical analysis, a sophisticated customer database, and parallel processing to optimize customer relationships and expand their business. The confluence of these technologies is called *data mining*—a process that uses information as a key strategic asset to increase profitability.

Nowhere is data mining more beneficial than in its application to sales and marketing. Through data mining, industry leaders today are not only improving their marketing efficiency, they are leap-frogging the competition by offering new customized products and services specially tailored to market segments. Powered by information warehouses, these decision-support systems are allowing businesses to respond to market conditions in hours, rather than weeks, based on a clear understanding of customers and prospects.

This essay will explore Tessera's experience in creating state-of-the-art data mining solutions for Fortune 500 clients and will outline key business and technical issues. It addresses advanced statistical methods, such as neural networks, that model customer behavior more realistically than standard statistics. It will also demonstrate how data mining can improve your customer modeling and your marketing ROI (return on investment).

PREDICTING WHO WILL BUY

In 1993, a national consumer club wanted to increase marketing effectiveness and reduce costs through improving their targeted marketing. Their marketing universe was 70 million American households. Using minimal targeting, they mailed 5 million pieces per month. The mailings would generally add 100,000 new members per month, or 2 percent of the target. If they could better predict who would join, they could reduce the size of the monthly mailings yet still acquire the 100,000 new members. At 40 cents a piece, eliminating just 10 percent of the mailings would save over $2 million per year.

When it comes to capturing market opportunity, nothing is more valuable than knowing who is most likely to buy and what is most likely to induce an individual to become your customer. By precisely defining a target audience, marketers can spend less money reaching buyers or increase their customer base by improving the offer for the target. The principles of targeted marketing have been understood for decades, but targeting methods have traditionally been more art than science, driven too often by intuition and lore than by analysis.

Start with the Data

In contrast to manual targeting, computer-based models use customer and prospect data to predict who will buy. These data can include a wide range of information, such as demographics, psychographics, subscriptions, responses to past promotions, and customer purchase and payment histories. This information is sampled and summarized to present a consistent set of relevant data for each customer. Figure 8–1 shows the process flow for building and using a predictive model.

Figure 8–1

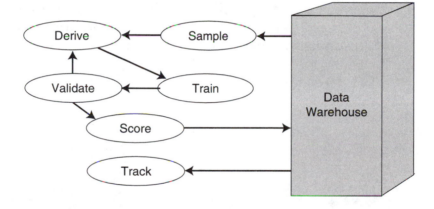

The best way to create a computer-based customer model for a new marketing campaign is to search the data warehouse for a previous campaign where similar products were marketed. This data source, called the *training set,* identifies all customers and prospects targeted by the campaign and whether or not they bought. The applicability of this historical data to the target audience is critical to the model's effectiveness in the new campaign. For instance, a retailer introducing a new line of swimwear is better advised to draw a training set from historical sales of swimwear than from winter coats. In cases when a relevant training set cannot be found, marketers, in the first stages of a campaign, will create one through non-targeted test mailings.

Linear Statistical Modeling

Linear statistical modeling was first used by database market-ers in the 1970s. Using training sets to automatically segment customers in two halves, linear models advanced marketers' targeting capabilities compared to manual estimates, but failed to account for significant exceptions, as Figure 8–2 explains.

Figure 8–2 illustrates a training set and how a traditional linear model predicts behavior. Each dot on the scatter plot represents an individual in the training set. Each individual's position is determined by two variables—the individual's age (horizontal position) and income (vertical position). The shape and color of the dots indicates whether the individual accepted the offer. In this example, black triangles are buyers, and gray squares are non-buyers.

Figure 8–2

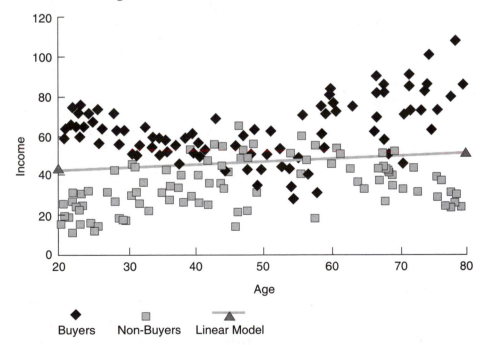

The line running through the graph depicts a linear predictive model. The line separates buyers into two regions: individuals above the line are predicted as buyers, and individuals below the line are predicted as non-buyers. The model in Figure 8–2 is fairly accurate, since the training set population divides neatly across the model boundary. The model expresses the fact that most buyers have higher income and that income rises with age. It is interesting that the training set contains a set of individuals who violate the model: a cluster of middle-age, moderate-income buyers. The existence of this cluster exemplifies a key shortcoming of linear modeling because of the profit potential these customers represent.

In practice, linear statistical models incorporate a dozen or so variables in an attempt to capture as much information as possible. However, models more complex than this suffer from the "curse of dimensionality," whereby computational and data resources grow exponentially for accurate modeling. To compensate for this, traditional modeling creates "derived variables" that combine many features into a single dimension.

Linear statistical modeling techniques have two major weaknesses. First, the simplicity of the models does not accurately reflect the complexity of data, causing market segments, such as the middle-age, moderate income buyers in Figure 8–2, to be completely overlooked. Second, the models cannot exploit the wide variety of potentially relevant data. To compensate for this, human modelers make assumptions that simplify the data used, often reducing the model's accuracy.

Non-Parametric Modeling

In case after case, Tessera has found that new analytic methods, such as neural networks, decision trees, and example-based methods, are more accurate and flexible than traditional methods. These *non-parametric methods* allow a model to classify discrete regions for prediction, as illustrated in Figure 8–3. This figure contains the same data set as Figure 8–2, but the model is indicated by trapezoids. The area inside the polygons denotes buyers; outside the polygons are non-buyers.

Although imperfect, this model more accurately reflects training data than the linear model. Today, there are three promising non-parametric data mining techniques: neural networks, decision trees, and example-based methods—all of which are superior to traditional linear techniques.

Figure 8–3

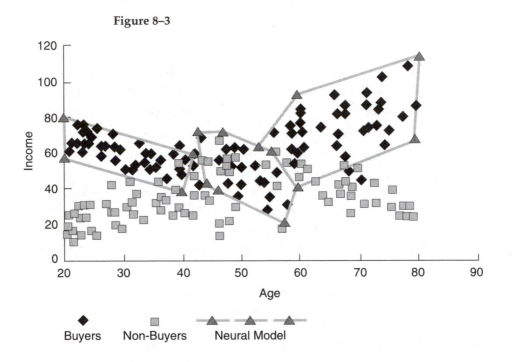

The following describes the capabilities and benefits of neural networks, decision trees, and example-based modeling.

Neural networks

Introduced in the 1980s, neural networks are today's most popular advanced modeling technique. Analogous to the workings of the brain, neural networks compute predictions using a set of "neurons" (computations) and their interconnections (weighted inputs). Neural networks use nonlinear relationships between variables, enabling marketers to update models continuously as customer behavior and/or demographics change. Figure 8–4 illustrates a neural network that predicts responses based on an individual's age, income, home ownership, and so on.

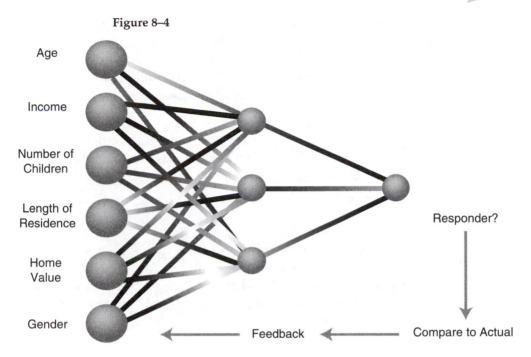

Figure 8–4

For each individual, the values of the above variables are input at the left of the network and combined in two stages to produce a prediction on the right. Mathematically, the spheres represent combining functions, and the size of the connections represent variable coefficients called "weights." The functions predict response based on input values and weights, giving more importance to variables with greater weights. The middle spheres or "hidden nodes" take the same inputs, but weigh them differently, allowing each hidden node to focus on a particular segment of values. This allows the neural network to model many discrete regions in the training set.

Creating a neural network requires two critical steps: structuring the network, such as the choice of input variables, and the numbers of hidden nodes. Network structure is determined by the modeler, but weights are automatically learned by analyzing the training set as follows: first, a random set of weights is assigned to the network. Then, for each individual in the training set, inputs are propagated through the network and a prediction is made. The prediction is then compared to the actual result. If they match, weights in the network are adjusted to make this prediction more likely the next time the individual is seen. If they disagree, the network is adjusted to make the prediction less likely. After many iterations over the training set, the network "learns" patterns in the data, becoming increasingly intelligent with continued use.

Despite neural networks' growing use, they can be expensive to compute and hard to understand. Still, if performance is your top priority, their accuracy is consistently better than linear statistical methods and can make a significant contribution to your marketing.

Decision trees

Like the game Twenty Questions, decision trees break the prediction task into a sequence of decisions. For each individual, a decision tree model asks a series of questions, each question determined by the answer to its predecessor, as illustrated in Figure 8-5.

Figure 8–5

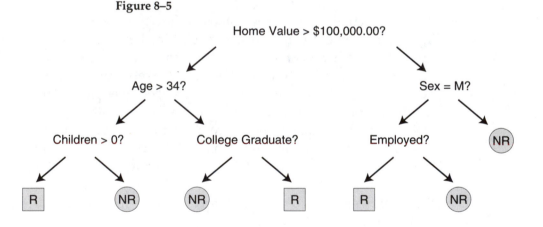

Decision tree methods such as CART, CHIAID, and C4.5 build models by training on a data set. For decision trees, the training set determines the questions asked, such as the split-point for income, when to stop asking questions, and when to make a prediction. Decision tree models use efficient scoring methods, such as simple "if-then-else" statements, and offer easy-to-understand predictions.

Example-based

In these methods, the training set *is* the model. Techniques such as k-nearest neighbors and memory-based reasoning compare individuals to records in the training set, using a function that defines similarities between two individuals. The most similar member of the training set is used to predict how the matching individual will behave. Example-based methods can be efficient to score and easy to explain (for example, "John will respond because he is just like Joe"), but it may require substantial real memory to hold the training set during scoring.

MEASURING THE BENEFIT

The goal of modeling is to pick all the buyers and none of the non-buyers. And again there is a measurable method—though imperfect—called *lift* that marketers can use to compare the accuracy of models. Lift is the ratio of the density of responders accurately predicted for each population segment by a modeling technique compared to the level of accuracy achieved using non-modeled data.

Figure 8–6 illustrates the cumulative lift of a traditional linear model and a neural network.

In this chart, the target audience is sorted from left to right by individuals most likely to buy as predicted by the models.

This sorted group is lumped into ten bins, called "deciles"; the left-most decile is the 10 percent of the target predicted most likely to buy. The height of the bars in each decile represents the number of buyers predicted if the audience from that decile on down were mailed to.

For example, consider the third decile. The chart shows that if 30 percent of the target audience were mailed to, the neural network would capture 70 percent of possible buyers, while the linear model would capture 50 percent of buyers. The baseline titled "Random" represents no modeling, where a 30 percent mailing would capture 30 percent of buyers. The lift ratio quantifies how much more accurate a model is than

Figure 8–6

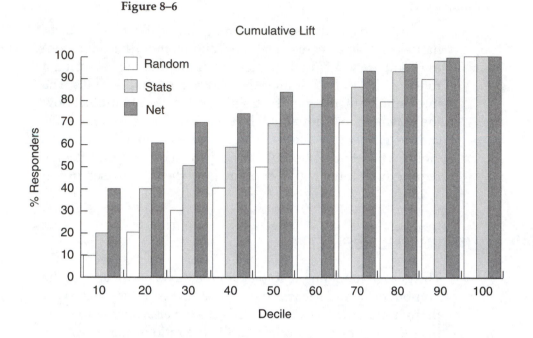

Cumulative Lift

with no modeling. In the first decile, the neural network has a lift of 4, and the linear model has a lift of 2.

This chart shows that a more accurate model can be used for more efficient marketing, a better return, or both. For example, a neural network can capture 70 percent of buyers by mailing only 30 percent of the target audience, while the linear model requires 50 percent and no modeling requires 70 percent. Similarly, a mailing to 20 percent of the target will result in a 60 percent response using the neural, 40 percent using the linear model, and 20 percent return without modeling.

RETURN ON INVESTMENT

The final and most critical step in data mining is to turn accurate modeling into effective marketing decisions. By combining the model scores above with a business model of costs and the value of acquiring buyers, marketers can decide how to maximize their profits. A simple return on investment calculation is shown in the following equation.

$$\text{ROI} = \frac{(\text{Response x Target Audience}) \times \text{Customer Value}}{\text{Fixed Costs} + (\text{Per Customer Cost} \times \text{Target Audience})}$$

In this equation, the revenue of a campaign is the number of buyers acquired multiplied by their individual value; the cost of the campaign is the sum of fixed costs and variable costs multiplied by the target size. The ROI (return on investment) is simply the ratio of revenue to cost.

Figure 8–7 depicts the cumulative profit from a marketing campaign based on the predictive models in Figure 8–6. This marketing campaign has the characteristics of a telemarketing effort to acquire new customers for a long-distance carrier. This campaign targets 200,000 individuals with a total expected response rate of 4 percent (8,000 individuals). The value of each acquired customer is $125—only annualized average calling is considered. On the cost side, the program costs $100,000 to launch and $4 per targeted individual.

Figure 8–7

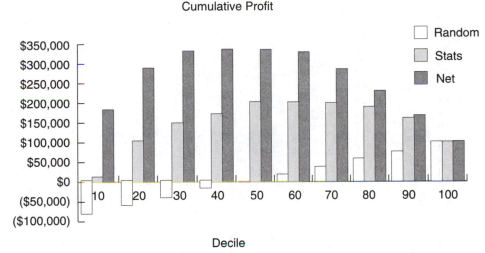

The cumulative profit graph shows several interesting things. First, better modeling means higher profits. The $320,000 earned by using the neural network model outperforms non-targeted mailings by more than 300 percent. Second, more profit is earned with a smaller target—the neural model achieves maximum earnings by reaching less than 40 percent of the target audience. In contrast, the statistical model must reach more than 50 percent of the audience to maximize profits, and non-targeted mailings must reach everyone. Savings due to effective predictions, therefore, reduces overhead costs and frees up money for other programs.

This method allows marketers to optimize the return on their marketing campaigns. In fact, marketers can treat their campaigns as a portfolio of investments and make informed decisions to maximize their returns. Figure 8-8 illustrates the ROI for each decile and shows that mailing to the second decile with the neural network has the highest return. For marketers with a variety of campaigns and a fixed budget, this type of ROI analysis forms the basis for a marketing strategy that allocates dollars to maximize overall return.

Figure 8–8

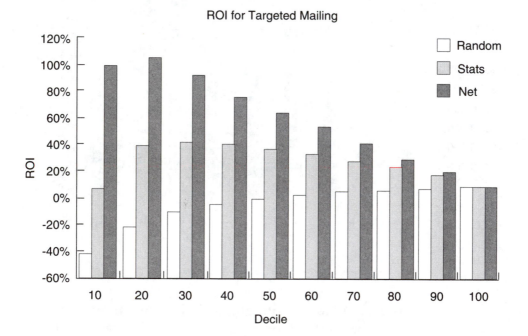

ROI for Targeted Mailing

SUMMARY

Used effectively, advanced data mining can maximize ROIs by building complete models that accurately capture the complex indicators of customer behavior. Data mining can increase customer acquisitions and cross-selling revenues, as well as upgrade, retain, and recapture customers. It can even be used to optimize pricing. To achieve this performance, data mining requires three key components. The first of these is a data warehouse containing a full range of customer information, such as purchase histories, responses to previous marketing campaigns, past modeling scores, demographics, and so on. This information should go back a minimum of five years, enabling marketers to use all the customer interaction data they have acquired to support their marketing decisions.

Coupled with the data warehouse, marketers also require high-performance computers that can explore the wide range of variables needed to predict customer behavior accurately. This computing power will be used to house the data warehouse and drive highly focused marketing programs with a measurable ROI. The computers will also be used to score the database once models are developed—a critical capability in light of the fact that the number of people scored can be a hundred times larger than the group used to create the model. At present, parallel processor computers are the only systems able to deliver the thousands of I/Os and megaflops per second that are needed for this level of scoring. Companies, therefore, must explore parallel systems and vendors to determine the solution that best satisfies their data warehousing needs.

Finally, the predictive power of the warehouse and data mining system must be coupled with production systems that reach the customer. This integration allows marketers to transform the wealth of information gathered from data mining into customized direct mail and highly targeted telemarketing campaigns. As customer touch points become more interactive via interactive TV, the Internet, and ATMs, the link between data analysis and operations will become even more valuable. Companies that integrate these systems in a strong data mining infrastructure will ultimately be poised to capture their marketplace and fully optimize their large-scale data warehouse investment.

Scalable Data Mining

Robert D. Small and Herbert A. Edelstein

Two Crows

INTRODUCTION

Data mining can yield exciting results for almost every organization that collects data on its customers, markets, products, or processes. By discovering hidden patterns and relationships in the data, data mining enables users to extract greater value from their data than simple query and analysis approaches.

To discover the hidden patterns in data, we need to build a model consisting of independent variables (such as income or marital status) that can be used to determine a dependent variable (such as credit risk). Building a data mining model consists of identifying the relevant independent variables and minimizing the predictive error. To identify the model that has the least error and is the best predictor may require building hundreds of models in order to select the best one.

It is fortunate that we have reached a point in terms of computational power, storage capacity, and cost that enables us to gather, analyze, and mine unprecedented amounts of data. While some data mining problems are amenable to a desktop or simple client/server approach, many problems—due to their size or complexity—require a scalable data mining product.

Literally, scalability means that as a system gets larger, its performance improves correspondingly. For data mining, scalability means that by taking advantage of parallel database management systems and additional CPUs, you can solve a wide range of problems without needing to change your underlying data mining environment. You can work with more data, build more models, and improve their accuracy by simply adding additional CPUs. Ideally, scalability should be linear or better. For example, if you double the number of CPUs in a parallel system, you can build twice as many models in the same amount of time, or the same number of models in half the time.

The rest of this essay will examine in detail the reasons scalable data mining solutions are needed and the main methods of achieving scalability. While our discussion will be based on the problem of predicting which groups or classes a case (or row of data) falls into, the need for scalability covers all categories of data mining. We'll use many real examples drawn from a variety of organizations to illustrate the breadth of applications to which scalable data mining may be applied as well as the universality of the issues.

USERS NEED SCALABLE DATA MINING

The primary reason for scalable solutions is to be able to build a good data mining model as quickly as possible. This offers two benefits.

First, there is value in being able to deploy and use the model sooner rather than later. In the second example below, finding a good model will immediately increase the payoff of the product promotions included with bills. The credit card vendor doesn't want to let many billing cycles pass without taking advantage of the data mining results.

Second, faster turnaround times yield better models. As we shall see, mining large databases and constructing complex models call for lots of computing power, as do sampling, testing, and validating. If analysts have to wait hours or overnight for a model to run, their effort is going to be very different than if they can get a model trained in a few minutes. Time previously spent waiting for results can instead be devoted to finding the model that results in the best, most reliable solution.

For example, if in a few minutes analysts can create a group of models and graph their forecasts, they can pick from a large number of model possibilities. If they have to wait overnight for each model, they will take steps to reduce the number of models investigated, such as studying smaller sampled databases and including fewer columns. It is not surprising that their results will be different and quite likely not as useful.

While model building can be accelerated through the use of judicious sampling, such sampling—especially if complex (such as stratified or clustered)—itself requires substantial power. In the end, nothing is more useful than adequate computer power, and nothing so changes the analyst's approach as inadequate power.

> *Example:* The marketing department of a research-intensive company decides to investigate the possibility of using data mining techniques on several of their databases. They acquire some data mining software and request that some of the statisticians in Research assist them as analytic experts. The statisticians have work stations that are excellent for the analyses they usually do on modest-size research databases, and they usually get immediate response to virtually any request for analysis or processing or graphical displays. The statisticians are initially excited by the novelty of the data mining assignment and dealing with huge, complex databases. Their interest quickly wanes, however, when they are dealing with response times in excess of a few hours. They report that data mining methods are cumbersome and useless, and they do not find pat-

terns in the data. They recommend that the effort be terminated.

If these statisticians had had a data mining tool that scaled to handle the larger amount of data they were now using, on appropriately sized parallel hardware, they would have stayed enthusiastic about data mining.

The size of a database is not the only reason to use scalable tools; other factors in building, testing, and deploying a data mining solution may come into play. In the example below, we see how, within a single database, one problem dealing with a large portion of the data requires a scalable solution because of the number of cases, while the complexity of another portion leads to the requirement for a scalable solution.

Example: A credit card vendor includes a product offer in each month's statement. It would like to mine its extensive customer database to increase the number of people who take advantage of the monthly offer. Relatively simple preliminary analysis shows that the card holders split into two groups with different buying patterns.

The first group is relatively large and responds to moderately priced offers at a low rate. Because the group is so large, a modest percentage increase in the response rate will easily pay for the data mining effort. Also, the effort promises to be a relatively simple exercise since no more than five variables account for a large part of the differences between purchasers and non-purchasers. Although there are a huge number of customers, only a few columns will be analyzed, which simplifies the model building. Scalability means the model may be created quickly despite the large number of rows.

The second group presents a different challenge. While small relative to the larger group, it is still of substantial size. The response rate in this group is very low, but the items purchased are expensive. Therefore, even a modest increase in response rate will have a large payoff, justifying the effort required to mine this data. Yet, to determine what is unique about this second group of purchasers will require all of the data available on each customer and several complex models. For this problem, scalability permits building a large number of models to adequately explore the data and find the unique characteristics of this second group.

It is important to remember that the amount of data you are going to mine is likely to increase over time. Furthermore, other problems to which you wish to apply data mining may be larger or more complex than your current problem. Thus, a system that is scalable can not only meet your current requirements but grow with them. In some cases, it is difficult to know your precise requirements before you get well into the application. This will not be a problem with a scalable tool, which can accommodate a range of requirements.

TECHNICAL FACTORS REQUIRING USE OF SCALABLE DATA MINING TOOLS

Database Size

To find the patterns hidden within a database, enormous amounts of data may need to be processed. The optimum platform for accomplishing this is to run parallel data mining algorithms and parallel DBMSs on parallel hardware.

The following example illustrates how the size of a database to be investigated can quickly grow. It also shows how mining your data may require many different models.

Example: A chemical manufacturing plant is not satisfied with the yield or quality of a product and wants to investigate the various factors that might affect these two variables. An online database stores variables such as temperature, pressure, and time for each six-hour run. These observations are taken at one-second intervals. The plant runs seven days a week, twenty-four hours a day, with one batch run on each shift. Thus, more than 20,000 observations per shift yield a tremendous amount of data.

The chemists and chemical engineers identify several variables that, they are certain, affect the yield and quality. They speculate that other environmental conditions such as ambient humidity may affect results. A decision will have to be made if such items are to be investigated, since that data will have to come from an outside source such as the weather bureau.

They define their problem as lower-than-acceptable product yield and quality. They decide that a minimal 20 percent improvement in yield and a 10 percent improvement in quality is an acceptable goal for their data mining project. They list all the variables they will investigate and what models might be useful to them. They write all this information in a protocol that guides their investigations over the coming weeks.

Data analysis approaches and computer storage and processing requirements are affected by database size. A useful measure of database size is the number of rows and columns. Rows refers to the number of units or cases—customers, transactions, products, patients, items on an assembly line. Columns refers to the number of different measurements taken on each item. For example, a mail-order catalog house transaction would be a row, and the columns might include customer information, catalog numbers of items ordered, their price, the credit card used, whether the customer wanted expedited delivery, and so forth.

Rows and columns are a better indication of the amount of time it will take to build a model than simply the aggregate number of bytes. When the number of rows in the database is large, either all of the rows will need to be processed or a random sample of the rows will need to be taken. In either event, the amount of time to build a model will be greater than if there is a smaller number of rows which can be quickly processed.

The attributes of the columns can also add to size. For example, a categorical variable such as GENDER has only two values, but one such as STATE may have fifty-one or more values. Some algorithms, such as neural nets, prefer to have categorical variables split up into multiple columns so that each value becomes a column with a value of Yes or No. Thus STATE might be broken into fifty-one columns, with Alaska having a value of Yes or No, and so on. Not only does the size of the database swell, but the amount of searching that the algorithm must do goes up dramatically.

The number of columns and the attributes of those columns will also influence the complexity of the data mining model, and hence the time it takes to build.

Data subsets and samples

In almost all data mining applications the data is divided into a number of subsets, or samples. The sample might be from a database that's too large to process in full, for example, or it may have been selected for a pilot. Sample selection must be done carefully to ensure the sample is random.

Training and testing the data mining model will also require sampling the data to split it into at least two groups: one for model training (i.e., estimation of the model parameters) and one for model testing. If you don't use different training and test data, the accuracy of the model will be over-estimated. After the model is generated using the training database, it is used to predict the test database, and the resulting error rate is a good estimate of how the model will perform on future databases. There are other more complicated ways to estimate error, but, as we shall see, they also involve sampling the data in a random way.

For most problems, an appropriate sample of 10 percent of the data or even less can give excellent results when training a model. Straightforward calculations show that for most business problems there is virtually no loss in information when this is done. Numerous models could be investigated on a small sample of the data and only the best few be trained on the whole database. Though such approaches do not eliminate the need for powerful computing, they can speed up the model effort.

There are times when business requirements necessitate sampling. For example, suppose that every record in the analysis set had to be reviewed by a panel of experts to determine the value of an unrecorded data item. This is often the case with exact cause of death in epidemiological studies. To have such a panel of experts review 100,000 records might take months or years, but a 10 percent sample may be done in an acceptable time.

> *Example:* A software vendor develops a model that can be used to control the settings of a vat in a chemical plant to increase yield. Once every three minutes, the model uses thirteen characteristics of the raw materials and readings of five vat conditions and three ambient conditions as inputs. It then outputs values for three vat conditions that are used to regulate the process in real time.
>
> After pilot projects at three different plants the vendor begins to sell the software model and a computer that accepts the readings, trains the model, and automatically sets the vat conditions. The company finds that one group is very happy with the unit while the other group is so upset with performance that they have disconnected the unit and returned to manual setting.
>
> The vendor finds that the complaints all come from companies who have new plants or have had new equipment recently installed. The new equipment takes a reading every second instead of every three minutes. The computer is much slower processing 180 times as much data and, in fact, delivers forecasts for what was happening two minutes earlier. This often leads to unstable feedback that results in lost batches.
>
> To respond to the unhappy chemical manufacturers, the vendor puts together a group of three analysts to study the problem and implement a solution. They note that the conditions in the vat do not change much in a second or even in a minute. The device that records the data every second is a bit of technological excess. They write a short piece of software that takes a systematic sample of one point in every sixty, which they use as the input to the computer. Although three times as much data is

entered as before, the model can produce forecasts quickly enough.

Had they written their software to take advantage of parallel computing, they would have been able to solve the problem by simply adding CPUs.

There are also times when sampling is not appropriate. This is particularly true when we are trying to discover subtle effects that may be exhibited by only a small portion of the population. In such a case, sampling can lose the information necessary to find the pattern for which we are searching.

Deployment

Even after the data mining model is built, there may be a need for parallel computing to apply the model. In some situations, the data mining model is applied to one event or transaction at a time, such as scoring a loan application for risk. The amount of time to process each new transaction, and the rate at which new transactions arrive, will determine whether a scalable algorithm is needed. Thus, while the loan applications can probably be easily evaluated on modest-sized computers, monitoring credit card transactions or cellular telephone calls for fraud would require a scalable system to deal with the high transaction rate.

Often a data mining model is applied to a batch of data such as an existing customer database, a newly purchased mailing list, or a monthly record of transactions from a retail store. In this case, the large quantity of data to be processed would also require that a scalable solution be deployed.

Model-Building Complexity, Performance Monitoring and Tuning

Building a complex model with many variables, even when the number of rows is small, may be computationally intensive and will therefore benefit from parallel data mining algorithms. In all data mining applications, extra variables can introduce noise and reduce the accuracy of your model. At the same time, you don't want to leave out important variables that can increase your accuracy or simplify the application of the model to new data. Consequently, you often need to do additional analysis and build different models to ensure that you are using the right columns.

Furthermore, searching for the best model may require building and testing many different models, sometimes numbering in the hundreds, before the best solution can be found. For example, neural nets are a popular data mining technique that often require building many different models with slightly different architectures in order to find the one with the lowest error rate. Not only must you often build multiple models, but you need to do it with different algorithms. Not all algorithms are suitable for every purpose, nor can each find all the patterns for which you are searching. This can further extend the length of time it takes to find the right model.

Another problem arises from the fact that the increase in time for some data analytic techniques is worse than linear. For example, the time to complete a simple linear regression increases approximately linearly for the number of observations (i.e., rows), but increases approximately with the square of the number of columns in the model. Thus, fitting six columns will take four times as long as fitting three columns. Similar calculations apply to neural nets, k-nearest neighbor methods, most time series methods, and any regression technique.

Although all data mining techniques are computer-intensive, some are particularly so. For example, for k-nearest neighbor the calculation time increases as the factorial of the total number of points, and the calculation must be made every time the model is used. If each model you build requires even an hour, let alone a day, you will be unable to test all the variations you would like to.

Clearly, if it takes a long time to build each model, or the number of models you must build to find the one you want is large, the only way to effectively mine your data is with a scalable tool.

Even when you think you are finished because your model works well, you must continually monitor the performance of the model. Over time, all systems evolve and the data they produce changes. Salespeople know that purchasing patterns change over time. External variables such as inflation rate may change enough to alter the way people behave and the factors that influence that behavior. Even precise manufacturing systems age and cause drift in the data they produce. Thus, from time to time, the model will have to be retrained and possibly completely rebuilt. Control charts of the residual differences between the forecasted values and the observed variable are an excellent way to monitor model results. Control charts are easy to use and understand, not computationally intensive, and could be built into the software that implements the model. Thus, the system could monitor itself.

For many data mining applications, you are never completely done.

> *Example:* A financial institution wants to reduce the number of delinquent and fraudulent transactions it processes. The managers believe that most delinquencies and some of the fraud can be relatively easily detected by checking a few variables associated with each transaction. On the other hand, there is a class of fraudulent transactions carried out by knowledgeable individuals that are detectable but much more subtle.
>
> The staff meets with a data mining consultant and financial modeler to describe the situation and available data. The consultants suggest that a relatively simple logistic regression model effort using only three predictors can handle delinquencies. The forecasted error rate is only 3 percent.
>
> The fraudulent model is much more complicated, and a neural net proves to be the best possibility. The model detects 52 percent of the fraud cases. To improve the number of frauds caught, the consultants suggest a policy change. In six months, the model will be re-evaluated in light of the policy change.

Training and Validation

Training and validating a model may require large amounts of data manipulation, and up to thousands of training sessions. Data mining error rates must be determined by testing rather than calculation, and all the methods used are computing-intensive. Newer techniques are likely to be even more so. As you will see, in applying these testing methods scalability is a key to efficient model development.

A model built by any technique needs to be *validated*, which means calculating an error rate based on data independent of that used to estimate the model. This exercise gives a statistically valid estimate of the true error rate that the modeling procedure produces. It does not guarantee that the model is correct in any way. It simply says that if the same technique were used on a succession of databases to build a model, the average error rate would be close to the one obtained this way.

Because data mining model-building is so complex, you cannot simply calculate the error rate. Instead the model needs to be tested against other data. The testing may reflect the complexity of the model being developed. One of the ironies of data mining is that complex testing methodologies are required when you have only a few cases or samples on which to build the model. As we shall see, complex testing schemes make heavy use of the computer and are one of the reasons scalability is required.

The most basic testing method is called *simple validation*. To carry this out, we set aside a percentage of our database and do not use it in any way in the model building and estimation. This percentage is usually small, perhaps 5 percent to 20 percent, but there is no fixed rule. For a very large database, we may set aside 50 percent or more of the data. For all the future calculations to be correct, the division of the data into two groups must be random.

After building and estimating our model on the main body of the data, we use the model to predict the classes of the validation database. We then count up the number of correct and incorrect classifications and calculate an error rate.

In building a single model, even this simple validation may need to be performed dozens of times. For example, when using a neural net, each training pass through the net is tested against a test database. Training stops when the error rates on the test database no longer improve with additional iterations. In such a case, being able to perform the training and testing cycle using many CPUs instead of just one will help you arrive at a model sooner.

Even small databases present challenges that require major computing power. In a small database, setting aside some data for testing and validation makes the estimation less precise. To address this situation, *cross validation* was developed. In this method, we randomly divide the data into two equal sets. We estimate on the first set and predict the second. But since the data were randomly divided, we can reverse the situation and estimate on the second database and predict the first. We now have two independent (because we randomly divided) estimates of error rates. We can take the average of the two and get a better estimate of the true error rate.

In cross validation we have estimated two models. Which do we use? Neither. Instead we generate a third model using all the data. The error rate for the model using all of the data is the average of the error rates for the two halves. Thus we have a model using all of the data for estimation and all of the data for error calculation.

In practice, a database is usually divided into more than just two groups to improve error estimation, and the more general *n-fold cross validation* is used. In this method, we randomly divide the data into *n* disjoint groups. For example, suppose we divided the data into ten groups. The first group is set aside for prediction and the other nine are lumped together for estimation. The model built and estimated on the 90 percent group is then used to predict the group that was set aside. This process is repeated a total of ten times as each group in turn is set aside and the model built and estimated on the remaining 90 percent of the data. The model is used to predict the set-aside group each time. Finally, we take the mean of the ten independent error rate predictions as our error rate.

Clearly these more complex methods require much more computing. In ordinary cross validation, we have to estimate three models and forecast on two sets of data. The amount of computing required by most models is governed more by the number of variables in the model than by the number of observations. Therefore, the model estimated on each half of the data requires *more* than half the computing of fitting one model to all of the data. With the fit to all of the data, cross validation requires at least three times the computing as does simple validation. N-fold cross validation, on the other hand, requires at least n times as much computing as simple validation. Since n is usually around 10, this means an order of magnitude increase in computation. The increase in accuracy and precision is usually worth the effort, however.

> *Example:* Some physicians studying a large epidemiological database have developed a model for predicting the eventual expression of a debilitating disease in patients. Though the model fits the data well, a correct error-rate calculation is crucial. If the patient is likely to develop the disease, he must submit to a strict, expensive, and in part unpleasant dietary and medicinal regime. So it is important to minimize false positives. If the patient does not submit to the regime and later develops the disease, there is no later treatment and he is doomed. So it is important to know the false negative rate.

> Although the database is large, the physicians use n-fold cross validation to split the data into ten groups, repeatedly estimate the model on nine tenths of the data, and predict the final tenth. In this way, they use all of the data for both training and testing their model. Based on the error rate calculation, they decide that on close calls (i.e., patients who are not firmly in one of the two groups) additional blood and genetic tests be carried out. They build a more complicated model for such patients and lower the overall error rate to an acceptable level.

The next method, *bootstrapping*, requires even more computing to validate a model than does n-fold cross validation.

Briefly, when applying the bootstrapping algorithm you take a random sample, *with replacement*, of the data of size equal to the whole database. In other words, if you had 1,000 rows of data, you would build a sample of 1,000 rows by picking one row at random. After putting it back, you would pick another row, put it back, and keep on doing this until you had a total of 1,000 rows in your sample. Note that this means that some rows may appear more than once and some may not appear at all. You split the sample into two groups: one for training and one for validation. You repeat this cycle of model building at least 200 times—and in some cases up to 10,000 times. The mean error rate is the mean over all of the repetitions (bootstraps). By building enough models, you will converge on a very low error rate.

The bootstrap is extremely powerful as it gives not only the error but also give the variance of the error as the variance over all of the bootstraps. This is an unbiased and usually efficient (lowest possible variance) estimate of the variance of the error rate.

Because we are going through the training-test cycle conceivably thousands of times, clearly bootstrapping is computationally intensive. Furthermore, the large number of samples may put an I/O burden on the computer. Only with modern parallel hardware and algorithms can we hope to use bootstrapping effectively.

> *Example:* In a manufacturing process, the only way to absolutely determine if an item is defective is to test it to destruction. Based on some test data, a model has been developed that will predict the status of an item without destructive testing. Only a few variables are used in the model. Although the form of the model remains constant, the parameters change with each new shipment of raw material. The model is sensitive to slight changes in some of the parameters, so it is important to use as much data as possible to estimate these parameters. However, since the raw material is expensive and testing of the items is destructive, the plant wants to use as little material as possible for testing.

A data mining consultant recommends a technique called bootstrapping to estimate and validate the model. This method, which attempts to use every possible split of the data by repeatedly taking samples from the data, is computer intensive and must be run on a moderate sized computer overnight. For faster model building, or to handle more data, they will need to move to a parallel computer.

Making Data Mining Tools Scalable

Hardware Scalability

We have talked about the need for parallel hardware for data mining algorithms and database access. As we have seen, many data mining problems involve large, complex databases, complicated modeling techniques, and substantial computer processing. In addition to the actual computation, a great deal of processing is needed to select and reformat data for the data mining database. Various selection and subsetting functions are needed, and display functions are used to view data and results. All of these operations take considerable power for databases that store millions or possibly tens of millions of rows. Without adequate processing power, a large or complex data mining effort will come to a halt.

The goal of hardware scalability is to provide high performance by adding modestly priced processor building blocks (or nodes) in such a way that performance scales linearly. For example, by doubling the number of processors you can process twice as much data in the same time or the same amount of data in half the time. The hardware vendors have taken two complementary approaches of using multiple CPUs: symmetric multi-processing (SMP) and massively parallel processing (MPP).

It is important to understand the different routes to achieving hardware parallelism as they are most frequently used in data mining. A company beginning a data mining effort has to decide whether its computing facilities are adequate, and if not, what steps to take.

Example: A small trucking company decided to mine their databases to explore scheduling their delivery trucks more efficiently. Their corporate computer, though perfectly adequate for the existing transactional databases, proves totally inadequate when analysts attempt to merge them into one large analysis database. Furthermore, the data analysis and data mining applications make it impossible for the corporate computer to maintain its level of transaction throughput.

The company has to off-load its databases to a data warehouse running on an SMP parallel computer with a parallel DBMS optimized for decision support and data mining. The analysts then work on the data warehouse computer rather than on the corporate transaction computer. As the database size grows, they will add additional processing units. At some point, they may need to consider migrating to an MPP architecture.

In an SMP computer, there is a collection of processing nodes, each with its own private local cache memory. However, there is only a single instance of the operating system, and the disks and main memory are shared through a common bus. The amount of time for any processor to access main memory is equal. A major appeal of SMP is that it is relatively easy to administer, in part because it looks like one computer with a single operating system. It can be used by a DBMS with little if any reprogramming, simply by assigning tasks to CPUs, although modifications such as multithreading based on small-grained, light-weight threads can let the DBMS take better advantage of SMP.

Even greater degrees of scalability can be achieved by moving to one of a variety of MPP architectures. For example, in the so-called "shared nothing" MPP architecture, each node has its own main memory and I/O subsystem, but shares a backplane over which data or requests for services (called functions) can be shipped. Each node in a shared nothing system can be an SMP node, and these can be coupled together to bring hundreds of CPUs to bear on a problem. These are sometimes called SMP clusters, and should not be confused with clustered disk access systems in which a group of CPUs share an I/O system.

Parallel Algorithms

Data mining algorithms written for a uniprocessor machine won't automatically run faster on a parallel machine; they must be rewritten to take advantage of the parallel processors. There are two basic ways of accomplishing this. In the first method, independent pieces of the application are assigned to different processors. The more processors, the more pieces can be executed without reducing throughput. This is called *inter-model parallelism*. This kind of scale-up is also useful in building multiple independent models. For example, a neural net application could build multiple models using different architectures (e.g., with a different number of nodes or hidden layers) simultaneously on each processor.

But what happens if building each model takes a long time? We then need to break this model into tasks, execute those tasks on separate processors, and recombine them for the answer. This second method is called *intra-model parallelism*.

Native Database Access and Parallel DBMSs

As we saw earlier, large data mining problems can require large amounts of database access. This requirement can come from such operations as mining a large amount of data, needing to sample a large database, building many different models, or needing to retrieve many samples when testing and validating the model.

If the data from an existing database can be mined, then native DBMS access will provide the best possible performance. Most data warehouses today make use of parallel database management systems. However, because the data mining process may involve data from multiple databases, or subsets of data from a data warehouse, it is usually a good idea to create a datamart for purposes of mining that data. This avoids the problem of consolidating data every time you want to use it.

While in some cases the datamart may use a special-purpose DBMS developed for the data mining tool, in most cases it will use a standard DBMS. In either case, the size of the datamart or allowing for growth in the size of the datamart will require the data store to be parallelized.

A scalable data mining tool should be able to directly access the datamart DBMS, rather than require that the data to be mined be written to a flat file. Ideally, the tool uses the native SQL of the database server, which maximizes performance and takes advantage of individual server features such as stored procedures and SQL extensions. No single product, however, can support the large variety of database servers, so a gateway must be used for all but the four or five leading DBMSs. The most common gateway supported is Microsoft's ODBC (Open Database Connectivity).

A parallel DBMS can assign individual SQL statements to CPUs. This is called *inter-query parallelism*. Alternatively, it may break up a large SQL statement and assign pieces of it to different CPUs. This is called *intra-query parallelism*. Both of these approaches are analogous to how data mining models are parallelized.

If there is more than one data stream, it's possible for some operations to proceed simultaneously. For example, a customer database being mined could be spread across multiple disks, and a thread could process each subset of the customer data. This is called *partitioned parallelism*. Because data can be partitioned into many subsets, this technique provides a much greater opportunity for performance improvement.

All of these types of parallel processing can happen in either SMP or shared nothing MPP architectures. The algorithms for good SMP performance, however, are different than those for good shared nothing performance.

A good partitioning scheme is an essential part of designing a database that will benefit from parallelism. Partitioned data benefits from indexed access just like non-parallel databases do. The indexes may also be partitioned. To get the best results of partitioning, the allocation scheme must be carefully designed to minimize skew and data movement. The choices will largely be determined by the queries run against the database, and the inevitable tradeoffs will mean some queries will run faster than others. In particular, any partitioning scheme can run afoul of unanticipated queries, and the parallel optimizer needs to be able to deal with these variations. A good parallel optimizer has a host of techniques to minimize the need for data shipping, but, even in a shared nothing architecture, sometimes considerable amounts of data will need to be shipped. There are so many variables among the hardware configurations and data partitioning that it is impossible to draw conclusions from vendor benchmarks.

CONCLUSION

Data mining is an important method for extracting valuable information from all sizes of databases: large and small. Data miners need fast response time when building their models so they can construct the most effective model. Three factors, however, make developing a data mining model a potentially lengthy process:

1. The enormous amount of data that must be processed when mining or sampling massive databases.
2. The large number of models that must be built to explore complex databases.
3. The intricacies of testing and validating models.

The solution to these large-scale problems is through applying parallel technology. Scalable data mining tools take advantage of hardware parallelism, including parallel algorithms as well as direct access to parallel DBMSs.

SCALABLE DATA MINING REQUIREMENTS

The following is a list of items to consider when evaluating the need for scalable data mining solutions.

1. Database size
   - Number of tables
   - Required storage in bytes

- Number of rows in each table
- Number of columns in each table
- Number of samples
- Type of samples (e.g., stratified, clustered)
- Model deployment
  - Arrival rate of new transactions
  - Processing time per transaction
  - Response time required
  - Size of batches to be processed

2. Model complexity

- Number of columns
- Data types for columns (continuous, categorical)
- Categories of problems to be solved
  - Classification
  - Clustering
  - Association
  - Sequences
  - Value forecasting
  - Other
- Types of algorithms
  - Decision trees
  - Neural nets
  - k-nearest neighbor
  - Memory based reasoning
  - Other

3. Training and testing

- Simple validation
- N-fold cross validation
- Bootstrapping

SCALABLE DATA MINING TOOLS

The following list summarizes those features of a data mining tool that make it scalable.

1. Parallel algorithms

   - Inter-model parallelism
   - Intra-model parallelism

2. Database processing

   - Sequential file
   - Native database access
     - DB2
     - Informix
     - Oracle
     - Sybase
     - Other
   - ODBC
   - Support of parallel DBMSs

3. Hardware support

   - SMP computers
   - MPP computers

Chapter 10

Updating the Data Warehouse

J.D. Welch

PRISM Solutions

The data warehouse is defined as being subject-oriented, integrated, time variant, and non-volatile. These characteristics are an important distinction from operational systems and data. However, non-volatility does not mean that the data warehouse is never updated, or that data in the data warehouse cannot be updated. Indeed, in order to be time variant (that is, historical), the data warehouse must be updated at regular intervals.

This chapter discusses some of the approaches to updating the data warehouse in order to capture new or changed data, identify a particular point in time in the data warehouse's data, and preserve historical integrity of the data warehouse's data.

HISTORICAL INTEGRITY

Historical integrity is as important to a data warehouse as referential integrity is to an operational system's data. Historical integrity means that the time variant data in the data warehouse is accurate whenever it is being accessed, whether that data is one month, one year, or infinite years old. Without historical integrity, users will not be able to trust the data in the data warehouse, since the accuracy of that data will fluctuate and be unreliable. Therefore, both the extract of data from operational sources and the loading of that data into the data warehouse must be designed in such a way that historical integrity is preserved. There will be times when the values of certain data will or must change, based on changing business rules or the correction of incorrect or incomplete data previously loaded into the data warehouse. Therefore, the non-volatility characteristic of the data warehouse is not to be interpreted as a strict rule, but as a goal and a guideline. Once data has been determined to be accurate, given the information and business rules available at the time it is captured from an operational source and loaded into the data warehouse, then that data should not change unless it is under extraordinary circumstances. If a change does need to be applied to a static, time variant piece of information, then a description of that change and the business reasons for it should be added to the metadata about that data. In this way, even though the data may need to be changed, the historical integrity of the data is preserved through the metadata. Historical integrity does not mean, therefore, that data never changes, but that accuracy of data is preserved over time, and that if data must change, it do so for valid business reasons and those reasons be recorded as metadata.

TYPES OF SOURCE SYSTEM EXTRACTS

In order to update the data warehouse, it is necessary first to identify what data is required from the operational system in order to capture any new or changed data during a given time variant interval. Therefore, let us begin with identifying the triggers in the operational environment that determine when an extract should be taken. These triggers can be categorized as **point-in-time snapshots**, **significant business events**, or **delta data**.

Point-in-Time Snapshots

The simplest way to preserve history is to take a point-in-time snapshot of the operational data. Snapshots are typically scheduled for very specific points in time, such as the end of a calendar week or month, and they preserve the historical relationship between different data elements and subject areas. For example, if it is important to know a customer's status, discount plan, and account manager responsible for service to the customer's account, then a point-in-time snapshot will preserve the specific values for all of these data elements whenever a snapshot is taken.

From an access standpoint, snapshots are a very effective and efficient way for users to pinpoint specific points in time or ranges of time. A snapshot is a very effective way to determine deltas between different points in time, as well. For example, if monthly point-in-time snapshots of customer data are taken from an operational source and loaded into the data warehouse, a determination of the changes in the customer base can easily be determined from month to month, or any time period. New accounts, canceled accounts, and changes in account attributes can be easily determined by comparing two different points in time, without having to capture and store the specific changes to each account during the same time interval.

The most significant problem with a snapshot is that it requires a complete read of virtually the entire operational source of data. The impact here can be reduced by selectively targeting and filtering data to be extracted in the snapshot. For example, some data in the operational system will typically be static, while other data will be more dynamic in nature. Likewise, some data may be relatively static, but knowing the specific values at a point in time is more of a determining factor than whether it might change. Address data tends to be relatively static, so while the majority of the data warehouse is based on weekly or monthly points in time, address data may need to be extracted only quarterly. Likewise, status code and discount plan may be static or dynamic, depending on any given customer's behavior and other factors; however, ensuring the accuracy of these data elements at the specified points in time will require that a snapshot of them be taken at each time interval. An account manager may be very static, but since preserving the relationship between status code, discount plan, and account manager is a high priority, capturing account manager in a snapshot along with status code and discount plan is essential to preserving the historical integrity and accessibility of the relationship between these data elements.

Another problem with snapshots is the possibility for uncontrolled growth or unmanaged redundancy of data. While the specific relationships between different data elements and subjects is historically preserved, a tremendous amount of redundancy of static data also results from snapshots. This can be offset by the ability to determine delta data, rather than storing changes in the data warehouse, as noted above.

Significant Business Events

Significant business events (SBEs) are actually an event-oriented variation of point-in-time snapshots. Unlike a point-in-time, which is an easily predetermined date such as the end of a calendar week or month, an SBE cannot be accurately predicted; it must occur for the snapshot to then take place. For example, an SBE might be the successful completion of a billing cycle. There may be several billing cycles during a calendar month, each with a predetermined cutoff date. Nevertheless, the successful completion of the billing cycle is dependent on a number of factors and cannot be predetermined; it may take anywhere from one to three days to complete the cycle. The actual completion event is determined by a set of success criteria, usually judged by the person or group responsible for quality assurance or other similar business function. Once the cycle has been deemed successful, bills can be mailed to the customers. It is at this point, this significant business event, that a snapshot of the billing data and any related or artifacted data can take place.

Another example might be the end of an accounting period. There may be a need for a snapshot of the same data at the end of each calendar month and at the end of each accounting period. The accounting period may be a 4-4-5 week cycle, which only occasionally corresponds to calendar months. The accounting period may be a calendar month, but the actual completion of the accounting close may not take place until sometime between, say, four and seven days after the end of the calendar month. It is not until the controller declares the books closed for the month that the accounting period snapshot can be taken. In this case the SBE is the actual closing of the books, not the end of the last day of the calendar month.

SBEs may need to capture some or all of the data that is also captured by a point-in-time snapshot. For example, a point-in-time snapshot may capture dynamic and vital customer information at the end of each calendar month. This snapshot would include such potentially dynamic and otherwise important month-end data as status code, discount plan, and account manager. With a monthly series of point-in-time snapshots, an exact profile of the customer base by discount plan and account manager can be accessed. Changes in terms of new accounts, canceled accounts, and migrations from one discount plan to another, or reassignment of accounts between account managers, can also be determined, but on the basis of net changes during the month, not specifically when a change took place. This satisfies the business requirement for information of knowing the net change of accounts from one time period to the next, and preserves historical integrity for that data. And for each billing cycle during the month, it is also important to know exactly which discount plan and geographic location apply to each customer. In this way revenue and other billing-related data can be analyzed by customer profile attributes. The discount plan may change at any point during the month. While discount plan is captured once a month in a point-in-time snapshot, it must also be captured at the successful completion of each billing cycle for those customers on that billing cycle. Therefore, discount plan would be an example of managed redundancy, in that it is captured at least twice in any month for each customer account, but for different reasons based on significant business events that take place in the operational environment and based on different end-user access requirements. The historical integrity of both events, the end of the calendar month and the successful completion of each billing cycle, is maintained.

Delta Data

Delta data is also known as "new and changed data"; that is, data that represents changes (deltas) from one point in time to the next. Delta data can be captured in a number of ways: as **operational events, change data capture, date last modified,** or **point-in-time comparisons**.

Operational Events

An operational event creates delta data by passing a record of the event either to a holding file or to a data warehouse updating process. This will result in an accurate record of the changes that take place in the operational system at a limited cost in terms of processing. Figure 10–1 illustrates this approach.

Figure 10–1 Operational Events

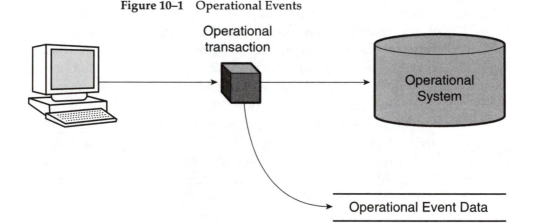

There are two major concerns with this approach:

1. The operational system will need to be modified to write out the transaction to the data warehouse operational event repository. This can be difficult and time-consuming to accomplish, as any enhancement to an operational system should be thoroughly evaluated and then tested to ensure that it does not jeopardize that system's functionality.

2. Data warehouse operational event transactions must not interfere with either online or batch transaction

processing. If several processes are writing to the data warehouse operational event repository, be it a file or a process, there is a very real risk of locking contention that may cause an operational process to seize.

After the operational event data has been captured, it will be necessary to determine which is the correct record to update to the data warehouse. For example, for any single instance in the operational system there may be several transactions during a time variant interval. One technique for deriving the data for the data warehouse is to take the net change during a time interval, rather than accumulating all of the changes to a data element during that interval. Therefore, if there were several changes to the same data element for the same source system record, then only the last operational event need be updated to the data warehouse.

Changed Data Capture

Changed data capture (CDC) refers to the process of reading a database or other operational change logs and extracting the appropriate changed data for updating the data warehouse. For example, the database change log of a transaction-based operational system will preserve all of the changes that were applied to the database during a given processing period. A CDC process will read that log and write to an output file those changes that are pertinent to the informational requirements of the data warehouse. The changes can then be applied to the data warehouse as additions of new data or as updates to existing data. Figure 10–2 illustrates the CDC approach.

As with the operational event, in some cases only the last record identified from the CDC process will be needed to update the data warehouse, adding an additional preprocessing step to the CDC-based data acquisition. But unlike the operational events, which are being accumulated to the data warehouse operational event repository in real time, CDC data must be processed for each operational time interval. Since most database and other operational logs are backed up and "cleared" nightly, this will necessitate nightly CDC processing, regardless of the time interval required by the business requirements for information that are driving the data warehouse.

Figure 10–2   Changed Data Capture

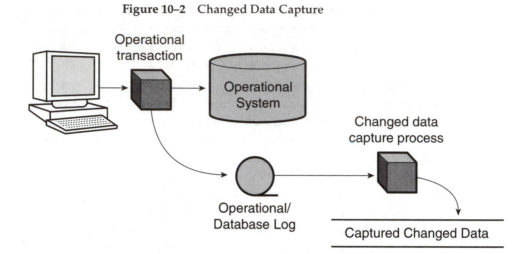

Date Last Modified

A very efficient means of extracting new and changed data from operational sources is to interrogate a date last modified (DLM) in the operational tables or files. This DLM data element is updated with the current system date whenever a record is modified by the operational system, usually for whatever reason. (It is unfortunate that many legacy systems do not have an effective DLM that can be used for this purpose.) In some cases a DLM does not exist, or if it does it is on a very large record that contains a wide variety of different data elements, most of which were not changed. For example, a record in a flat-file-based legacy system may contain customer profile information, status, and services purchased or used data, most recent billing data, and Receivables data. A change to any one of these areas will result in the DLM being updated and the entire record being extracted. This will result in excessive update processing when loading the data warehouse. Whenever possible, the data being extracted from the operational source should be filtered to include only that data that should be updated into the data warehouse. Such an example would better benefit from a point-in-time comparison, an operational event, or a CDC approach.

Point-in-Time Comparisons   An overlooked approach to extracting delta data from an operational system is the point-in-time comparison. This can be especially effective when the time variant interval is not daily, but weekly or monthly. Point-in-time comparisons are in general not considered a legitimate approach to generating delta data because they require a complete read of the operational source to create a full snapshot file that is then compared to the previous period's full snapshot. In many systems, however, especially flat-file systems, this can be a very fast and efficient process.

(Note: Serious consideration should be given to the stated need by users or others for daily extracts. The data warehouse is an analytical environment, and in most cases monthly time intervals are sufficient, followed by weekly. If there is a legitimate business cause for daily extracts, consider the length of time that daily data needs to be retained in the data warehouse. In most cases, daily data becomes stale very quickly, and it loses its value as an analytical tool after ninety [90] days at the most. Also, the need for daily detailed data may be better resolved by an Operational Data Store [ODS], rather than by a data warehouse.)

In one case a Multiple Virtual System (MVS)-based customer order processing and billing system required this approach. Half a million records were extracted nightly and compared to the previous night's full extract. The extracted records were more than 2,500 bytes in length. The entire process of extract and compare consistently took approximately 15 minutes, regardless of the size of the output file. Also, since this large source system record contained a variety of different types of related data (as described in DLM above), the DLM was not an effective approach. The extracted record was broken into a series of records, each corresponding to a table or set of tables in the data warehouse. The comparison process effected on this partitioned record generated *only* new and changed records *specific* to the target environment, resulting in very efficient loading of the data warehouse. The source system, likewise, was not adversely affected due to the efficiency of the simple duplication of its data. See Figure 10–3 for an illustration of this point-in-time comparison.

Figure 10–3 Point-in-Time Comparison

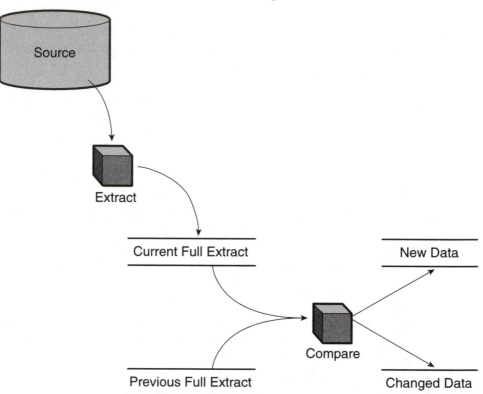

Summary of Source System Extract Types

Operational data can be extracted from its system of record as either a point-in-time snapshot, a significant business event snapshot, or as delta data. Delta data can be derived a number of ways, from operational events (transactions), changed data capture of operational or database logs, from a date last modified in the system of record, or as the result of comparing two different points in time. Each approach is valid and has merits, based on a number of factors. First, what are the business requirements for information that the users of the data warehouse have, and how will their need to access the data in questions affect the decision of which extract approach to take? Then, what is the most efficient and economical approach to extracting data from its operational source? And finally, what is the most historically accurate approach to extracting data from its operational source?

TYPES OF EXTRACTED DATA

Since point-in-time snapshots and significant business events are essentially both forms of a snapshot, they will be considered the same type of data for update purposes. Conversely, delta data should be broken down into new data and changed data. Therefore, for a discussion of the different types of updates, extracted data will be categorized as **snapshots**, **new data**, or **changed data**.

Snapshots

In this simplified view of extracted data, snapshots represent any point in time, be it a specific, predeterminable calendar date or an event-driven date where the determination to take the snapshot is based on some significant business event. Snapshots of operational data preserve all of the historical relationships between the different data found in all of the systems snapped, ensuring a high degree of historical integrity and ease of access for a specific point in time or time range. Snapshots do, however, tend to result in high and, in some cases, extraneous amounts of redundant data. This can be mitigated to some degree by selectively filtering either records or data elements that are not essential to the business requirements for information for which the snapshot is being made.

Snapshots also present the challenge of managed redundancy. As noted, snapshots may represent both a point-in-time and an SBE, and may contain similar or identical data for these different time variant purposes. For example, a point-in-time snapshot may contain the following information:

ME Snapshot Date	Customer ID	Customer Status Date	Customer Status	Customer Address State	Customer ZIP Code	Customer Type	Discount Plan	Account Manager
6/30/96	AZ12345	3/15/95	Active	UT	84094	Corp	A	Smith

And an SBE for a billing cycle run on May 20th might contain the following:

Customer ID	Billing Cycle Month	Billing Cycle Year	Bill Cycle	Customer Status	Customer Status Date	Discount Plan	Account Manager	Prev Bal	Payments Received	New Chrgs	Curr Bal
AZ12345	7	1996	4	Suspend	7/12/96	B	Smith	$425	$425	$100	$100

Both extract records contain status, discount plan, and account manager data because these can change at any time during the month and it is important to know their values at the time of billing for each customer. As we can see, this customer's status changed on July 12, 1996, from "Active" to "Suspend." Nevertheless, the previous month-end point-in-time still shows him as "Active." If it were not contained on the billing or on SBE snapshot record, in order to capture the correct customer profile information for the time of billing, it would need to be extracted daily from its operational source. The result would be significantly more processing and resulting changed data than the small amount of managed redundancy represented by status, discount plan, and account manager data being captured on both snapshot records, representing two different points-in-time based on different business events (end of calendar month and billing cycle number 4), serving different business requirements for information.

New Data

New data is made up of records that did not previously exist in the operational system as of the extract immediately prior to the current extract, and will therefore be new to the data warehouse. Examples of new data include new customer accounts and transactions made during the time variant interval between extracts. New data is related to changed data in that the existence of a new record is a "change" from the standpoint of the operational source. New data is usually much simpler to load into the data warehouse than changed data. So from a data warehouse perspective, we want to distinguish new from changed data wherever possible.

Changed Data

Changed data consists of changes to existing records in the operational data source. These changes may be a full representation of the changed source system record, including unchanged data, as well as all of the changes that took place during the time variant interval. This is the simplest output of a DLM-based extract. Table 10-1 is an example of this kind of changed record.

Table 10–1 Change Data Comparison Results

Record	Customer ID	Customer Status Date	Customer Status	Customer Address State	Customer ZIP Code	Customer Type	Discount Plan	Account Manager
Previous 1	AZ12345	3/15/95	Active	UT	84094	Corp	A	Smith
Previous 2	BA34567	10/22/95	Active	NJ	07920	Govt	A	Wilson
Current 1	AZ12345	7/12/96	Suspend	UT	84094	Corp	B	Smith
Current 2	BA34567	10/22/95	Active	NJ	07920	Govt	A	Wilson
Current 3	BX98765	7/12/96	Active	OH	45701	Indvl	C	Jones
Delta 1	AZ12345	7/12/96	Suspend	UT	84094	Corp	B	Smith
Delta 2	BX98765	7/12/96	Active	OH	45701	Indvl	C	Jones

In Table 10-1, the example above, new and changed records have been identified and extracted from the operational source, represented by files "Previous" and "Current." When compared, the resulting "Delta" file contains the changed record for customer ID AZ12345, which contains three changes. Since there were no changes to the record with customer ID BA34567, there is no record with this key in the delta file. And, since customer ID record BX98765 is new as of the current extract, it is in the delta file as well.

This approach is fairly straightforward and preserves all of the relationships between the data elements in a given source system row. It does not distinguish between new and changed records, merely the difference between the previous and the current files. An alternative approach might be to alter the compare process so that new and changed records are distinguished from each other to simplify input processing by separating it from update processing, as shown in Table 10-2.

Table 10–2 Changed and New Data from Comparison

Record	Customer ID	Customer Status Date	Customer Status	Customer Address State	Customer ZIP Code	Customer Type	Discount Plan	Account Manager
Delta 1	AZ12345	7/12/96	Suspend	UT	84094	Corp	B	Smith
New 1	BX98765	7/12/96	Active	OH	45701	Indvl	C	Jones

Another approach would be to identify changed data as a before/after image of a given data element associated with the key value of the record, as depicted in Table 10-3.

Table 10–3 Delta and New Data from Comparison

	Customer ID	Customer Status Date	Customer Status	Customer Address State	Customer ZIP Code	Customer Type	Discount Plan	Account Manager
Column	1	2	3	4	5	6	7	8

Record

	Customer ID	Customer Status Date	Customer Status	Customer Address State	Customer ZIP Code	Customer Type	Discount Plan	Account Manager
Previous 1	AZ12345	3/15/95	Active	UT	84094	Corp	A	Jones
Previous 2	BA34567	10/22/95	Active	NJ	07920	Govt	A	Wilson

	Customer ID	Customer Status Date	Customer Status	Customer Address State	Customer ZIP Code	Customer Type	Discount Plan	Account Manager
Current 1	AZ12345	7/12/96	Suspend	UT	84094	Corp	B	Smith
Current 2	BA34567	10/22/95	Active	NJ	07920	Govt	A	Wilson
Current 3	BX98765	7/12/96	Active	OH	45701	Indvl	C	Jones

Delta Records	Customer ID	Column Changed	Previous Value	Current Value
Delta 1	AZ12345	2	3/15/96	7/12/96
Delta 2	AZ12345	3	Active	Suspend
Delta 3	AZ12345	7	A	B

New Record	Customer ID	Customer Status Date	Customer Status	Customer Address State	Customer ZIP Code	Customer Type	Discount Plan	Account Manager
New 1	BX98765	7/12/96	Active	OH	45701	Indvl	C	Jones

In this situation only the changes to customer ID record "AZ12345" are recorded, each change including an identification of the column where the data changed and the previous and current values for that column. A separate output file contains the new record with the customer ID of "BX98765." This will allow for the simplified input of new records, but the more normalized output of changed data will result in a more complicated update process. For example, since "Customer Status Date" and "Customer Status" are related to each other, both must be applied at the same time in an update of the data warehouse. But since they exist as separate records in the normalized delta file, the update process must have a more complex set of processing logic to understand which columns are related to each other, and therefore they must be processed together so as not to create unclear or illogical "interim" records in the data warehouse. Also, it may not be sufficient merely to record changes in the data warehouse, as these by themselves are not conducive to clear understanding of the data from an access perspective.

Summary of Extracted Data Types

The different types of extracts essentially produce one or a combination of three different types of data: snapshot data, new data, and changed data. These three categories of data provide different means of capturing changes in operational sources and retaining those time variant differences in the data warehouse. Like the different extract methods, which extracted data type is appropriate is based on the business requirements for information, efficient and economical processing, and ensuring historical integrity.

TYPES OF DATA WAREHOUSE UPDATES

Updating the data warehouse can be addressed by one, variations, or combinations of **Insert**, **Replace**, or **Update**. In addition, these updates have different application when used with each of the different types of extract data.

	Insert	Full Replace	Partial Replace	Update	Update Plus Insert	Insert With Update	Replace And Insert
Snapshot	X	X					
New Data	X	X				X	X
Changed Data		X	X	X	X	X	X

Insert

Perhaps the most straightforward approach to updating the data warehouse is simply to insert the extracted data into the appropriate table or tables. This is particularly effective with snapshot and new data, since by definition both of these types of data are "new" from a time variant perspective. Figure 10-4 illustrates the insert process.

An example of a series of snapshot data that has been inserted into the data warehouse can be seen in Table 10-4. In this example, extracts are made at the successful completion of each billing cycle for every customer on that billing cycle.

Figure 10–4   Simple Data Warehouse Insert

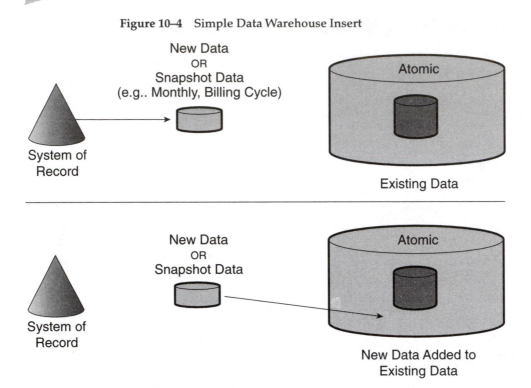

Table 10–4 Series of SBE Snapshot Data

Monthly Billing Table	Row 1	Row 2	Row 3	Row 4	Row 5
Customer ID (PK)	AZ12345	AZ12345	AZ12345	AZ12345	AZ12345
Billing Cycle Month (PK)	3	4	5	6	7
Billing Cycle Year (PK)	1996	1996	1996	1996	1996
Billing Cycle	3	3	3	4	4
Customer Status	Active	Active	Active	Active	Suspend
Customer Status Date	6/1/95	6/1/95	6/1/95	6/1/95	7/12/96
Discount Plan	A	A	A	A	B
Account Manager	Jones	Smith	Smith	Smith	Smith
Previous Balance	$250	$225	$400	$425	$425
Payments Received	$150	$0	$125	$175	$425
New Charges	$125	$175	$150	$175	$100
Current Balance	$225	$400	$425	$425	$100

The SBE snapshot records contain a combination of the billing cycle data itself (represented by the columns "Previous Balance" through "Current Balance") and customer profile information, including status, discount plan, and account manager information. The reason for this is that any of these data elements could change during the course of a calendar month, and it is important for informational purposes to preserve the status of each of them as they existed at the time of each billing cycle. While it would be possible to locate and align the appropriate profile records from another table for any one instance of a customer, connecting sets of billing data records that span a wide time period to the appropriate profile records is an extremely complex activity. Since one of the objectives of the data warehouse is that users be able to access the data in order to turn it into information, the additional redundant data is a small price for historical integrity and ease of use. Managed redundancy, of which this is an example, while consuming more disk per customer per month than a more normalized approach, ensures historical integrity of important data from different subject areas and is simpler for users to access in the set-at-a-time processing that is characteristic of informational processing.

Snapshot data inserted into the data warehouse can be very efficient to access, as demonstrated by this sample SQL query to satisfy the business question "What was revenue by discount plan for the last 13 months?"

```
Select billing_cycle_year, billing_cycle_month,
                discount_plan, sum(new_charges)
From Monthly_Billing
Where (billing_cycle_year = 1995 and
                billing_cycle_month GT 5) or
                billing_cycle_year = 1996
Group by billing_cycle_year, billing_cycle_month,
                discount_plan;
```

Inserts can also be used to apply changed data to the data warehouse. In this case a time variant identifier must be part of the primary (unique) key in the target data warehouse table. (Note: A time variant identifier should always be part of the primary key of data in the data warehouse.) In this situation, the full extracted changed record will be the most efficient to insert into the data warehouse. In the following example, the full extract record of containing changed data is inserted into the target data warehouse table.

Existing data warehouse data:

	Row 1	Row 2	Row 3	Row 4
Customer ID (PK)	AZ12345	AZ12345	AZ12345	AZ12345
Record Change Date (PK)	1/15/94	5/1/95	6/1/95	3/15/96
Customer Status	Active	Suspend	Active	Active
Customer Status Date	1/15/94	5/1/95	6/1/95	6/1/95
Customer Address State	UT	UT	UT	UT
Customer ZIP Code	84094	84094	84094	84094
Customer Type	Corp	Corp	Corp	Corp
Discount Plan	A	A	A	A
Account Manager	Jones	Jones	Jones	Smith

Changed data from the operational source in snapshot form:

Record	Customer ID	Customer Status Date	Customer Status	Customer Address State	Customer ZIP Code	Customer Type	Discount Plan	Account Manager
Delta 1	AZ12345	7/12/96	Suspend	UT	84094	Corp	B	Smith

Changed data simply inserted into the data warehouse target table results in a new row (number 5):

	Row 1	Row 2	Row 3	Row 4	Row 5
Customer ID (PK)	AZ12345	AZ12345	AZ12345	AZ12345	AZ12345
Record Change Date (PK)	1/15/94	5/1/95	6/1/95	3/15/96	7/12/96
Customer Status	Active	Suspend	Active	Active	Suspend
Customer Status Date	1/15/94	5/1/95	6/1/95	6/1/95	7/12/96
Customer Address State	UT	UT	UT	UT	UT
Customer ZIP Code	84094	84094	84094	84094	84094
Customer Type	Corp	Corp	Corp	Corp	Corp
Discount Plan	A	A	A	A	B
Account Manager	Jones	Jones	Jones	Smith	Smith

Delta data can also be used to insert changed data into the data warehouse. In this situation the corresponding current record must be read from the data warehouse, all of the changes from the operational source must be applied to the output from the data warehouse, and the resulting record can then be inserted into the data warehouse. The following example describes this process.

Where the existing data warehouse data in the target data is as follows:

	Row 1	Row 2	Row 3	Row 4
Customer ID (PK)	AZ12345	AZ12345	AZ12345	AZ12345
Record Change Date (PK)	1/15/94	5/1/95	6/1/95	3/15/96
Customer Status	Active	Suspend	Active	Active
Customer Status Date	1/15/94	5/1/95	6/1/95	6/1/95
Customer Address State	UT	UT	UT	UT
Customer ZIP Code	84094	84094	84094	84094
Customer Type	Corp	Corp	Corp	Corp
Discount Plan	A	A	A	A
Account Manager	Jones	Jones	Jones	Smith

And changed data from operational source in delta data form is:

Delta Records	Customer ID	Column Changed	Previous Value	Current Value
Delta 1	AZ12345	2	3/15/96	7/12/96
Delta 2	AZ12345	3	Active	Suspend
Delta 3	AZ12345	7	A	B

The last row from the target table is read from the data warehouse, the changes are applied, and the resulting row is inserted into the target table. The result is a new row (number 5) in the data warehouse target table:

	Row 1	Row 2	Row 3	Row 4	Row 5
Customer ID (PK)	AZ12345	AZ12345	AZ12345	AZ12345	AZ12345
Record Change Date (PK)	1/15/94	5/1/95	6/1/95	3/15/96	7/12/96
Customer Status	Active	Suspend	Active	Active	Suspend
Customer Status Date	1/15/94	5/1/95	6/1/95	6/1/95	7/12/96
Customer Address State	UT	UT	UT	UT	UT
Customer ZIP Code	84094	84094	84094	84094	84094
Customer Type	Corp	Corp	Corp	Corp	Corp
Discount Plan	A	A	A	A	B
Account Manager	Jones	Jones	Jones	Smith	Smith

Although this can be an efficient means of updating the data warehouse with changed data, accessing a specific point in time becomes increasingly difficult as more changes are inserted into the target table. One approach to improving access of time variant data is to include an "end date" in addition to the "start date" ("Record Change Date" in the example above). This requires an update to the previous row in the target table (Row 4 above) and is explained below in "Insert Plus Update."

An additional consideration with all inserts is whether uniqueness needs to be enforced. For the most part, snapshot and new data will, by definition, be unique, since they represent either a unique point in time or data that does not exist in the data warehouse. Therefore, to increase the speed and efficiency of an insert to the data warehouse, consider eliminating a unique key on the target table. If there is a need to preserve referential integrity and/or ensure uniqueness beyond a doubt, then a unique key can be applied in a staging area. But remember that since the time variant nature of the data warehouse means a significant amount of data will be accumulating over time, unique keys for inserted data will quickly become a performance bottleneck in most cases.

Full Replace

The full replacement of existing warehouse data with data extracted from an operational source is a somewhat radical means of updating the data warehouse. This can be applied to any of the data types: snapshots, new data, or changed data. A full replacement of data in a data warehouse table with a new complete snapshot of operational data will result in a loss of historical data in the data warehouse. Figure 10-5 illustrates this.

This full replacement snapshot may be subject-oriented and integrated with data from other operational sources, satisfying some of the characteristic criteria of the data warehouse. The result, however, is merely a snapshot of the operational systems and does not provide any time variance for historical analysis. One solution to this problem is to have the operational system maintain any necessary history. This, however, defeats the purpose of the data warehouse and causes the operational system to maintain historical data for informational purposes, something that is not the operational system's primary responsibility. Therefore, except in extremely unusual circumstances, a full replace of data warehouse data by itself, while relatively simple, is not an effective means of providing the informational capabilities for which the data warehouse is intended. It can, however, be a useful method in conjunction with other, history-providing updating techniques, as described below.

Figure 10–5   Data Warehouse Table Full Replace

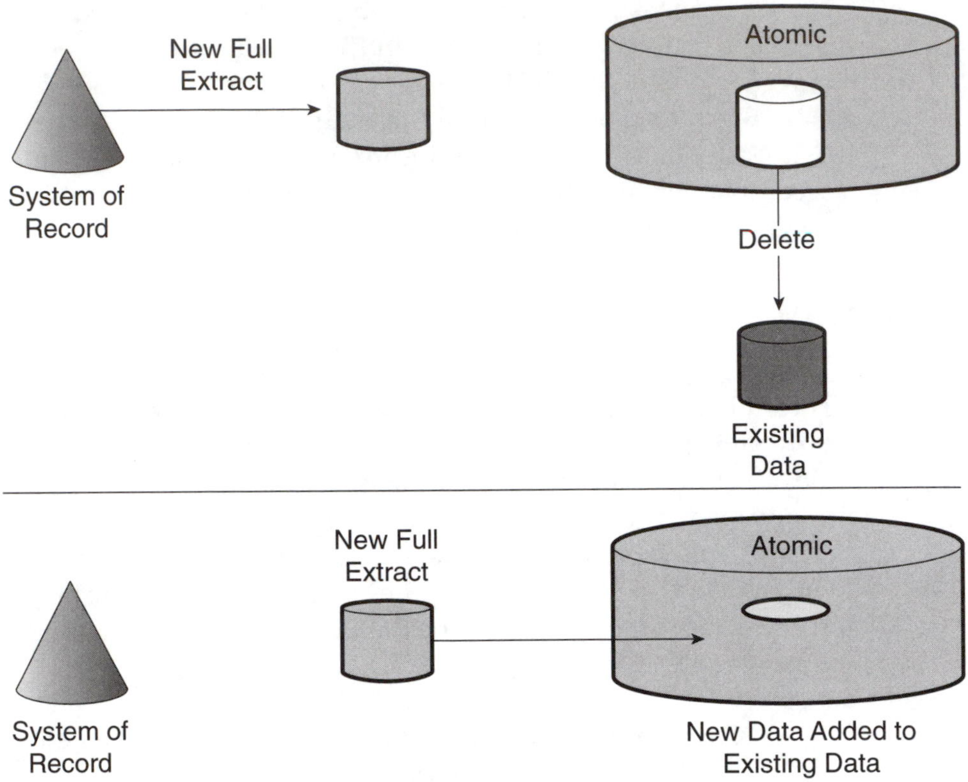

Partial Replace

A partial or selective replacement of existing warehouse data with new data extracted from an operational source is a variation on an update (see below). In this situation, the output of the extract from the operational source(s) is used to identify those records in the data warehouse that have changed in the operational system(s). Those identified records are then deleted from the data warehouse, and the changed data is inserted into the target table. Figure 10–6 illustrates the partial replace.

Although this results in an efficient load of the data warehouse target table, the identification and row deletion process can be very complex and/or processing-intensive. Even so, depending on the complexity of the process and the

Figure 10–6   Partial Replace

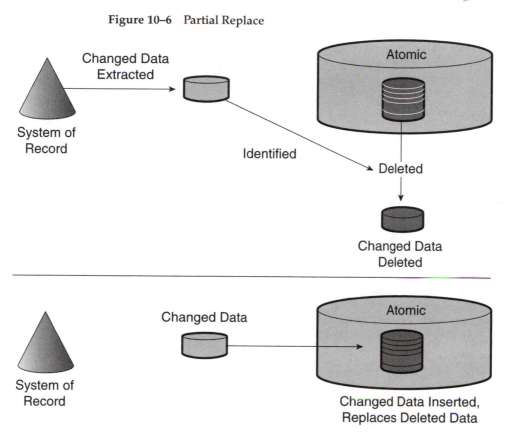

update performance of the data warehouse's RDBMS, this may be a more efficient process than an update.

Update

Applicable only to changed data, an update of data in the data warehouse overwrites an existing row, or existing data elements on a row, with the changed data extracted from the source system. Figure 10–7 illustrates the updating of a data warehouse table.

The problem with an update is that there is no historical preservation of the existing data or of the change that took place. In some cases this is acceptable. For example, some organizations may not need to record changes such as customer address to certain data; it is only relevant to know the customer's current address, not retain a history of changes.

Figure 10–7 Data Warehouse Table Update

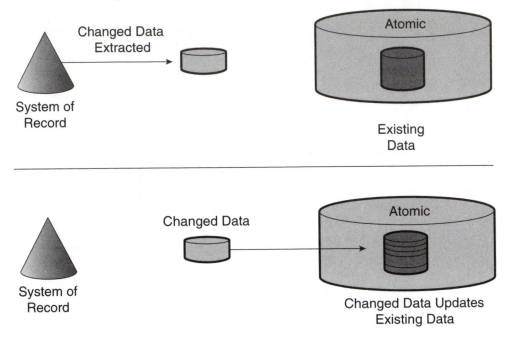

(Note: This may not apply to your organization's informational requirements, it is provided only as an example, not as a standard approach to warehousing addresses.)

Update Plus Insert

As noted above, an update alone does not retain an historical record of the change(s) to the operational source of the data. One way to update existing data and retain a history of the change is with an update plus insert (Figure 10–8).

In this approach to updating the data warehouse, the target data is partitioned into a "current" table and a "history" table, where the current table contains all the data for a given subject, and the history table contains only those data elements that are either volatile (constantly changing), or those data elements that need to be artifacted with other data elements when either changes, or both. Also, the current data table maintains a single instance of each unique record from the operational source, such as customer account, while the

Figure 10–8 Update Plus Insert

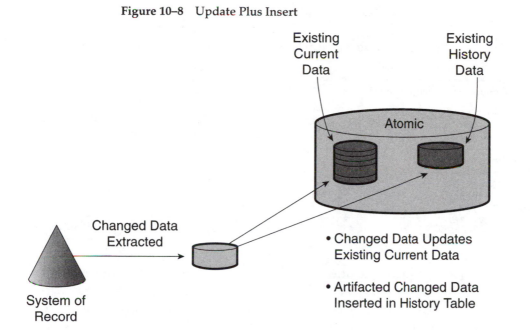

history data table retains a row for each change or set of changes to the dynamic data for each single instance of operational data. For example, a single instance of a unique record in the operational source would have one row in the following current data warehouse table, reflecting the current state of the operational data:

Customer Information	Row 1
Customer ID (PK)	AZ12345
Customer Status	Active
Customer Status Date	3/15/96
Customer Address State	UT
Customer ZIP Code	84094
Customer Type	Corp
Discount Plan	A
Account Manager	Smith

The history table for the same data would have a row for every change or set of changes that have taken place to the single instance of unique data in the operational system:

Customer Information History	Row 1	Row 2	Row 3	Row 4
Customer ID (PK)	AZ12345	AZ12345	AZ12345	AZ12345
Customer Info Change Date (PK)	1/15/94	5/1/95	6/1/95	3/15/96
Customer Status	Active	Suspend	Active	Active
Customer Status Date	1/15/94	5/1/95	6/1/95	6/1/95
Discount Plan	A	A	A	A
Account Manager	Jones	Jones	Jones	Smith

This partitioning of current and history data into similar but separate tables in the data warehouse serves several purposes. First, it reduces the amount of redundancy needed to be managed by separating the dynamic from the static data so that static data does not need to be replicated every time a dynamic data element changes. Second, it facilitates better access to current or historical data based on user requirements for information. Separating current data from historical data makes it simpler to identify the current profile of data. In most cases, users will begin their queries by selecting a set of data based on the current values, and then conduct an historical analysis based on the result set from the selection of current profile data. While this approach does necessitate a join between the current and historical data tables, the reduced redundancy and ability to "drive" a query based on simplified selection of the current data profile will, in most cases, result in simpler access.

For example, where the existing current data in the data warehouse is as follows:

Customer Information	Row 1
Customer ID (PK)	AZ12345
Customer Status	Active
Customer Status Date	3/15/96
Customer Address State	UT
Customer ZIP Code	84094
Customer Type	Corp
Discount Plan	A
Account Manager	Smith

And the existing history data in the data warehouse for the same customer is:

Customer Information History	Row 1	Row 2	Row 3	Row 4
Customer ID (PK)	AZ12345	AZ12345	AZ12345	AZ12345
Customer Info Change Date (PK)	1/15/94	5/1/95	6/1/95	3/15/96
Customer Status	Active	Suspend	Active	Active
Customer Status Date	1/15/94	5/1/95	6/1/95	6/1/95
Discount Plan	A	A	A	A
Account Manager	Jones	Jones	Jones	Smith

And the changed data from the operational source in snapshot form is:

Record	Customer ID	Customer Status Date	Customer Status	Customer Address State	Customer ZIP Code	Customer Type	Discount Plan	Account Manager
Delta 1	AZ12345	7/12/96	Suspend	UT	84094	Corp	B	Smith

Then the updated current record in the data warehouse will be:

Customer Information	Row 1
Customer ID (PK)	AZ12345
Customer Status	Suspend
Customer Status Date	7/12/96
Customer Address State	UT
Customer ZIP Code	84094
Customer Type	Corp
Discount Plan	B
Account Manager	Smith

And a new row (number 5) will be inserted into the history table in the data warehouse:

Customer Information History	Row 1	Row 2	Row 3	Row 4	Row 5
Customer ID (PK)	AZ12345	AZ12345	AZ12345	AZ12345	AZ12345
Customer Info Change Date (PK)	1/15/94	5/1/95	6/1/95	3/15/96	7/12/96
Customer Status	Active	Suspend	Active	Active	Suspend
Customer Status Date	1/15/94	5/1/95	6/1/95	6/1/95	7/12/96
Discount Plan	A	A	A	A	B
Account Manager	Jones	Jones	Jones	Smith	Smith

The major problem with this approach to preserving history is that, although it is relatively simple to perform an update plus insert to update the current data and insert a new history record, accessing the historical data described above can be complicated. This is due to the fact that there is only one time variant component in the history record ("Customer Info Change Date") to facilitate point-in-time access. For individual record access, this is not a problem. But for set-at-a-time access, simple SQL statements will not return the appropriate set of data; cursor processing is required to "step back" from a candidate record to evaluate the previous record and determine if the correct record has been selected. Nevertheless, for the atomic level of the data warehouse, this may be the most appropriate and efficient means of capturing data and ensuring historical integrity of the data. More efficient access of the data may be facilitated at a departmental level (datamart).

Insert with Update

An insert with update also addresses the problem of retaining history for changed data. While this approach is somewhat more complex than an update plus insert approach, accessing the resulting data is much simpler for either a point-in-time or a date range perspective. Figure 10-9 depicts an insert with update.

For example, if the existing target table in the data warehouse is as follows:

Customer Information History	Row 1	Row 2	Row 3	Row 4
Customer ID (PK)	AZ12345	AZ12345	AZ12345	AZ12345
Customer Info Change Date (PK)	1/15/94	5/1/95	6/1/95	3/15/96
Customer Info End Date	4/30/95	5/31/95	3/14/96	null
Customer Status	Active	Suspend	Active	Active
Customer Status Date	1/15/94	5/1/95	6/1/95	6/1/95
Discount Plan	A	A	A	A
Account Manager	Jones	Jones	Jones	Smith

And the changed data from the operational source in snapshot form is:

Record	Customer ID	Customer Status Date	Customer Status	Customer Address State	Customer ZIP Code	Customer Type	Discount Plan	Account Manager
Delta 1	AZ12345	7/12/96	Suspend	UT	84094	Corp	B	Smith

Figure 10–9 Insert with Update

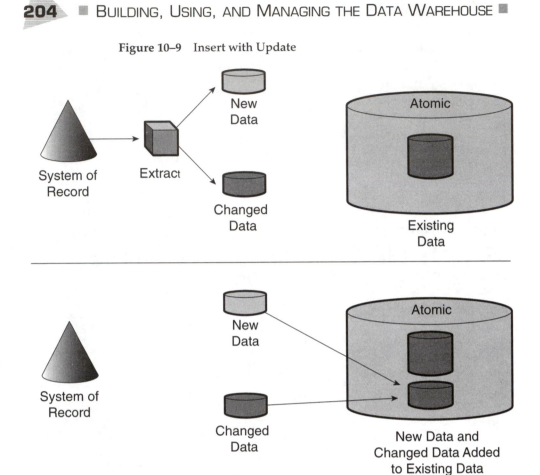

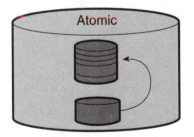

Changed Data Used to
Update Previous
Instance of Existing Data

Then the applicable data will be assembled from the extract snapshot record and a new row (number 5) will be inserted into the history table in the data warehouse:

Customer Information History	Row 1	Row 2	Row 3	Row 4	Row 5
Customer ID (PK)	AZ12345	AZ12345	AZ12345	AZ12345	AZ12345
Customer Info Change Date (PK)	1/15/94	5/1/95	6/1/95	3/15/96	7/12/96
Customer Info End Date	4/30/95	5/31/95	3/14/96	null	null
Customer Status	Active	Suspend	Active	Active	Suspend
Customer Status Date	1/15/94	5/1/95	6/1/95	6/1/95	7/12/96
Discount Plan	A	A	A	A	B
Account Manager	Jones	Jones	Jones	Smith	Smith

After row 5 has been inserted into the history table, the value of "Customer Info End Date" of the previous row (number 4) must be updated, set to the day before the most recent changes that are recorded in row 5:

Customer Information History	Row 1	Row 2	Row 3	Row 4	Row 5
Customer ID (PK)	AZ12345	AZ12345	AZ12345	AZ12345	AZ12345
Customer Info Change Date (PK)	1/15/94	5/1/95	6/1/95	3/15/96	7/12/96
Customer Info End Date	4/30/95	5/31/95	3/14/96	7/11/96	null
Customer Status	Active	Suspend	Active	Active	Suspend
Customer Status Date	1/15/94	5/1/95	6/1/95	6/1/95	7/12/96
Discount Plan	A	A	A	A	B
Account Manager	Jones	Jones	Jones	Smith	Smith

Accessing this data from a point-in-time perspective is now relatively simple. For example, to answer the question "What is the current distribution of customers by discount plan?," a simple SQL statement can be employed:

```
Select discount_plan, count distinct(customer_id)
From Customer_Information_History
Where customer_info_end_date is null
Group by discount_plan;
```

(Note: This assumes that the Relational Data Base Management System [RDBMS] being used for the data warehouse supports null dates. If not, the value of "Customer Info End

Date" can be set to an unrealistic future date, such as 1/1/3000, and the "where" clause changed to "Where customer_info_end_date = '01-jan-3000'.)

The above example will return the current profile of information, regardless of the current date. Likewise, comparing the results of the above, current-oriented query with an historical view of the same information is also simple. For example, to compare the current distribution of customers by discount plan with the distribution from the previous year, save the results of the above query and compare them with the results of a query that answers the question "What was the distribution of customers by discount plan last year at this time?" (assume current date to be July 15, 1996):

```
Select discount_plan, count distinct(customer_id)
From Customer_Information_History
Where customer_info_change_date LE "15-jul-1995" and
            customer_info_end_date GE "15-jul-1995"
Group by discount_plan;
```

Note that, unlike inserted snapshots, selecting a range of dates with this data structure becomes somewhat more complicated. For example, answering the question "What was the distribution of customers by discount plan by month for the last 13 months" cannot be easily accomplished with a single SQL statement. Each individual month can be returned quite easily, but returning the entire 13-month range becomes somewhat more complex. Rather than building a single complicated SQL statement with nested subqueries or a complex *where*-clause, the best approach would be either to execute a series of SQL statements, one for each month, saving the result sets so they can be assembled and presented as a single set of data, or to construct a "union," labeling each month in the "select" statement.

```
Select "June 1995", discount_plan,
            count distinct(customer_id)
From Customer_Information_History
Where customer_info_change_date LE "30-jun-1995" and
            customer_info_end_date GE "30-jun-1995"
Group by "June 1995", discount_plan
Union
```

Select "July 1995", discount_plan,
                count distinct(customer_id)
From Customer_Information_History
Where customer_info_change_date LE "31-jul-1995" and
                customer_info_end_date GE "31-jul-1995"
Group by "July 1995", discount_plan
Union
(etc.);

Replace and Insert

The replace and insert is an example of a compound approach to updating the data warehouse, driven by a combination of different business requirements to access tactical and strategic data, the behavior of the data in the source system, and the business processes that affect the use of the source system.

In this example, customer orders need to be tracked as they move through the fulfillment process—from the placing of an order, to pulling inventory, to the loading dock, to the shipping vehicle until it arrives at the customer's location.Orders in process need to be tracked for tactical analysis purposes, and completed orders need to be analyzed historically for strategic purposes to show, among other things, what factors might affect the organization's ability to deliver orders "on time." The users who need to access the data for tactical purposes, while the orders are still "in process" or "open," are different from those who need to do historical, strategic analysis of completed or "closed" orders.

The problem was how to identify those records that needed to be extracted from the operational system, which records were still "open," which records were considered "closed," and which records did not need to be extracted from the operational system at all. In addition, adjustments could be made to orders well after they might otherwise be considered "closed." A combination update approach was developed whereby all orders that were "open" were extracted into one output file. "Open" orders were defined as any order that had not gone into a status of "billed" (the final state of any order), plus those orders that were in a status of "billed" but had been so for less than 45 days. Once an order had been "billed" for exactly 45 days, it was considered "closed" and extracted to another output file. This allowed for a "stabilization period" when adjustments could be applied to "billed" orders. Those orders that had been in a state of "billed" for 46 days or more were not extracted from the operational system (that is, they were "filtered" from the extract). Since there was a need for tactical analysis of "open" orders, extracts had to be run against the operational source daily to provide daily changes to "open" orders. This allowed for the ability to pinpoint orders that had been in a state of "billed" for exactly 45 days.

The result of the extract is two output files, one containing "open" orders and the other containing stabilized "closed" orders. In the data warehouse, both the "open" and "closed" orders target tables are virtually identical. The "open" orders are then processed against the data warehouse with a full replace, where all previous "open" orders are deleted and the new "open" orders inserted into the "open" orders table. "Closed" orders are then inserted into the "closed" orders table. Since the definition of "closed" is precise to 45 days after being "billed," there should be no duplicate records either in the "closed" history table, or between the "open" and "closed" tables.

Figure 10–10 depicts this example of replace and insert.

This approach allows for "open" and "closed" orders to be partitioned based on how they are used for different analysis purposes, and how they behave in the operational source. It allows data to "stabilize," eliminating the problems that post-dated changes and adjustments can have on historical integrity. Only those records that need to be are extracted from the operational source, and the update processing on the data warehouse is as simple as it gets.

Figure 10–10   Replace and Insert to the Data Warehouse

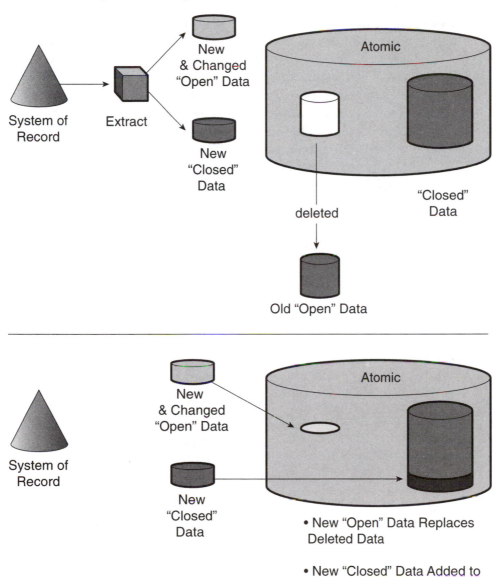

Summary of Data Warehouse Updates

Updating the data warehouse is a combination of the approach taken to extract data from its operational source, the kind of extract data generated, and how that data should be loaded into the data warehouse. Rarely does one extract approach, one type of extracted data, or one update approach meet all of an organization's requirements for turning its available data into information. Determining which approach is best will be based on each combination of subject area of data, operational source of data, and business requirement for accessing that data. Combinations of different approaches may be needed for the same subject area, source, or informational processing requirement. And those requirements will more than likely change over time, possibly necessitating a modification to the selected approach to updating the data warehouse.

MANAGING THE
DATA WAREHOUSE

Chapter 11

Managing and Staffing the Data Warehouse

Dr. Narsim Ganti

Boeing Corporation

This chapter describes the managing and staffing aspects of a large data warehouse. The size of a data warehouse is arbitrary. For our purposes, a "large" data warehouse is one that may obtain data from more than one source. More than twenty simultaneous users may be accessing a gigabyte-sized database. It is also possible to have multiple, and varied, applications accessing the same physical data warehouse.

The key messages of this chapter are conveyed through simple models and metaphors. Models help by focusing issues, and metaphors assist by clarifying ideas. A model at best is an idealization; rarely is it absolutely correct. A metaphor, if extended beyond a certain point, will also be inadequate to include all aspects of an idea. Therefore, it is important to maintain the context in which these models and metaphors are introduced.

"Data warehouse" is a metaphor borrowed from the physical world, where tangible assets are stored in a secured building. A data warehouse secures facts about business in a secured computing systems environment. Therefore, common attributes such as sizes, accesses, storage efficiencies, and so on are the basis of an architecture and warehouse metaphor. The metaphor connects two different disciplines: electronic computing and civil structures.

Complex computing systems are, typically, designed by defining logical aggregations of features and functions required by an application. These logical aggregations are realized through physical mappings on hardware and software components. In the civil engineering discipline, an architecture is defined for the desired features and functions of a structure. A design blueprint consistent with the architecture is physically realized by constructing the structure of bricks, mortar, steel, timber, and so on. These similarities suggest the use of an architecture metaphor to explain the design and construction processes of a complex computing system such as a data warehouse.

Data warehouses supply meaningful data to applications. The data-meaning is obtained by transforming and mediating transactional data from disparate systems. The data transformation supports specific and ad hoc information constructs. In general, users need more meaningful information and less raw data. Data warehouse-based applications serve such functions effectively.

Computing applications typically have evolved around functional groups. Critical information for making operational decisions vital to business operations is essentially cross-functional. Data warehouses do not support traditional stove-pipe applications. To the contrary, they integrate cross-functional data in support of specific business processes. Therefore, it is very important how we staff and manage data warehouse projects.

Conventional information systems organizations have been organized in a central batch and queue model. Managing massive amounts of data produced by transactional systems is ideally suited for such an organizational model. We, however, require a different and new model based on value chains (value-added transformed data) and pull mechanisms (organic and business-driven applications) for managing and staffing data warehouse projects.

Information-Delivery Model

A data warehouse, if designed correctly, serves as infrastructure for delivering information. Rarely is it a rigid, inert product. A useful data warehouse evolves organically with the superstructure of applications built on it. A practical information-delivery model is shown in Figure 11–1. Data from the warehouse is processed through a set of data access middleware that connects cross-functional applications, which in turn deliver information for action.

Figure 11–1 A Data Warehouse Information Delivery Model

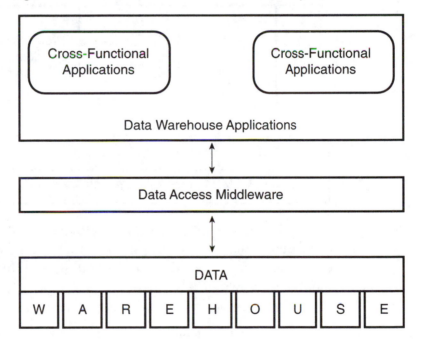

Structure of the Chapter

The contents of this chapter are organized around three key ideas. The first is understanding awareness of management and staffing. The second is understanding the issues of people's skills, attributes, and the tools and techniques to do so. Finally, the third is to integrate the previous two ideas holistically.

These three ideas are treated in a structured manner and arranged as eight architectural elements in Figure 11–2.

Figure 11–2 Structural Elements of the Chapter in an Architectural Context

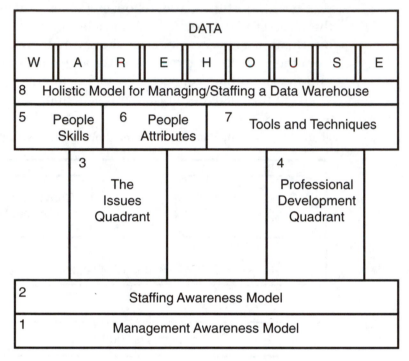

A functioning data warehouse will require all these eight elements. A mapping of the models to manage and staff a data warehouse, and the corresponding architectural elements, are shown in Table 11-1.

Table 11–1 Architectural Elements Described in This Chapter

Element	Data Warehouse Model	Architecture Metaphor
1	Management Awareness	Bedrock
2	Staffing Awareness	Amorphous Soil
3	Issues Quadrant	Supporting Pile-1
4	Professional Development Quadrant	Supporting Pile-2
5	People Skills	Foundation
6	People Attributes	Foundation
7	Tools and Techniques	Foundation
8	Holistic Model for Managing and Staffing	Footing

These eight elements are discussed sequentially in the following paragraphs.

1. MANAGEMENT AWARENESS MODEL

Managing information systems involves people and technologies. Information systems are pulled by business drivers. These pulls and technology pushes are best understood by an awareness model. An awareness model shows formal relationships along several dimensions which change in concert with the problem domain and business norms.

Managing the Data Warehouse

To manage, we have to comprehend all the possible interactions of people, technologies, and business realities. Accordingly, management awareness for data warehousing is in three dimensions. These dimensions are identified as styles or patterns: management style, perception style, and thinking style. In practice the three styles intersect and are not mutually exclusive.

Figure 11-3 shows the essence of each style. Most information systems are managed using the "most prevalent" characteristics. In many large enterprises, the functional orientation of applications is tightly coupled with transaction data. Controlled and proprietary architectures are inherently rigid and brittle.

Data warehouses by demand contain cross-functional data. This is particularly true in business processes that cut across functions. The "desirable" characteristics shown in the right half of Figure 11–3 are closely aligned with data warehouse management. An organization should have both halves of the model in some proportion. Let us examine these three styles in detail.

Management Style

In the most prevalent situation, the management style is controlled and oriented according to functional lines. The more

Figure 11–3   Management Awareness Model for Managing Data Warehouses

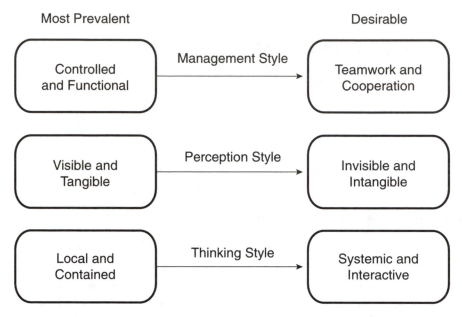

desirable model encourages teamwork and cooperation. Table 11-2 compares the dominant characteristics the two styles in the context of all management aspects, such as design, construction, maintenance, and change management. Changes to a data warehouse are essential for promoting continued reuse of data assets in an enterprise.

Table 11–2   Dominant Characteristics of Management Style

Dominant Characteristics: Controlled and Functional	Dominant Characteristics: Teamwork and Cooperative
System ownership is at the top of a functional group such as manager of sales, vice-president of marketing, director of accounts payable, and so on. Information is passed down and rarely crosses functional departments.	The data is drawn from various functional units. This requires teamwork and cooperation for periodic updates to warehoused data. Ownership is less proprietary because everyone owns a part of the whole.
Decisions for building systems or what data should be warehoused are centralized. There is little tendency to be all things to all people. The rate payers and charge-backs are the primary concern. Decisions are passed through the management chain for implementation.	Decisions are made across functional organizations. Access to data is facilitated by the participants for satisfying business-demands vital to meeting goals. The hierarchy, though present, is virtually flattened by a participatory decision-making process.

Table 11-2 Dominant Characteristics of Management Style (Contd)

Data and information are very controlled. The system access and security controls for warehoused data are designed to embody such control.	The data in the warehouse becomes a shared information resource. This will perhaps move the enterprise closer to the promises of data as a resource.
Failures are suppressed. Damage-control strategy is routinely practiced to lessen blame.	Missed targets are discussed to gather "lessons learned" for enhancing the team's knowledge.
The flexibility needed to make a data warehouse relevant to market conditions is usually impaired by rigid bureaucratic procedures. The control model of management is inherently rigid.	The cooperative environment reduces time lag in making decisions. Data warehouses change according to business conditions. Decision-support systems evolve to use the most recent data from transaction systems.
A data warehouse is viewed as a functional resource.	A data warehouse is viewed as cross-functional, not just a cross-system product.

Perception Style

Perception styles for the two management styles are shown in Table 11-3.

Table 11-3 Dominant Characteristics of Perception Style

Dominant Characteristics: Visible and Tangible	Dominant Characteristics: Invisible and Intangible
The functional group owns the data and strives to benefit itself exclusively.	The data flows smoothly as a resource. Sharing is the governing consideration.
Profits and benefits are related to functional units and systems.	The whole system works at maximum efficiency as quality data flows through the system.
Limited data is released through lengthy policies and procedures.	Data is made accessible by up-front agreements.
Functional divisions drive business decisions.	The attitudes, beliefs, and usefulness of the data shared are the underlying parameters for making decisions.

Thinking Style

Thinking styles for the two management styles are shown in Table 11-4.

Table 11–4 Dominant Characteristics of Thinking Style

Dominant Characteristics: Local and Contained	Dominant Characteristics: Systemic and Interactive
Every system is viewed as a separate and essential entity. A dedicated group of people is associated with a warehoused product and the application. Different applications rarely draw data from a warehouse. Stove pipe warehouse implementations are a natural outcome of the warehousing efforts.	The data warehouse is viewed as a resource for cross-functional applications. Cooperation and negotiation with key business stakeholders are the dominant behavior norm. The thinking is enterprise-oriented and results in synergy among functional units. Individual system optimization is discouraged. Resources are shared.
The business drivers are local and contrived.	The business drivers are real. Everybody works to align systems continuously.
Each system is tuned to perform at maximum efficiency. All systems as a total must, therefore, operate at peak rates.	The integrated data in the warehouse is organized for overall performance by selectively denormalizing tables. If the whole is optimized, the individual data segments obtained from different systems need not be suboptimized.
The information systems are functionally understood. A complete picture emerges only upon synthesis.	The design is based on understanding how the disparate data sources interact with each other. The emphasis is on the big picture. Such understanding leads to specifying optimal data refresh cycle times.
Operational problems are solved by producing a list of options.	The system is tuned for maximum leverage and is connected to business drivers.
Individual functional systems are the sole pursuits for increasing efficiencies.	Systems lose value when these are taken apart. A complete meaning of the warehouse is in appreciating the data interaction in a process-driven context.
Each system is managed as a unit, and problems are solved in isolation.	The "big picture" of business permeates through the whole design process.

A Hybrid Awareness Model

A good model for awareness can be obtained by combining the preceding two management styles as shown in Figure 11–4. The source systems carry the rational style of transactional systems. The derived or transformed data will benefit from the intuitive features of the second management style. The models shown here can be used for creating general guidelines in managing data warehouses. Individual variations are possible for specific situations.

Figure 11–4 Hybrid Awareness Model for Managing Data Warehouses

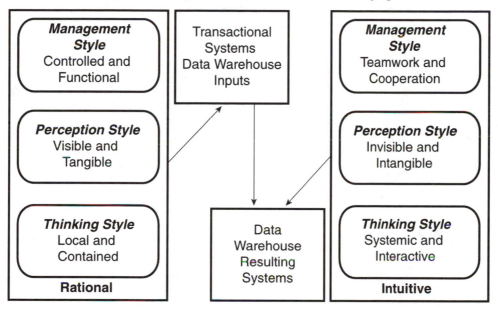

Building and managing data warehouses exclusively on the "command and control" management style will certainly result in a short shelf life for the resulting data warehouse. This is so because the policies make the data warehouse rigidly brittle. Consequently, the data warehouse is sapped of its vitality and its business relevance.

2. STAFFING AWARENESS MODEL

The data warehouse should be staffed by taking into account the special requirements and qualifications of available resources in the enterprise. First, the people's skills and attributes have to be mapped in a systematic fashion. A staffing awareness model depicts these resources.

Staffing the Data Warehouse

The staffing awareness model is simpler than the management awareness model. Here we deal with issues in an organized manner in a very pragmatic approach. Figure 11–5 describes a staffing awareness model.

Figure 11–5 A Staffing Awareness Model for Staffing Data Warehouses

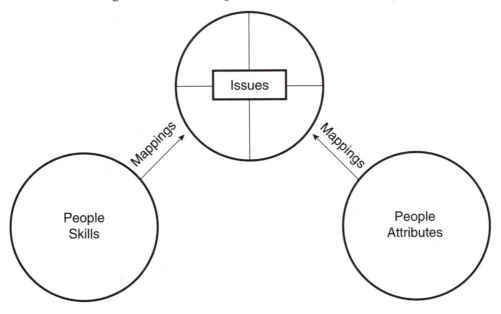

The model has three key elements: issues, people skills, and people attributes. The issues are classified into mutually exclusive categories, each of which is considered in the context of people's skills and people's attributes. The context of the model is preserved by mapping people's skills and attributes onto each category of issues. Let us expand the issues element into components appropriate to staffing a data warehouse.

3. ISSUES-GROUPING MODEL

The principal issues of staffing a data warehouse can be classified into four groups with equal influence. The grouping is usually determined by considering the local environment.

There are two key aspects in understanding these issues in the context of staffing the data warehouse. The first, scope, describes the boundary of the issue. The second is to outline different scenarios to show what happens within the specific issue's boundary. The four issues are drawn from a number of practical situations and are shown in Figure 11-6.

Figure 11–6   The Issues Quadrant for Staffing Data Warehouses

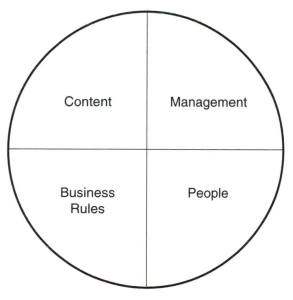

The Content Issue

The first issue deals with what the data warehouse will contain and the specific purposes it will satisfy. This in turn will suggest what data-sources should be used and who has the knowledge about these systems. The data warehouse application is designed to satisfy specific business objectives, so current needs *and* future requirements should be incorporated in the planning.

An effective way to understand issues is to relate them to actual scenarios or business situations. Sometimes understanding and uncovering different scenarios helps in alleviating staffing problems, such as lack of appropriate skills or knowledge. Different situations will generate a separate set of scenarios. For the "contents" issue, seven representative scenarios are identified and shown in Figure 11-7.

Figure 11–7   Content Issues for Staffing Data Warehouses

- What should be warehoused?

- Is this a report generator replacement?

- Is this a data clean-up operation?

- Is this BPR data reclamation?

- Is this a point or global solution?

- Is this an architecture transition?

- DSS, or a conduit for obtaining cross-functional data?

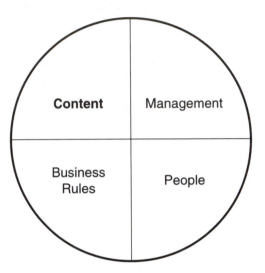

What should be warehoused?

This is the most important consideration because including too much would increase the scope to an unmanageable size and perhaps require a cast of thousands. The design sessions should reduce the data requirements during each design iteration. The process is analogous to writing a good technical paper. With fewer words, we can deliver a succinct message; more words distract the reader.

In practice, the data scope can be increased gradually by using an extensible architecture. Data aggregation reduces size of a data warehouse. How the data is aggregated is related to the granularity of the information. Hence, we should be able to relate these two considerations meaningfully. These aspects immediately guide us in choosing the correct skills and staff.

Is this a report generator replacement?

In many situations, a data warehouse may be designed to replace several special-report–generation applications. In these situations, we are altering the behavior of a number of support personnel who were responsible for producing these reports. Potentially, some may no longer be required. In staffing a data warehouse project, this possibility should be considered up front and alternate opportunities planned for the affected personnel. Although several can be part of the new project, a potential problem can be a mismatch of the technologies used in older systems and the data warehouse.

Is this a data clean-up operation?

Transaction systems, for the most part, supply the data to build a data warehouse. Historically, certain data about the same facts may have changed over time. The data therefore needs to be cleaned or resolved before it can be loaded in a data warehouse, and many projects unknowingly become major data-cleansing operations. For staffing, people who have a historical knowledge about source systems must be included in the project teams. Automated tools help in this regard, but may demand new skills.

Is this BPR data reclamation?

Business process reengineering (BPR) is a consideration when we design new processes for improving overall business performance. Data warehouses are very useful in reclaiming data from older production systems. Therefore, staffing the project will require people who understand cross-functional systems.

Data warehouses, if designed well, improve old processes and help in deploying new ones. Such simple objectives are BPR efforts. We may not use the term "BPR," but we are actually doing it in the data warehouse project.

Is this a point or global solution?

A data warehouse can be a point solution used to satisfy a specific need. In a bigger or global scope, it can be a common data resource for a number of functional groups. Point solutions are easy to implement with minimal data modeling effort. Global solutions require coordination with several data-naming standards and enterprise-modeling considerations. The issue is to select the right people who will pragmatically use such design procedures and complete the project on time.

Is this an architecture transition?

Technology shifts cause major changes in computing systems architecture. Data captured in older, arcane formats may have to be used in new systems. Occasionally, data warehouses satisfy data transition requirements from mainframe systems to distributed servers. When a project takes these dimensions, the staff operates in two different computing paradigms. The staff is selected and trained on this basis.

DSS, or a conduit for obtaining cross-functional data?

Decision-support systems (DSS) traditionally espoused concepts similar to data warehousing, albeit in a point solution domain. Only recently we have seen a broadening of the scope. This is facilitated by data warehousing technologies such as multi-dimensional data structures, parallel machines, and bit-mapped indices. The DSS-based data warehouses are potential primary sources for providing cross-functional data. If a project evolves around such concepts, the staffing is accordingly modified to include "systems"-level thinkers as opposed to point solution providers. The above scenarios provide substantial insights into understanding the content issue for selecting team members for a data warehouse project. Individual project mangers may use the same technique in identifying situations relevant to their specific situations.

The Management Issue

Management issues (shown in Figure 11–8) contributing to the staffing of data warehouse projects are generally concerned with the overall life cycle of the information produced and the quality of data in a warehouse. At a minimum, include policies, ownership issues, distribution rights, configuration, and data validity. Specification of roles and the responsibilities of key individuals are also important. The following seven representative scenarios are taken from actual data warehouse business situations.

Figure 11–8   Management Issues for Staffing Data Warehouses

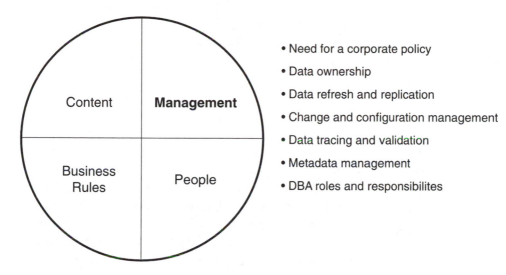

- Need for a corporate policy
- Data ownership
- Data refresh and replication
- Change and configuration management
- Data tracing and validation
- Metadata management
- DBA roles and responsibilites

Need for a corporate policy

Data warehouses consume substantial investment in time and funding. Initial start-up funding may be easy to justify, but to sustain, enhance, and maintain a data warehouse that is not owned exclusively by one functional group, a corporate policy that provides a funding mechanism is essential. A corporate policy will state the general guideline for qualifying data warehouses as a corporate resource. It will also define who the shareholders are in a given business context and the roles and responsibilities of management. Funding and charge-back policies are put in place to manage the investments. If a policy does not exist, we have to select individuals who can define a policy and get the required approvals to make it a reality.

Data ownership

Data ownership for warehoused data is an important issue, particularly when cross-functional data is involved. In a data warehouse, derived or aggregated data can be regarded as new data. An ownership facilitates quality programs taking hold, and the information produced will be of high quality.

An ownership board is a viable tack. The staff should be able to negotiate data instance definitions, changes, and maintaining configuration control. Data-auditing skills are needed to ensure accuracy of results. The staff should be able to trace inaccurate data to its source and put appropriate actions in place. The staff should have good interpersonal skills to smooth over data ownership "turf" battles.

Data refresh and replication

Data refreshing and replication involves negotiating operation windows with centralized data centers. The issues are mostly centered around job scheduling, back-up, and recovery. While these issues are not much different from conventional production systems, a data warehouse can tie up a number of source systems simultaneously during data transformation and loading operations. If any contention arises, the staff should be able to partition data into logical and physical databases to resolve the problems. Database design skills take on a new dimension for data warehouses.

Change and configuration management

Data warehouses deal with persistent data with long life cycles. Errors or changes in data are common. Configuration management requires good trace-back recording tools, date stamps, log books, and so on. The staff should be able to design altered procedures in a cross-functional and multi-data ownership situation.

Data tracing and validation

Data tracing and validation is an issue that cuts across metadata and data quality management processes. The sources from which a data warehouse accesses data should be made visible. Certain quality issues are corrected ad hoc. However, it is preferable to have standard operating procedures. These skills should reside with the data warehouse staff.

Metadata management

"Metadata" describes the data. Data structure, syntax, and semantics are typical key elements of metadata. Other system-related data (e.g., present in a dictionary, directory, or a repository) can also be regarded as metadata. The responsibility for managing metadata lies with warehouse staff, but its ownership is distributed and external. Therefore, the selected staff should include a dimension of negotiation skill.

DBA roles and responsibilities

The last consideration is to define the roles and responsibilities of the database administrators, including those who manage source systems. The data warehouse DBA has little control on upstream source systems, but they affect the downstream data warehouse data with regard to data integrity and data quality. The warehouse staff should be able to devise enough process-control-points to tune the rate of changes with the timeliness of warehouse data supplied to the users.

The Business Rules Issue

Business rules define controls (such as log transaction if credit is preauthorized) and impose constraints (such as notify supervisor if account is delinquent) on a process. Business rules are arbitrary and change. Business rules should not be confused with application logic. Application logic manipulates data according to the expected behavior or business laws (for example sales tax = sales price multiplied by a percentage). In production applications, business rules and application logic are encoded in the application. Sometimes the data has no meaning if extracted directly from a data store (flat files, relational data, and so on). The situation depends on how the source system was designed.

A data warehouse has to be faithful to such embedded data meanings. This may necessitate storing all rules along with the data during the data warehouse design-and-building phase. Three scenarios (depicted in Figure 11–9) explain the impact of business rules on staffing the data warehouse.

Relationship between business rules and data

Business rules change according to people norms, market supply-and-demand conditions, and finally process-changes (work flow). The same data instance or value in a source-transaction system acquires new meaning over time. A temporal relationship between business rule and data is an essential data warehouse design parameter.

Figure 11–9   Business Rules Issues for Staffing Data Warehouses

- Relationship between business rules and data
- Metadata and business rules
- Business rules change impact on data

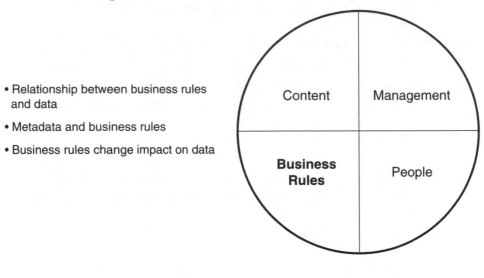

The data warehouse staff should have people who track, understand, and report the changing relationship between source data and warehoused data. This is a very different function from configuration control or change management. A data warehouse is a historical record of business rules changes. The history might reveal trends. Therefore, a specialized function and a corresponding skill are required of the staff.

Metadata and business rules

Metadata is impacted by changes to business rules. A historical record of metadata facilitates increased data quality and data sharing. Correlating metadata with business rules completes the total data-picture. Such a synthesis is not required in a conventional transaction system. A new function—maintaining metadata and business rule changes—is required of the data warehouse staff.

Business rules change impact on data

Impact assessments of business rules on data sometimes reveal shortcomings in data refresh cycle times. Again, this a specialized function typical of a data warehouse application. The staff should include resources to perform this important activity.

People

The people issue is concerned with the impacts a data warehouse has on the current staff. This is a natural consequence of introducing change in an organization. The impact on the people who support the current systems challenges the warehouse staff (all people who support and use transaction systems involved in providing data to the data warehouse) in several ways. Six scenarios describe the situations that potentially impact warehouse staffing decisions.

1. Loss of control

The most immediate reaction to the implementation of a data warehouse, perceived as a replacement to anything in current use, is loss of control. The control and command management style (described earlier) is the primary reason for this reaction. The issue is not whether this is good or bad. It is, rather, how to deal with it while it is happening. Data served "cut and dried" to a controlled group is power. A data warehouse tends to open up lines of communication and unclog data arteries. The data is used in more flexible manners. Data is transparent, and information constructs can be more inquiry-driven. The user controls the flow, not a group of data-base application programmers. This is the classic loss-of-control situation.

2. Data niche players

Functional and monolithic transaction application systems are niche-oriented. The data community is organized around such niches. People define career paths along niche-transactional systems. It is natural to feel too comfortable and secure in such an environment, and to resist change.

Data warehouse projects more often than not disturb the status quo. The old data niche players may not be motivated to share their knowledge. Data niche players require much "storming" and "norming time" before a team can really form. This is the greatest challenge in staffing a data warehouse.

3. Applications, data, and DBA

The source systems used for constructing a data warehouse are usually mainframe-based transaction systems. Such systems come with a community of application programmers, data owners, and database administrators. This community has its own subculture. Recognizing this community and the subculture is important, for without their cooperation, a data warehouse project is doomed to fail. This also is a significant data warehouse staffing issue.

4. PC clan

Personal computers and local area networks have redefined the way information flows in an enterprise. Instead of building report generator applications on mainframes, the users now download data from the mainframes by using any available tool and manipulate the data using desktop applications such as spread sheets. Some download data into PC-based databases, which act as surrogate data warehouses. This situation creates another group of people, threatened by a much broader scoped data warehouse. We need to consider this as a significant staffing issue.

5. Fictitious customers

Large "data food chains" create customers and suppliers almost instantaneously. The data middle-people, regardless of value, are part of the data family. The family has some fictitious customers who get exposed in a data warehouse information and data flow chain. Obviously this situation creates a data warehouse staffing issue.

6. Data broker and mediators

The last situation is related to the previous scenario. When data flows through a long path of data owners and administrators, we encounter several data brokers and mediators. Data brokers provide replicas of data in exchange for resources. Data mediators redefine data ownership territories to suit their data sharing enterprise model. While these people in their own right are useful, the data warehouse staff should devise special models of cooperation and behavior to see that the process does not break down.

4. PROFESSIONAL DEVELOPMENT MODEL

A model for professional development is shown in Figure 11–10. There are four key groupings: knowledge sources, behaviors, activities, and observations.

Figure 11–10 Professional Development Quadrant Model

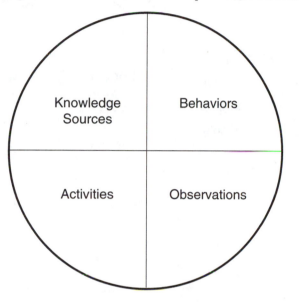

5. PEOPLE SKILLS AND ISSUE MAPPING

In the previous section, we discussed the four issue groupings using several business scenarios. In this section, we will map the required skills on the issues. The business situation and scenarios help us to understand the mapping rationale. A data warehouse staff should have the following desirable skills.

Required People Skills

The required skills for each issue category are discussed briefly. In the tables, the first column describes the mapping component, the second column, the corresponding skill set required.

Issue: Content

Figure 11–11 and Table 11-5 show and describe the mapping details.

Figure 11–11   Mapping People Skills on Content Issues for Staffing Data Warehouses

- Process and data relationship
- Metadata collection and definition
- Aggregation and abstraction skills
- Understanding real requirements from solutions
- To live in a denormalized world

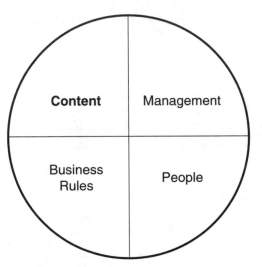

Table 11–5 People Skills and Data Warehouse Contents

Mapping Component	Desirable Skills and Attributes
• Process and data relationship.	• Process definition methodology, data modeling, conceptual thinking.
• Metadata collection and definition.	• Systems knowledge, structured thinking, process knowledge.
• Aggregation and abstraction.	• Analytical skills, big-picture thinking style.
• Understanding real requirements from solutions.	• Ability to separate solutions and pose these as requirements.
• To live in a denormalized world.	• Knowledge of data structures suitable for decision support.

Issue: Management

Figure 11–12 and Table 11-6 show and describe the mapping details.

Figure 11–12   Mapping People Skills on Management Issues for Staffing Data Warehouses

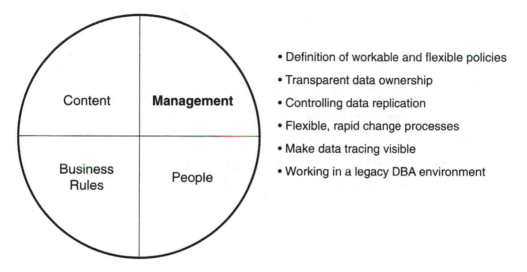

- Definition of workable and flexible policies
- Transparent data ownership
- Controlling data replication
- Flexible, rapid change processes
- Make data tracing visible
- Working in a legacy DBA environment

Table 11–6 People Skills and Data Warehouse Management

Mapping Component	Desirable Skills and Attributes
• Definition of workable and flexible policies.	• Team-leading experience in proposing ideas and obtaining consensus.
• Transparent data ownership.	• Ability to map processes on data, and identifying right ownership of data.
• Controlling data replication.	• Negotiation skills, ability to promote data-sharing culture.
• Flexible, rapid change processes.	• Pragmatic thinking, ability to differentiate DSS with OLTP.
• Make data tracing visible.	• Information dissemination skills.
• Working in a legacy DBA environment.	• Patience, ability to deal with strong, opinionated personalities.

Issue: Business Rules

Figure 11–13 and Table 11-7 show and describe the mapping details.

Figure 11–13 Mapping People Skills on Business Rules Issues for Staffing Data Warehouses

- Capturing business rules from user dialogs
- Mining business rules from legacy systems
- Metadata and business rules
- Change/manage business rules

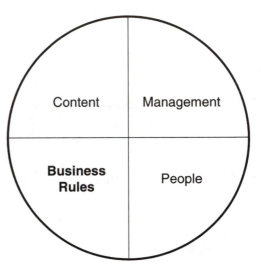

Table 11–7 People Skills and Data Warehouse Business

Mapping Component	Desirable Skills and Attributes
Capturing business rules from user dialogs.	Listening, research, note-taking, follow-up, process knowledge.
Mining business rules from legacy systems.	Analytical skills, correlating facts and data with observations.
Metadata and business rules.	Process knowledge, understanding business views of data.
Change/manage business rules.	Negotiation skills, ability to simplify cumbersome old processes.

Issue: People

Figure 11–14 and Table 11-8 show and describe the mapping details.

Figure 11–14   Mapping People Skills on People Issues for Staffing Data Warehouses

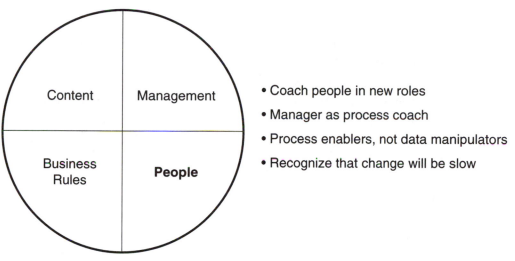

- Coach people in new roles
- Manager as process coach
- Process enablers, not data manipulators
- Recognize that change will be slow

Table 11–8   People Skills and Data Warehouse People Issues

Mapping Component	Desirable Skills and Attributes
• Coach people in new roles.	• Team-leading skills, positive thinking, effective communications skills.
• Manager should be a process coach.	• Leader, not a controlling-personality; effective listener.
• Select process enablers, not data manipulators.	• Coaching skills, open to new ideas, ability to think abstractly.
• Recognize that change will be slow.	• Pragmatic, deliberate, and patient.

6. PEOPLE ATTRIBUTES AND ISSUE MAPPING

People attributes should be understood in the context of staffing and managing a data warehouse project.

Required People Attributes

The issue quadrant is used to map the various desirable attributes of people who may be working in designing and constructing a data warehouse. The following paragraphs will assist the data warehousing practitioner to deal logically with a very complicated set of interrelated issues.

Issue: Content

Figure 11–15 and Table 11-9 show and describe the mapping details.

Figure 11–15 Mapping People Skills on Content Issues for Staffing Data Warehouses

- Balance between abstract and concrete thinking

- Minimize available data to needed data

- Transaction people are consultants, not designers

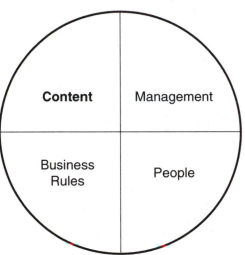

Table 11–9 People Attributes and Data Warehouse Content

Mapping Component	Comments
• Practice balance between abstract and concrete thinking.	• This quality helps in establishing meaningful denormalization of transaction data.
• Minimizing proposed data to needed data.	• A drill-down thinking and process's orientation will result in identifying the optimum data for a purpose.
• Use transaction people as consultants, not as designers.	• The data-modeling process will rapidly converge with such a staffing strategy.

Issue: Management

Figure 11–16 and Table 11-10 show and describe the mapping details.

Figure 11–16   Mapping People Attributes on Management Issues for Staffing Data Warehouses

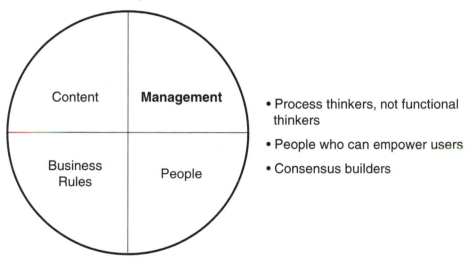

- Process thinkers, not functional thinkers
- People who can empower users
- Consensus builders

Table 11–10   People Attributes and Data Warehouse Staffing

Mapping Component	Comments
• Staff with process thinkers, not functional thinkers.	• Cross-functional systems need process orientation. Functional thinkers rarely meet these criteria.
• Empower the users.	• Team may include senior managers as mentors to help when required.
• Build consensus.	• This is a key attribute for staffing and managing the data warehousing project.

Issue: Business Rules

Figure 11–17 and Table 11-11 show and describe the mapping details.

Figure 11–17 Mapping People Attributes on Business Rules Issues for Staffing Data Warehouses

- Communicators

- Processes people, not computing experts

- People close to core competencies

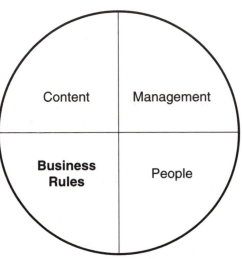

Table 11–11 People Attributes and Data Warehouse Business Rules

Mapping Component	Comments
• Select communicators for tasks requiring customer interaction.	• The staff should be able to identify business rules from production applications. Much communication is needed to verify opinions.
• Computing folks should follow, not define, business processes.	• Business processes are known to the actual people who use them. Computing systems follow processes, not the other way around.
• Select people having core competencies.	• Data warehouses are created to exploit core competencies. People with these skills should be part of the staff.

Issue: People

Figure 11–18 and Table 11-12 show and describe the mapping details.

Figure 11–18   Mapping People Attributes on People Issues for Staffing Data Warehouses

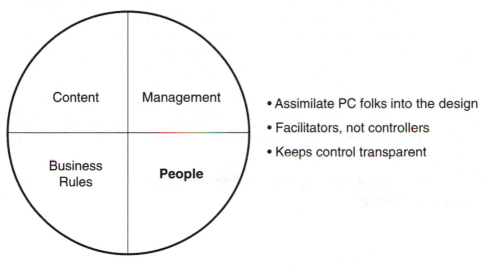

- Assimilate PC folks into the design
- Facilitators, not controllers
- Keeps control transparent

Table 11–12   People Attributes and Data Warehouse People Issues

Mapping Component	Comments
• Include PC folks into the design and assimilate them into the processes.	• PC-based DSS analysts know business-views (information models) well. These folks must be part of the team. A data warehouse should assist them in creating quick applications for their customers. At times a data warehouse is seen as a threat. This strategy removes negativism.
• Leaders act as facilitators, not controllers.	• Data warehouse lead analysts should facilitate the process. This requires coaching skills.
• Controls are transparent to users.	• The background processes to assure data quality should be transparent. This requires using good abstraction skills and appropriate tools that do not bring arcane computer-code languages to the user interface.

7. TOOLS AND TECHNIQUES FOR PROFESSIONAL DEVELOPMENT

Professional development is an integral part of staffing and managing a data warehouse. The underlying computing technology in building a data warehouse is developing rapidly. Technology pushes are common in the information-delivery application development business. We do make changes for technology's sake, and a continual renewal is required to ward off obsolesce.

Technology is only half the picture. The other half has to do with people and the strategies utilized in staffing and maintaining a data warehouse and applications.

Tools and Techniques Mapping on Professional Development Model

The professional development will be used to map the various aspects.

Knowledge Sources

Figure 11–19 shows key features for this mapping.

Figure 11–19   Knowledge Sources for Professional Development Model

• Seminars

• Vendor products

• Published sources

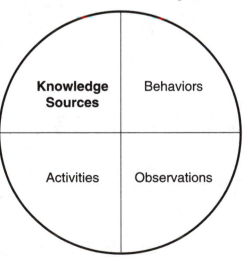

Besides generally available training, the three most effective sources are as follows.

Seminars and conferences: Seminars and conferences are useful in keeping current with technology shifts and also provide a forum for professional communication with peers and experts.

Vendor product overviews: Vendors generally advertise their products through mailings, seminars, and local visits. While a level of optimism is generated for any product by its vendor, we must carefully evaluate it against our needs and test it before committing to a large-scale implementation. It is very common to hear from a vendor that the most required feature by us will be in their next product version.

Published Literature: The last source is published literature in trade magazines and journals. The publishing rigor and philosophy of each article determine the accuracy of information.

Behaviors

Figure 11–20 shows key features for this mapping.

Figure 11–20   Behaviors for Professional Development Model

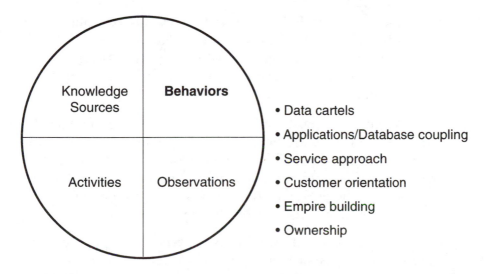

- Data cartels
- Applications/Database coupling
- Service approach
- Customer orientation
- Empire building
- Ownership

Data cartels, information is power: Data is controlled by functional groups. People's behavior is molded along those lines. Information is power. When we staff a data warehouse project, we have to recognize that these are the key motivators. The teaming concept has many intangibles in its value stream. The management must be, accordingly, open and ready to make changes for overall good as opposed to individual good. If the whole system is optimized, the individual parts are no longer the focus.

Application and database seen as one: An application in conventional systems and its database are considered an integral, inseparable unit. In a data warehouse, applications evolve based on what story the data is telling us. We have to staff the data warehouse with people who understand such abstraction. The throw-away part is the application (relatively speaking). The valuable part is the underlying data warehouse. The managing considerations are data-centric as opposed to being application-centric.

Service approach: A data warehouse is a service, an infrastructure item. No single function should own it. The management is best conducted by steering committees and consensus; autocratic management styles are not conducive to data warehouse growth. Similar personal attributes are required of the staff as well.

Customer orientation: The data warehouse application should have a customer orientation. Customer orientation is accomplished through a customer pull process. This requires that the staff have full participation and support of the customers.

Empire building: Data warehousing should be managed and staffed as infrastructure service. It should not be a reason to build a huge stand-alone functional department or empire. Stand-alone departments and empires become aloof and miss the point of the project. Corporate policies to build data warehouses should be recognized at the highest level.

Payee owns resources: Functional systems are paid for by the local unit; as such they own it. A data warehouse is a cross-functional resource which everybody can use, so ownership is virtual. This fundamental aspect must be kept in mind when we are staffing and managing a data warehouse.

Activities

Figure 11–21 shows key features for this mapping.

Figure 11–21   Activities for Professional Development Model

- Case histories
- DBA retraining
- Lessons learned
- Cross-pollinate ideas
- Network with others
- Supplier connections
- Colocation of personnel
- Share information
- Vendor presentations
- Manage success

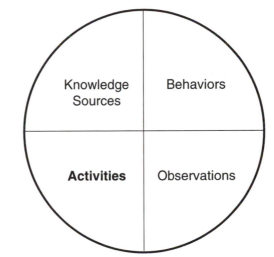

The following activities list, while not all-inclusive, is suggested for meeting challenges of a data warehouse project.

1. Study case histories, particularly of downsized projects.
2. Rethink the application and DBA method of management.
3. Share lessons learned generously.
4. Cross-pollinate ideas and knowledge with people of different skill sets.
5. Network with other data warehouse practitioners.
6. Establish supplier connections for efficient procurements.
7. Locate design/build teams close to the users.
8. Share information to grow professionally.
9. Have vendors present products and services frequently.
10. Learn to manage success and expectations.

Observations

Figure 11–22 shows key features for this mapping.

Figure 11–22   Observations for Professional Development Model

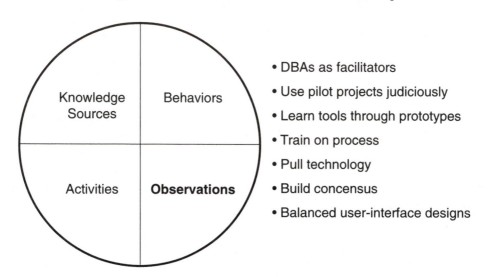

- DBAs as facilitators
- Use pilot projects judiciously
- Learn tools through prototypes
- Train on process
- Pull technology
- Build concensus
- Balanced user-interface designs

The observations presented below are in the context of the prior discussion of issues in staffing and managing a data warehouse.

DBAs are facilitators, not controllers: DBAs should act as facilitators to convey data, data structures, and information to the designers of the data warehouse. If they tend to control the process, there may be a tenuous relationship among the various team members.

Use product evaluation pilots judiciously: Product evaluations and pilots are expensive, but used judiciously, they help to access challenges and uncover potential problems.

Prototypes should be a tool for learning and scale-up: Prototypes are a scaled-down working version of the larger data warehouse. In a distributed architecture, we should be able to scale up by adding processors or storage media transparent to the user. Prototypes provide an opportunity to verify the choice of physical components of the warehouse design.

Process training is a must: Data warehousing is a set of processes. Each process consists of specific tasks. A robust process-definition methodology yields a successful project. The team should be trained in process-oriented thinking.

Problem solution approach should pull technology: It may be very tempting to chase technology, but a data warehouse project is about data. Data is seldom in friendly usable formats. Technology is only a small part of the overall effort. Data cleaning and validation are a major part of the project. Tools used in this regard should be driven by the project, not by technology.

Cross-functional applications require consensus and teaming: A data warehouse is a mostly cross-functional product, using data from various vertical functions. Several data owners and database administrators are part of the process, which will require a teaming approach. The intangible aspects of the management awareness model (described earlier) are extremely important. The data warehouse should be managed using systemic thinking models.

Balance between hidden and exposed technical information: A balance in background and foreground data should be attained when designing user interfaces, reports, and query applications. A perfect balance will probably be achieved by using iterative design methods, as opposed to doing everything in one big step. Incremental benefits are afforded at the end of each iteration.

8. A HOLISTIC MODEL FOR MANAGING AND STAFFING A DATA WAREHOUSE PROJECT

A data warehouse is a cross-functional resource, potentially supplying data to a number of functional applications. Most source systems support transactions and run on a mainframe host.

We have observed, in prior sections, two different management styles. Cross-functional systems are systemic in nature. A successful data warehousing project should be staffed and managed by using best practices. A holistic model combining the two management styles may provide such practice. A holistic model for staffing and managing a data warehouse project is shown in Figure 11–23. The foundation of the data warehouse is subjected to several forces.

Figure 11–23 Holistic Model for Managing and Staffing Data Warehouses

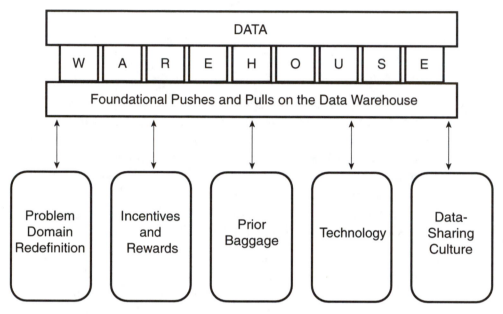

Foundation Forces on a Data Warehouse

A data warehouse is an organic entity. It grows or shrinks in direct proportion to the value provided to the enterprise. The data warehouse responds to the forces generated by the people responsible for building and using it. It can be either a pull force generated by the users or a force pushed by the support or development group responsible for the service. These pulls and pushes influence the data warehousing staffing and management considerations. The pulls and pushes are events. Response to these forces depends on the outcome of business case analysis for each event.

The dynamic nature of business assesses newer expectations from a data warehouse. These changes are the basic stimuli for ongoing actions. We will examine the system stimulus and the corresponding pushes and pulls on the foundation of a data warehouse for all the elements.

Elements Producing Pushes and Pulls on the Foundation

A data warehouse's foundation is constantly pulled and pushed by business forces generated by five key elements. People cause the environment in which these basic elements interact.

1. Problem domain
2. Incentives and rewards
3. Prior baggage
4. Technology
5. Data-sharing culture

Problem Domain Redefinition

A problem domain defines the scope of data, query structure, reports, and application requirements of a data warehouse. The problem domain of a particular data warehouse changes according to its popularity. A few system stimuli are described below.

Inclusion of data sources: The scope of data is perhaps the most dynamic stimulus. At any moment, the volume of data included is generally scrubbed down. This is due to a practical scheduling consideration for the project. Providing incremental benefits to the users is better than delayed perfection. The pushes result in providing new data that was out-prioritized in the current version. The pulls are strictly customer-generated.

Enhanced query capabilities: The information access products hide complex SQL from the end-user. In many cases, nested queries have to be designed by analysts who understand the underlying data structures and how these are selectively denormalized. A common technique is to provide preplanned queries. At times, users can pick ranges of values within a pre-designed query.

As the understanding of the data increases, so does the need to ask more succinct questions of the database.

Replicate data: Replication of data is emerging as a practical solution to resources and network capacity issues, as distributed computing takes hold. Replication tools are more sophisticated then the old hand-crafted extract programs of yesterday. A data warehouse contains replicated and transformed data. The foundation pulls and pushes are an emerging problem in the overall information delivery process.

Developing new applications: The need for new vertical applications (aligned around a process or function) is a business-driven requirement. In time, data warehouses will contain clean, historical data. All the possible ways of using these spawn a variety of specific applications containing specialized analytical algorithms.

Data-aggregated data warehouse: Data aggregation is a delicate balancing act between storage capacity and user appetite for most data. Users create newly derived data to support their processes. It is conceivable to have several derived clusters suitable for a new aggregated data warehouse.

Inclusion of derived data: Derived data is obtained by applying analytical rules to the raw data in a data warehouse. The computations result in new data elements not originally in the data warehouse. A need can be seen for storing and managing these data.

Table 11-13 correlates the stimuli with the pull and push forces on the foundation of a data warehouse.

Table 11–13 Pulls and Pushes of Problem Domain Redefinition

System Stimulus	Pull Force on Foundation	Push Force on Foundation
• Include new data sources	• Users demand more data for supporting additional queries or analysis. • Data sources are external to the enterprise, and are needed by users to understand such as competition or trends. • Users demand replacing old sources with alternate or better sources to combat data quality or performance problems.	• Support group tries to justify additional hardware by increasing data volume. • Enterprise initiatives being pushed to support large data or process modeling projects. • Justification for obtaining additional resources in anticipation of user demand.

Table 11–13 Pulls and Pushes of Problem Domain Redefinition (Contd)

• Enhance query capabilities	• Users find current queries inadequate to meet previously unforeseen need. • Users may be really understanding the data as it is not in a raw form, but useful information is beginning to emerge.	• Support group has understood new tools to exploit further the previously unknown capabilities. • Routine performance improvement may require this capability.
• Replicate data	• Data remoteness is causing delays. Users feel having data in proximity may improve system productivity. • Inadequate data management policies, as perceived by the users, may be alleviated by data replication.	• Developers may be lobbying for control on data or indirectly own data of a different functional group. • Could be a work around for architecture transition deployment.
• Develop new applications	• Users are seeing the value of the data warehouse and want to exploit it. • Users are finding old applications inadequate as data knowledge is increased by drill-down queries.	• Could be part of normal work-statement driven by local conditions. • New tools and technology may require some pilot projects that are requested by user community.
• Produce more aggregated data warehouse	• Users are thinking value and better resource utilization. • DSS processes may have matured as a result of availability of cross-functional data.	• A data archiving function. • A solution for optimizing storage. • Expanding warehousing state of practice in self-interest.
• Warehouse derived data	• Users are finding the original data definitions inadequate and are augmenting it by storing derived data. • Users cannot write new data into the "read only" data warehouse. This could be work-around.	• Augmenting inadequate designs, not yet perceived by the user community. • Accommodating a design philosophy.

Incentives and Rewards

Incentive and rewards augment quality information sharing and decrease data copies. We gradually become information rich. Each new strategy to reward sensible data management and information delivery advances the cause of prudently managing information resources.

Resource rewards: Rewards are structured around increasing human and computing resources.

Value-added rewards: Rewards are based on measuring the actual value a data warehouse information systems affords the organization. The metrics could be increased sales, profits, and market share enhancement.

Data quality rewards: The data quality problems are a consequence of inadequate processes at the point where data is collected. In addition, it is also a result of the management style. If occurrences of errors are punished, they are never reported. Instead, a positive environment can be created by encouraging error correction and defect removal as a normal-health business process. The team owns an error, not an individual.

Data sharing incentives: Data warehouses encourage data sharing. Incentive (such as training, new technology pilots, and so on) affords the enterprise with tangible benefits.

Discourage data cartels: Data cartels are a result of rigid functionally controlled organizations. Data cartels own and operate application-specific data supporting a function. One can get a copy of the data only rarely when a direct access is allowed. While nothing appears wrong in a local environment, these generally produce dysfunctional information delivery at a cross-functional level.

Use of standard technologies: Standard technologies reduce system design complexities. Rewarding use of corporate standards should be encouraged. Disparate technologies cause resource wastage.

Table 11-14 correlates the stimuli with the pull and push forces on the foundation of a data warehouse.

Table 11–14 Pulls and Pushes of Incentives and Rewards

System Stimulus	Pull Force on Foundation	Push Force on Foundation
• Resource rewards	• Successful user-driven data warehouses usually are sustained and resources are added to accommodate growth.	• Agenda-driven considerations could result in granting more rescues on politically savvy groups.
• Reward value-added benefits	• The value is measured by predefined metrics and rewarded accordingly.	• Rewards are based on projections that are rarely validated. The benefits may be impossible to measure in the environment the enterprise operates.
• Reward data quality	• Data quality efforts are measured and rewarded as quality problems decrease.	• Business as usual. • No metrics exist or defined.
• Provide incentives for data sharing	• Data sharing is measured by a reduction in data copies across the enterprise.	• Data sharing exists only in strategy documents.
• Discourage data cartels	• Cross-functional data is reused, and the departments are rewarded accordingly.	• There is a denial that data cartels exist.
• Encourage using standard technologies	• Reduction in variation of similar tools and technologies is rewarded by providing more training to increase overall capabilities of the staff.	• Too many standards and variety of similar tools are approved based on the lobbying strength of the group.

Prior Baggage

Information management organizations have several "data skeletons" in their closets. The CASE discipline has not served the community well. Tools and technologies are based on fundamentally flawed and impractical theories, and technology shifts are large and unstable. To expect a perfectly modeled data world has been repeatedly elusive, yet many still chase such lofty goals dogmatically.

A data warehouse is a pragmatic solution to a real business problem. Data idealism has enormous baggage. The following are some key items that act on the data warehouse foundation.

Data modeling: Data modeling is a very useful tool in understanding data, but practiced as a rigid discipline, it provides little value. A data warehouse rarely contains fully normalized data. Staffing and managing a data warehouse should consider the value of large data-modeling efforts with care and justifiably with some trepidation.

Enterprise models: Enterprise models are extremely difficult and time-consuming to complete. In practice, an enterprise is never static: only a few aspects may remain the same. The rest of the business facts change faster than the models can respond.

Information centers: Information centers are an old throwback from the early data warehousing days. The concept may be right, but we never had the proper technology to deliver these. In staffing and managing a data warehouse, similar mistakes have to be avoided.

Repository: Repositories fall in the same category with data models and enterprise data models. These are expensive and time-consuming. Tying a data warehouse to a repository project is a mistake. Staffing the data warehouse with enterprise repository proponents likewise is a mistake.

Metadata: Metadata, practiced in the same vein as data modeling, enterprise models, and repository, is a sure prescription for failure. The data warehouse staffing and managing tactics should be evaluated for the combined pulls and pushes of these baggage items.

Tools: Tools are a dynamic area. One new venture-backed tools firm materializes almost every week. Tools do not solve the problem of fundamental ignorance of business information needs.

Table 11-15 correlates the above stimuli with the pull and push forces on the foundation of a data warehouse.

Table 11–15 Pulls and Pushes of Prior Baggage

System Stimulus	Pull Force on Foundation	Push Force on Foundation
• Data modeling	• Provide denormalized models.	• Design fully normalized models.
• Enterprise models	• Provide bare bones models to understand big picture.	• Engage in producing detailed models of the "as is" situation. • Engage in producing vision models of the "to be" data warehouse—information delivery environment.
• Information centers	• Give us useful information, not raw data.	• Produce a grand information delivery vision without a viable execution plan. • Someone else will execute it, not us.
• Repository	• Tell us what the data means in our context.	• Produce a neutral model with all attributes. • Developers will need repositories to solve all data problems; therefore, build one.
• Metadata for all	• Tell us where the data originated and what processes-in our business context.	• We will give you a very rich set of metadata that will solve all your problems. • Metadata will encourage data sharing and enhance data quality; therefore, we will collect all metadata.
• Tools will solve all problems	• Provide us answers and information, not tools.	• We will reduce complexity by using tools. • Provide us resources to learn new technology tools.

Technology

Technology imparts strong and continuous stimuli on the foundation of the data warehouse. Technology is both pulled and pushed in organizations, as outlined in the following paragraphs.

Processors: Parallel processors and fast data-retrieval mechanisms are rapidly emerging in the marketplace and will have tremendous impact when large data warehouses are built.

Data structures: Specialized data structures for data warehousing are now available as standard products.

Desktop SQL: Desktop data access and information-building tools are emerging. The users need not work with low-level SQL coding for constructing queries.

Multimedia: Complex data types can be stored and queried by using variations of SQL.

Middleware: Clever encapsulation of data objects, application interfaces, SQL database gateways, and so on, are emerging as middleware. The rich variety of middleware will influence the data warehouse significantly.

Table 11-16 correlates the stimuli with the pull and push forces on the foundation of a data warehouse.

Table 11–16 Pulls and Pushes of Technology

System Stimulus	Pull Force on Foundation	Push Force on Foundation
• Processors	• Add more users and enhance capacity.	• Upgrade delivery platforms.
• Data structures	• Enhance access to large data warehouses and reduce data refresh and downloading time.	• Introduce new database engines and platforms as a matter of policy.
• Desktop SQL	• Users demand more direct control on creating their own information access applications.	• Introduce new tools to users.
• Multimedia	• Competitive pressure demands more effective information delivery mechanisms.	• Provide technology upgrades.
• Middleware	• Users ask for more flexibility in connecting to various applications and databases.	• Developers introduce this as architecture improvement initiative.

Data-Sharing Culture

Data sharing is often talked about but seldom actually occurs. Management styles and functional models get in the way. A data warehouse tends to encourage sharing because data is more understandable and available without too many barriers. Several factors causing pulls and pushes on the data warehouse are especially helpful to understanding the issues on selection of staff and how well to manage an ongoing data warehouse resource.

Distributed computing: Distributed computing puts resources in the immediate control of users. With more available resources, useful information is accessible for other functional groups to use. Alternatively, a data replication strategy may be used to share large clusters of data.

Interoperability: Distributed computing introduces variations in technologies. These need to be resolved, and appropriate techniques have to be deployed to make these work as a unit. System interoperability is at the core of facilitating data-sharing culture.

Group computing: Group computing is essential in introducing process management. In group computing, common messaging, file management, information flows, and finally workflow management is deployed across functional groups. The infrastructure to share data is enhanced by a data warehouse.

Table 11-17 correlates the stimuli with the pull and push forces on the foundation of a data warehouse.

Table 11–17 Pulls and Pushes of Data Sharing Culture

System Stimulus	Pull Force on Foundation	Push Force on Foundation
• Distributed computing	• Facilitate access to other functional data sources.	• Transition to distributed computing as an enterprise standard.
• Interoperability, unity in diversity	• Users demand transparent access to enterprise-wide resources.	• Transition to new technologies as a corporate initiative.
• Group computing	• Users are managing processes.	• Modernize e-mail and messaging infrastructures.

Impact of Foundation Stimulus on Managing and Staffing the Data Warehouse

The data warehouse changes over time. The various conditions of change were suggested by the five elements shown in Figure 11–23. We also have seen the pull forces on foundation and corresponding pushes. We now will summarize these to understand the impacts on staffing and managing a data warehouse. The four issue groupings defined earlier are used to list the impacts, as shown in Table 11-18.

Table 11–18 Staffing and Management Impacts

Foundation Push and Pull Element	Staffing and Management Impacts on People Skills and Attributes
Problem Domain Redefinition	**Content**: • Select people who can translate requirements into pragmatic solutions. • Phasing of capabilities in meaningful ways and proper versioning of the data warehouse can address the pushes and pulls effectively. • Patience in understanding user requirement is an essential attribute of the staff. **Management**: • Document agreements of what will be available when. • Policies are redefined to leverage lessons learned. • Map functions to processes, and discern new data requirements as these evolve continuously. **Business Rules**: • Change-management implementation skills are essential. • Summarization and ability to scrub data down to manageable level is a valuable asset of the team. **People**: • Communications skills are most needed. • Assimilate users at all levels into critical design reviews. • The key requirement is to negotiate a reasonable statement of work with the users.

Table 11–18 Staffing and Management Impacts (Contd)

Foundation Push and Pull Element	Staffing and Management Impacts on People Skills and Attributes
Incentives and Rewards	**Content:** • Have people who can map requirements and correlate to metrics defined by management. • Recognize the right people at the right time. **Management:** • Relate metrics to accomplishments. • Motivational skills are required. • Design effective analyst appreciation programs. • Open communications and ability to accept responsibility of shortcomings without punishing the team members are an invaluable skill and management technique. **Business Rules:** • Skills to reward people who improve business processes by understanding how current business rules impact data warehousing processes. • **People:** • Leaders who can remain invisible, yet can make positive changes are crucial in the success of a data warehousing project..
Prior Baggage	**Content:** • Practical pragmatic thinkers are a must. **Management:** • Select people who are gentle but firm in resisting dogmatic data disciplines. **Business Rules:** • Business rules taken to extreme in modeling should be avoided. We need big picture thinking skills. **People:** • Ability to balance risks and rewards.
Technology	**Content:** • Ability to understand vendor hype **Management:** • Pilot-project-management skills • Ability to introduce mature technologies in a planned manner **Business Rules:** • Skills to use new metadata management tools • Ability to use intelligent agents in information delivery **People:** • Select people who can train the rest of the team in specialized technologies

Table 11–18 Staffing and Management Impacts (Contd)

Foundation Push and Pull Element	Staffing and Management Impacts on People Skills and Attributes
Data-Sharing Culture	**Content:** • Team players are a valuable asset. **Management:** • Skilled in discouraging agenda-driven behaviors. **Business Rules:** • Documentation skills in explaining the business-rules impact to users. **People:** • Select secure open-minded people in leadership roles.

CONCLUSION

A data warehouse is a resource for cross-functional and validated data. Several applications can share some or all the data. The requirements change as the maturity level goes up in using the warehouse. Flexibility in architecture, selection of staff, and managing are the keys to success.

A data warehouse is a pragmatic solution. It is not a playground for practicing data resource management dogma that is yet to provide promised benefits.

APPENDIX

Job Title	Primary Responsibilities
Data Warehousing Project Leader	1. Lead and define various teams to fulfill all the design and building activities of data warehousing. 2. Obtain consensus from all systems and process owners. 3. Estimate and obtain budget for construction, sustenance, and maintenance of data warehousing applications. 4. Coordinate cross-team activities in providing reliable data warehousing services to the users. 5. Participate in project staffing activities.
Data Warehousing Policy Architect	1. Define, obtain approval, and document data warehousing policies across the enterprise. 2. Alter and fine-tune policies to suit changing user requirements, computing architecture, and funding mechanisms. 3. Communicate policies to users.
Data Warehousing System Architect	1. Define logical and physical architecture of the components of a data warehouse. 2. Perform business case analysis in selecting products from vendor-furnished components. 3. Specify data mapping, refreshing, replication, accessing middleware, archiving tools, and strategies. 4. Coordinate technical policy requirements with **Data Warehousing Policy Architect.**
Data Warehousing Relations Specialist	1. Identify and resolve issues of data applications and users across functional organizations. 2. Act as the principal focal point in advancing the data warehousing team and users. 3. Perform as the single point of first contact for the data warehousing team and users. 4. Coordinate and manage vendor contacts with the data warehousing team. 5. Coordinate with **Policy Architect**.

Job Title	Primary Responsibilities
Data Warehousing Production-Source Systems Mapping Specialist	1. Understand source systems data structure, syntax, and semantics, and translate those to corresponding mapping specifications for data warehousing. 2. Identify data-quality problems as discovered during the data warehousing process. 3. Specify data refreshing cycles.
Data Warehousing Applications Specialist	1. Build data warehousing applications using sophisticated information construction and delivery tools. 2. Coordinate with business views as specified by **Business-Views Analyst**. 3. Phase-in capabilities of application functionality in concert with data warehouse versions deployment.
Data Warehousing Maintenance Specialist	1. Specify error reporting and correction procedures. 2. Assure that all data back-up and application recovery processes are followed. 3. Record and define system, metrics in support of continuous quality-improvement efforts. 4. Communicate data warehousing effectiveness to management.
Data Warehousing Business Views Analyst	1. Translate user requirements to database views in support of all information constructs. 2. Assure scope of data is adequate to support business-driven information requirements. 3. Specify data manipulation, analyses, and display requirements.
Data Warehousing Data Structures Analyst	1. Construct denormalized models of warehoused data. 2. Specify appropriate use of alternate schemas such as star and snowflake, for satisfying specific user requirements. 3. Build appropriate fact tables and so on to deploy sophisticated data warehousing technologies, such as OLAP and multidimensional analyses.

Chapter 12

An Education and Training Program for Data Warehousing

Dr. Ramon C. Barquin

The Data Warehousing Institute

The last few years have seen data warehousing emerge as a solid discipline within the mainstream of information technology. In parallel with this phenomenon, several commercial organizations have offered seminars and tutorials on data warehousing and related topics. These offerings have usually been scheduled around the many data warehousing conferences that have been held since mid-1994.

But the quality of these courses, the professionalism of the instruction, and the content of each specific syllabus have varied substantially. It has not been rare to see the same basic material taught under different course titles, or to find courses with the same title covering a substantially different set of topics. While this is not necessarily uncommon when dealing with a new discipline, it illustrates that data warehousing is quickly reaching a threshold of maturity requiring a higher degree of rigor.

The Data Warehousing Institute has as its mission the advancement and professionalization of data warehousing. This places us foursquare on the subject of data warehousing training, and has led to the creation of a Committee for Data Warehousing Education. It is the intent of this committee to review data warehousing training in detail, and to recommend a curriculum for the discipline to serve as a guideline for the industry. This is the principal objective of this chapter.

WHY WE NEED A DATA WAREHOUSING TRAINING PROGRAM

Training is an essential component of most industrial pursuits. It is the process whereby an individual acquires the necessary skills to perform a specific job or carry out specific tasks. (The *Random House Dictionary of the English Language* defines "to train" as "to make proficient by instruction or practice, as in some art profession or work.") It is at the heart of both productivity and competitiveness.

There is a long tradition of training within the information industry. The need to learn and relearn new versions of programming languages, operating systems, word processors, spread sheets, database management systems, and the many more tools of the trade has made training a necessity since the early days of computers. Most large information systems (I/S) organizations have departments or functions responsible for the continuous training of their staff. This is necessary to ensure that they have the right skills at the right time to work with whatever new tools, or new versions of existing tools, the organization adopts at any given point in time.

As data warehousing starts to penetrate large numbers of enterprises—and it is currently doing so—it becomes critical that there be ample training resources to meet the demand generated by its widespread adoption and dissemination. Further, organizations and individuals in need of instruction should have some level of assurance that the training that they get is the right training, and they should be able to have access to a set of standards or guidelines through which to compare the various offerings.

In addition, new disciplines often bring with them a wealth of new terms unfortunately accompanied by multiple and ambiguous definitions for many of those terms. And also common, of course, is the usual debate between theoreticians and practitioners, and even among the different factions of practitioners themselves. It takes time and experience for vocabulary to stabilize and for the patterns of practice to emerge. Then, and only then, can a first common set of guidelines and standards be developed that will constitute the initial point of reference.

This is precisely where we are right now in data warehousing. There is the need to decide what topics will be taught, to what depth, and in what sequence. We also need to answer questions such as Which topics are prerequisites of which others? What should a core curriculum look like? Who should be receiving what training? What should the syllabus cover for this specific course?

WHAT NEEDS TO BE TAUGHT

Within data warehousing there are a number of major topics and an even larger number of secondary topics. In addition, there are a series of related subject matters that can be covered from the perspective of data warehousing, such as object-oriented methodologies, client/server technology, and the Internet.

It goes without saying that a minimum level of information systems studies and/or work experience is required for a proper understanding of many of these topics. For example, without the basics of systems design, systems architecture, and some programming, it would be difficult to grasp data warehousing database design or data warehousing architecture and topologies.

In addition to the *what*, it is important to note the *who*. Not everyone on the staff of an enterprise that is launching a data warehousing initiative need be proficient in every aspect of the data warehousing discipline. Further, there may be a number of individuals outside the I/S shops—executives, business users, and so on—who may also need to be trained in how to access or query the data warehouse.

Broadly speaking, we can divide the audience in need of training into five categories: I/S staff, I/S managers, business users, executives, and general. (A general audience is defined as an audience, independent of their job description, with no prior knowledge of data warehousing.) Table 12-1 attempts to indicate which categories need instruction in what aspects of the data warehousing process. We should also recognize that in each category there may be some individuals who already have some level of understanding of data warehousing and related concepts, and thus may start at a different point in the curriculum. There will also be some courses that can be classified as being targeted for a general audience.

Table 12–1 Who Should Be Trained in What Areas

	Awareness	Plan	Design	Implement	Manage	Use	Maintain
I/S Staff (S)	X	X	X	X			X
Business Users (B)	X	X				X	
I/S Managers (M)	X	X	X	X	X	X	X
Executives (E)	X				X	X	
General (G)	X						

THE PROGRAM

A data warehousing training program will consist of a series of courses, each of which will develop its own syllabus and have a suggested length, a target audience, and some prerequisites. The set of recommended courses are listed in Table 12-2, and their descriptions and length are listed in Table 12-3. In Table 12-4 we provide a listing by job category of what courses should be taught.

Table 12–2 Data Warehousing Courses

Class No.	Prerequisites	Course Title & Description	Duration
G1	NONE	An Introduction to Data Warehousing	Full day
T1	G1	A Roadmap to Data Warehousing	Full day
G4	G1	Developing a Data Warehousing Strategy for the Enterprise	Half day
T2	G4	Planning a Data Warehouse Project	Half day
T3	T2	Data Warehousing Architectures	Half day
T5	G1	Data Modeling for the Data Warehouse	Full day
G6	G1	Data Warehousing: An Implementation Case Study	Full day
G7	G1	A Practitioner's Guide to Data Warehousing	Full day
T7	G4	Critical Decisions for the Implementation of a Data Warehouse	Full day
G8	G4	Criteria for Successful Data Warehousing	Half day
T9	T3	Developing the Metadata Repository for Data Warehousing	Full day
T10	T3	Data Extraction, Cleaning, and Transformation Techniques	Full day
T14	T3	Database Design for Data Warehousing	Two days
G12	G1	An Introduction to Data Mining	Half day
G14	G1	Data Warehousing: A Management Perspective	Half day
T18	T3	Data Warehousing and the Internet	Full day
G19	G1	Decision Support in a Data Warehousing Environment	Full day
G22	G1	Data Warehousing and Business Strategy	Full day
G25	G4	How to Win Support for Your Data Warehousing Project	Full day
T22	T14	Parallel Computing for Data Warehousing	Full day

Table 12–3 Data Warehousing Course Descriptions (Page 1 of 4)

Class	Course Title & Description
G1	**An Introduction to Data Warehousing** This course provides an overview of data warehousing to introduce all audiences—managers, users and practitioners—to the basic vocabulary and concepts. It will ensure that participants know what data warehouses are, what they do, and why they are needed in today's business environment. It also sets the foundation for all other topics covered in depth in later courses.
T1	**A Roadmap to Data Warehousing** This course is similar in scope to G1, but is intended for I/S professionals and managers who will be involved in data warehousing projects. Hence it is taught at a more advanced level in providing an overview of the principal components of the data warehousing process, following The Data Warehousing Institute's widely distributed "Data Warehousing Roadmap."
G4	**Developing a Data Warehousing Strategy for the Enterprise** This course addresses the need to provide a blueprint for data warehousing at the enterprise level. It is very common to find organizations engaging in tool selection and data warehouse database design before they have looked at the basics of their data warehousing effort. Does the organization really need a data warehouse? What subject areas should be prioritized? Should departmental or functional datamarts be implemented? If so, who are the users that are going to be served? What are the business issues which the data warehouse is going to address and resolve? What is the quality of the data which is going to feed the data warehouse? What is the level of effort entailed? Who is going to staff it? How are you going to manage the production? These, and many other questions, mandate that professional organizations develop a strategy for the data warehousing initiative before they launch into the tactical aspects of the effort. This course lays out the groundwork and provides a methodology for developing such a strategy.
T2	**Planning a Data Warehouse Project** This course applies basic project management techniques to the data warehousing discipline in order to provide a framework within which to carry out data warehousing projects. It is intended primarily for senior I/S professionals and managers with data warehousing development responsibilities.
T3	**Data Warehousing Architectures** This course is intended for senior I/S professionals and managers with responsibility for the design and implementation of data warehousing environments. A robust architecture is essential for successful data warehousing projects. This course focuses on developing such an architecture by introducing the students to the principal data warehousing topologies and components.

Table 12–3 Data Warehousing Course Descriptions (Page 2 of 4)

T5	**Data Modeling for the Data Warehouse** This course addresses the need to have a data model to work with for the data warehouse. In many cases this data model already exists, or can be quickly put together from previous work. It is intended to introduce the data warehousing project team to the basics of data modeling, the difference between full enterprise data models and functional data models for data warehousing, and the basic data modeling tool set.
G6	**Data Warehousing: An Implementation Case Study** This course provides a general overview of how a successful data warehousing project is implemented from conception to full production, and puts it all together through a case study. It reinforces many of the concepts previously presented, and allows the students to ask specific questions of instructors who have had the responsibility and accountability of putting a data warehouse in place within their organizations. This is important because as I/S organizations embrace data warehousing, many are finding that there is more to worry about than just technology, and that the impacts on the business, the end-users, and the I/S organizations themselves were very much underestimated. This session provides insight into how best to establish and continuously evolve an enterprise-wide data warehouse environment.
G7	**A Practitioner's Guide to Data Warehousing** This course combines the features of a classical data warehousing case study with the lessons learned of veteran practitioners. It introduces the key concepts and blends them with the realities and experience of having to implement a data warehouse in a live environment and dealing with budget pressures, corporate cultures, vendor hard sells, and the usual array of personalities populating any enterprise.
T7	**Critical Decisions for the Implementation of a Data Warehouse** This course addresses the major issues that must be resolved to implement a data warehouse and answers the most common questions arising in such endeavors. It does so by looking at components, tools, tool selection criteria, and integration strategies in each key area. <u>Data extraction techniques</u>: Should the source data be extracted and managed using the facilities of a standard relational DBMS, or through the use of specialized data extraction tool? <u>Target database for data warehouse:</u> Should the database for a data warehouse be supported by a conventional relational DBMS, or by a specialized multi-dimensional DBMS? <u>Front-end data access tools</u>: Should the data be accessed from the data warehouse using general purpose client/server tools, end-user query tools, or special purpose DSS/EIS tools?
G8	**Criteria for Successful Data Warehousing** This course helps the data warehousing team—to include the technical staff, managers, and business users identify and discuss critical success factors involved in the data warehousing effort. It addresses these topics at a high level and provides criteria against which the team can track the project's performance.

Table 12–3 Data Warehousing Course Descriptions (Page 3 of 4)

T9	**Developing the Metadata Repository for Data Warehousing** This course addresses the metadata layer in a data warehousing environment. Every successful data warehouse is tightly coupled with a metadata repository which serves as the navigational tool for the system and its users. This repository provides business views of the data, triggers source data extractions and data warehouse refreshes, as well as serving a number of other purposes in the data warehousing environment. This course introduces the students to the repository concept, describes it, and provides a methodology for developing it.
T10	**Data Extraction, Cleaning, and Transformation Techniques** This course addresses one of the toughest and most laborious aspects of data warehousing. These deal with migrating data from legacy systems. Disparate databases designed with ambiguous business rules and often conflicting definitions and lax systems controls have frequently resulted in very poor quality of information. This presents a formidable challenge; and yet, accomplishing this migration while meeting basic standards of data quality is a mandatory precondition of successful data warehousing. This course provides the student with the necessary skill set to identify the problem, understand the available tools, and develop the strategies for engineering large-scale migration from legacy systems to a data warehouse environment, under a very high data quality standard.
T14	**Database Design for Data Warehousing** This two-day course introduces the student to the basic skill set necessary to design databases for data warehouses. Data warehouse database design is substantially different from transaction processing database design. Hence, what works for one area often does not in the other. This course starts by refreshing basic concepts of query versus transaction systems, data modeling, dimensional analysis, administration and management of a data warehouse; and focuses on how to design both relational databases as well as multidimensional databases. It covers some of the basic schema, such as the "star" and the "snowflake" and other related topics.
G12	**An Introduction to Data Mining** This course provides an introduction to data mining and knowledge discovery. Data warehousing is consolidating customer information at an unprecedented level, giving companies the raw data for understanding customer behavior and marketing effectiveness. However, identifying patterns in this mass of data can be a daunting task, and traditional statistical methods fail to take full advantage of it. This course addresses the basic approaches to data mining, including new modeling techniques that capture key predictors of behavior. Details about how to carry these techniques into production will be given, from the best data sources to start triggering models in on-line systems.

Table 12–3 Data Warehousing Course Descriptions (Page 4 of 4)

G14	**Data Warehousing: A Management Perspective** This course looks at data warehousing primarily from a management perspective. Planning and designing a data warehouse are basically technical endeavors that are central to the successful implementation of a data warehouse. But while these are necessary requirements, they are clearly not sufficient. The data warehousing initiative must be allowed to emerge and then be nurtured. This can happen only if top management understands the true contribution of data warehousing and is committed to its implementation. This half day session focuses on the management aspects of a data warehousing project through a series of lessons learned, mistakes to avoid, and tips to follow.
T18	**Data Warehousing and the Internet** This course addresses the utilization of the Internet as a key resource to deliver data warehousing services to both internal and external users in an organization. The Internet is emerging as a ubiquitous, low-cost approach to sharing data warehousing information. This class shows you how to use standard Internet technology to provide access to data warehouses. It focuses on secure web servers, Internet-aware DBMS, standard web browsers, and the firewalls, intranets, and advanced security features mandatory in this environment.
G19	**Decision Support in a Data Warehousing Environment** This course provides the basis for choosing decision-support front-end tools for your data warehouse. The basic purpose of data warehousing is to empower knowledge workers with information that allows them to make decisions based on a solid foundation of fact. Users who are business knowledgeable are not necessarily SQL savvy nor are they experts in statistical analysis techniques. Hence, it is essential that they be provided with the type of decision-support tools that will allow them to interpret the data in the warehouse rationally in order to reach sound conclusions.
G22	**Data Warehousing and Business Strategy** This course attempts to position data warehousing as a strategic weapon through which an organization can obtain competitive advantage. Basic aspects of strategy, business strategy, and the alignment of I/S with business strategy are presented and integrated with data warehousing applications and examples from the real world.
G25	**How to Win Support for Your Data Warehousing Project** This course addresses the issue of how to sell your data warehousing project to both end-users and management. It is an essential component of any data warehousing initiative. It identifies errors technologists make and shows how to correct them. In it you'll learn the eight most important keys to getting support.
T22	**Parallel Computing for Data Warehousing** This course presents the audience with an overview of parallel computing and high-end database applications. It introduces the necessary concepts to understand both the hardware and software architectures, and draws on a series of case studies to reinforce the conceptual framework.

Table 12–4 Courses by Job Category

Course Title & Description	I/S Staff	I/S Mgrs	Bus. Users	Execs	General
An Introduction to Data Warehousing	X	X	X	X	X
A Roadmap to Data Warehousing	X	X			
Developing a Data Warehousing Strategy for the Enterprise	X	X	X	X	
Planning a Data Warehouse Project	X	X			
Data Warehousing Architectures	X	X			
Data Modeling for the Data Warehouse	X				
Data Warehousing: An Implementation Case Study	X	X	X		X
A Practitioner's Guide to Data Warehousing	X	X			
Critical Decisions for the Implementation of a Data Warehouse	X	X			
Criteria for Successful Data Warehousing	X	X			
Developing the Metadata Repository for Data Warehousing	X	X			
Data Extraction, Cleaning, and Transformation Techniques	X	X			
Database Design for Data Warehousing	X	X			
An Introduction to Data Mining	X	X	X		
Data Warehousing: A Management Perspective		X		X	
Data Warehousing and the Internet	X	X			
Decision Support in a Data Warehousing Environment	X	X	X		
Data Warehousing and Business Strategy		X		X	
How to Win Support for Your Data Warehousing Project		X	X		
Parallel Computing for Data Warehousing	X	X			

WHO WILL TEACH THE COURSES?

There is already a sizable contingent of practitioners who have been involved in the implementation of data warehousing for a number of years. From this pool, a competent cadre of instructors is already emerging that will be able to teach the recommended data warehousing curriculum. Some of these instructors have already taught seminars and tutorials for The Data Warehousing Institute and other organizations. Table 12-5 lists all the individuals who have taught courses at Institute conferences, or as part of its Corporate On-Site Education Program, through the summer of 1996. If to this list one adds the competent pool of instructors who have taught elsewhere, or those on the staffs of product vendors, one can appreciate that there is already a seed community to start addressing the demand.

That demand is bound to grow exponentially for the next few years, and hence there will be the need to resort to two other sources of instruction: internal training and academia. Large organizations with sufficient training needs may opt to develop their own programs and possibly use their own trainers in situations where they (a) cannot find adequate outside trainers, (b) find it substantially less costly, or (c) need to develop the internal capability because of the sensitive nature of their operations.

Academia, on the other hand, has been lagging up to now in the surge of data warehousing activity, and will need to play catch-up in order to be able to play a role over the next few years. We are seeing a bit of this already through the current interest in data warehousing, primarily in the business schools.

THE DATA WAREHOUSING INSTITUTE'S ACCREDITATION AND CERTIFICATION PROGRAMS

Given the importance of data warehousing and the knowledge production to each enterprise, it will be important that the industry guarantee an ample supply of quality instructors. But equally important will be to establish a solid set of standards for the training itself. Only in this manner can an organization be assured that when they recruit an individual based on his or her data warehousing credentials, all courses will have a common meaning and that common instruction can be adequately compared.

The best way to guarantee this is through the well-tested and proven process of accreditation. This does not mean that only courses which are duly accredited have validity; of course not. But given the usual uncertainty and risk surrounding any contractual process, an organization can rely at least on the fact that a serious and competent body has reviewed both the trainer and the training, and gives testimony that they comply with an established set of standards. Likewise, individual practitioners can be certified as having completed the general curriculum and/or a specialized curriculum when they have taken all the courses that comprise an accredited training program.

The Data Warehousing Institute, through its Data Warehousing Training Committee, has started to consider certification of its own instructors, and may offer to certify and train other instructors and training programs. This would be an important part of the Institute's mission to professionalize data warehousing and knowledge production.

The accreditation program, as being considered by the Institute, would address three specific areas. It will certify:

1. Training Programs
   a. Do the course offerings comply with the Institute's recommended curriculum?
   b. Do the course syllabi reasonably follow the Institute's own?
   c. Are the instructors certified?
   d. What references can be provided, and what do they say?
   e. Are the trainees willing to comply with Institute testing standards and audit procedures?

2. Instructors
   a. What academic credentials, data warehousing training, or practitioner's experience does the instructor have?
   b. What programs has he or she already taught?
   c. What references can be provided, and what do they say?
   d. Are the instructors willing to comply with Institute testing standards and audit procedures?
3. Practitioners
   a. Who successfully complete courses certified by the Institute.
   b. Who successfully complete the Institute's general or specialized curriculum.

Table 12–5 Instructors Who Have Taught Courses for the Data Warehousing Institute

1.	*Herb Edelstein*, Two Crows
2.	*Dick Hackathorn*, Bolder Technology
3.	*Pieter Mimno*, Technology Insights
4.	*James Ford*, Connexus
5.	*Hugh Watson*, University of Georgia
6.	*Larry Meador*, MIT
7.	*Glenn Livingston*, Red Brick
8.	*Neil Raden*, Archer Decision Sciences
9.	*Doug Neal*, A. T. Kearney
10.	*Alan Paller*, The Data Warehousing Institute
11.	*Lloyd Belcher*, Conoco
12.	*Carol Burleson*, Naval Surface Warfare Center
13.	*David Tabler*, Naval Surface Warfare Center
14.	*Michael Haisten*, VITAL Technologies
15.	*Nagraj Alur*, DataBase Associates
16.	*Paul Barth*, Tessera Enterprise Systems
17.	*Stephen Brobst*, Cambridge Technology Partners

Table 12–5 Instructors Who Have Taught Courses for the Data Warehousing Institute (Contd)

18.	*Irv Robinson,* ATT GIS
19.	*Narsim Ganti,* Boeing
20.	*J.D. Welch,* PRISM Solutions
21.	*Mike Ferguson,* Consultant
22.	*Jim Thomann,* Consultant
23.	*Jeffrey Bedell,* MicroStrategy
24.	*Estelle Brand,* Two Crows
25.	*Rob Gerritsen,* Two Crows
26.	*Colin White,* DataBase Associates
27.	*Lowell Frymann,* Consultant
28.	*Diogenes Torres,* Migration Software
29.	*Ramon Barquin,* The Data Warehousing Institute
30.	*Adrienne Tannenbaum,* Database Design Solutions

CONCLUSION

The Institute is determined to play a role in professionalizing data warehousing and knowledge production. We believe that training is one of the essential vehicles for accomplishing this and have introduced a core curriculum for the discipline. This is our first draft at such a curriculum; and we will be updating it periodically as new techniques and products enter the industry and as innovative approaches are introduced by practitioners.

Chapter 13

Understanding Data Warehousing Strategically

NCR Corporation, 1996

Bernard H. Boar

NCR

It is obvious to anyone who culls through the voluminous information technology (I/T) literature (books, journals, alerts, flashes, newspapers, etc.), attends industry seminars, user group meetings or expositions, reads the ever-accelerating new product announcements of I/T vendors, or listens to the advice of industry gurus and analysts that four subjects overwhelmingly dominate the I/T industry attention as we move into the late 1990s:

- *I/T processing architecture*, embodied in the shift to client/server computing from the aging monolithic host-centered computing architecture.

- *Electronic commerce*, exemplified in the explosive growth of novel communication services-based ways of engaging in commerce as personified by the Internet.

- *Application developer productivity*, observed in the extreme interest in object-oriented technology in all its myriad of forms, e.g., object-oriented analysis, object-

oriented design, object-oriented programming and object-oriented distributed processing frameworks.

- *Knowledge management, decision making, and learning,* illustrated in the intense interest and implementation of data warehouses.

The fundamental strategic logic of the first three are fairly well understood. The strategic imperative that propels one to client/server computing is *maneuverability*. To cope with the extreme business turbulence of the 1990s and beyond, a company must be agile and fast. Client/server permits a business to respond quickly and forcefully to constantly changing times and circumstances in a cost-competitive manner.

The strategic imperative that supports the unparalleled interest and investments in the Internet is *reach*. Electronic commerce provides entirely new ways to distribute and sell to consumers: ways that are faster, cheaper, more informative, customer intimate, and customer empowering, and that compress time and space. The history of free market commerce is that suppliers irresistibly gravitate toward technologies that enable them to reach customers in more cost-effective and efficient ways. Customers naturally gravitate toward distribution channels that provide them with ease of use and convenience at a fair cost. Electronic commerce, the Internet, converges the interest of suppliers and consumers. The Internet replaces local and physical marketplaces with a global and virtual *marketspace*.

The strategic imperative that motivates interest in the object-oriented technology is *leverage*. Through the prospect of treating software as pre-engineered parts, new productivity levels can be achieved by shifting the unit of software development from a line-of-code to pre-assembled, reusable, and certified parts. So the strategic logic of the first three pervasive I/T trends is clear; they are, respectively, maneuverability, reach, and leverage (productivity).

Data warehousing is the last of the four dominant trends, but the underlying strategic logic has not been well articulated. What is the underlying deep and compelling logic of data warehousing? How are we to understand data warehousing strategically so that we may fully optimize the investment?

This essay will attempt to answer those questions. We will demonstrate that to understand data warehousing strategically, we must first understand strategy and strategic thinking. Once we understand those concepts, the strategic logic of data warehousing becomes clear and the path to an optimum implementation emerges. We will demonstrate that data warehousing is best appreciated as a realization of the deep and far-reaching strategic idea of a *raising-tide strategy*. The maximum return from data warehousing occurs when it is conceptualized, implemented, managed, and evolved within that context. Before doing that, however, it is beneficial to level set and review the data architecture origins of data warehousing.

STRATEGY, STRATEGIC THINKING, AND DATA WAREHOUSING

From an academic perspective, the purpose of strategic planning is to provide direction, concentration of effort (focus), constancy of purpose (perseverance), and flexibility (adaptability) as a business relentlessly strives to improve its position in all strategic areas. Strategy is mathematics and is equal to direction plus focus plus perseverance plus adaptability. At a very pragmatic level, strategy can be understood as finding a way short (the shorter the better) of *brute force* to accomplish one's ends. Strategy should be comprehended as the movement from a current position to a more desirable future position but with economies of time, effort, cost, or resource utilization. There is neither elegance nor insight in brute force, but there must be both in strategy.

My view is that the eternal struggle of business is the struggle for advantage. The one with more advantage wins; the one with less advantage loses. The purpose of strategy is the building, compounding, and sustaining of advantage. Consequently, business strategy must focus on:

- building new advantages that increase customer satisfaction and create distance from competitors;

- elongating existing advantages that increase customer satisfaction and create distance from competitors; and

- compressing or eliminating the advantages of competitors.

The lone purpose of business strategy is the nurturing of advantage. Advantage can be realized through infinite combinations of strategic moves. While there are many ways to build advantage, all advantages can be classified into five generic categories:

- **cost advantage:** the advantage results in being able to provide products/services more cheaply.

- **value-added advantage:** the advantage creates a product/service that offers some highly desirable feature/functionality.

- **focus advantage:** the advantage more tightly meets the explicit needs of a particular customer.

- **speed advantage:** the advantage permits you to service customer needs quicker than others.

- **maneuverability advantage:** the advantage permits you to adapt to changing requirements more quickly than others. Being maneuverable permits you to constantly refresh the other types of advantage. It is the only advantage that your competitors can't take from you.

So you win by being cheaper, unique, more focused, faster, or more adaptable than your competitors in serving your customers. At a minimum, your advantages must satisfy your customers and, at best, delight or excite them. Sun Tzu said:

> *The one with many strategic factors on his side wins . . . The one with few strategic factors on his side loses. In this way, I can tell who will win and who will lose.*[1]

If an action does not lead to the development of an advantage, it is of no strategic interest. The struggle always has been, and remains, the perpetual struggle for competitive advantage.

The culmination of advantage is the building of a set of sustainable competitive advantages (SCA) for the business. An SCA is a resource, capability, asset, process, and so on, that provides the enterprise with a distinct attraction to its customers and a unique advantage over its competitors. An SCA has seven attributes that are itemized in Table 13-1. Without a well-designed set of sustainable competitive advantages, a business engages in a frantic life-and-death struggle for marketplace survival; after all, there is no compelling reason for consumers to choose that company's products or services.

Table 13–1 Sustainable Competitive Advantage (SCA)

SCA Attribute	Definition
Customer perception	The customer perceives a consistent difference in one or more key buying factors.
SCA linkage	The difference in customer perception is directly attributable to the SCA.
Durability	Both customers' perception and the SCA linkage are durable over an extended time period.
Transparency	The mechanics/details of the SCA are difficult for competitors to understand.
Accessibility	The competitor has unequal access to the required resources to mimic the SCA.
Replication	The competitor would have extreme difficulty reproducing the SCA.
Coordination	The SCA requires difficult and subtle coordination of multiple resources.

To summarize, the key ideas of strategy are:

- The purpose of strategy is to build advantage.

- Advantage can be built in many ways.

- Advantage is classifiable into five categories.

- The culmination of advantage is the creation of sustainable competitive advantage (SCA).

- Those with more advantages win; those with fewer advantages lose.

The basic problem is, of course, From where do advantages emanate? How do we discover that which will be elegant and insightful so that we may win without using mindless brute force? The answer is that we postulate, analyze, and select strategic actions through *strategic thinking*.

STRATEGIC THINKING

Figure 13–1 illustrates three dimensions to thinking:

- Time: we think across time in the past, the present, and the future.

- Substance: we think between the concrete and the abstract.

- Carnality: we may think about one or more issues concurrently.

Figure 13–1   Mundane thinking. Most of the time, most of us engage in *point thinking,* where we think only about one issue in concrete terms in the present. (Source: Bernard H. Boar, *The Art of Strategic Planning for Information Technology,* John Wiley & Sons, 1994)

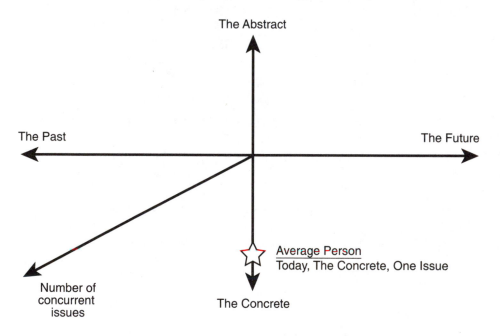

Most of the time, most of us, as illustrated in Figure 13–1, engage in *mundane thinking* to solve our daily problems. All we need to do, to meet our needs, is to think about one issue, in the present, and in the concrete, at a time. Anything more sophisticated would be overkill. This thinking pattern that we use to solve our daily problems is also referred to as *point thinking* because all our problem-solving efforts converge on one point.

Figure 13–2 illustrates strategic thinking. A strategist uses the same dimensions as the mundane thinker, but thinks dynamically within the thought bubble defined by those three dimensions. A strategist concurrently thinks about many issues in multiple dimensions, at many levels of abstraction and detail over time (past, present, and future). Strategic thinking is a creative and dynamic synthesis that is the exact opposite of point thinking.

Figure 13–2   Strategic thinking. Strategists think dynamically within the bubble of the three strategic dimensions. (Source: Bernard H. Boar, *The Art of Strategic Planning for Information Technology*, John Wiley & Sons, 1994)

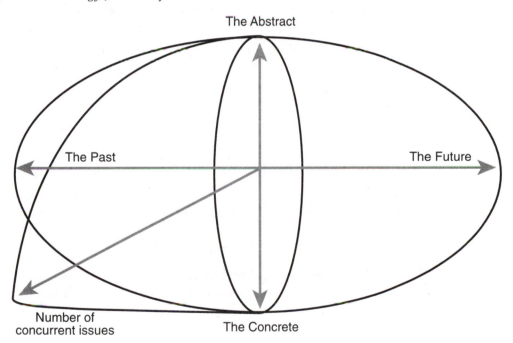

When looking at a problem, a strategist thinks about it in terms of certain established strategic ideas or themes. While new perspectives can always be developed, time and experience have demonstrated the power of looking at problems through certain enduring and tested strategic lenses. The following is a partial and representative list of powerful strategic ideas.

- *Assessment*: It is the responsibility of the leadership to fully assess the situation before committing its forces to conflict. Based on the assessment, an overarching strategy is adopted. Tactical maneuvers and adaptation take place within this strategy.

- *Alliances*: It is necessary to develop a community of allies. The strength of the alliance is stronger than the simple additive strength of the individual members.

- *Structure*: Structure depends on strategy. Forces are to be structured in a manner that enables the realization of the strategy.

- *Indirection*: Opponents should not be confronted directly. The maximum gain at the minimum expense is achieved by deception, surprise, and chipping away at the edges of the opponent. Exhaust them before you confront them.

- *Speed*: All matters require speed. Speed, alone, can compensate for numerous other shortcomings.

- *Strategic conflict*: The opponent is to be contested strategically. Attack and ruin his strategy, do not engage his advantages.

- *Self-invincibility*: The first order of business is to make oneself invincible. Before engaging in expansionist activities, be sure that you cannot be defeated at home.

- *Prescience*: The leadership must have deep and far-reaching foresight. Leaders must see and know what others do not. The height of prescience is to see the formless and act on it.

- *Formlessness*: The architecture of your advantages must be inscrutable. In this way, the opponent does not know what to attack and what to defend.

- *Positioning*: Forces must be pre-placed in winning positions by design. In this way, the actual confrontation is anti-climatic as you have already won by your superior positions.

- *Commitment*: All must share the same commitment to the objectives. Forces that do not share the same aims lack the will and resolve to overcome the endless barriers to victory.

- *Maneuver*: Maneuver means finding the best way to go. Forces must be able to maneuver to exploit gaps.

- *Leadership*: The leadership is responsible for the well-being of the community. Leaders must lay deep plans for what others do not foresee.

- *Efficiency*: Extended confrontations drain the community of wealth. The best victories are swift and at the absolute minimum cost.

- *Coordination*: The problem of coordination is the problem of managing the many as though they were one. The few can defeat the many if they act with one purpose. When perfect coordination is achieved, one cannot distinguish the will of the individual from the will of the many, nor the will of the many from the will of the individual.

- *Discipline*: There must be an impartial system of reward and punishment. Good leadership rewards the worthy.

- *Psychological conflict*: Victory and defeat occur first in the mind. Defeat your opponent psychologically so that even if he is intact, he lacks the will to contest you.

- *Foreknowledge*: All matters require competitive intelligence. Nothing is more important than understanding the plans of your opponents and the needs of your customers.

- *Love of the people*: True leadership is not a function of title, but a function of the love of the people. Leaders must share the struggle of their forces. We must win the affection of our employees so that they will extend themselves for us.

- *Learning*: One must continually learn and adapt based on that learning. All progress includes making mistakes, but the same mistakes should not be made twice.

All these themes, not surprisingly, converge on one grand strategic idea—the building, sustaining, and extending of advantage. So a strategic thinker:

- chooses a problem (or set of problems).

- samples strategic ideas (singularly and simultaneously).

- thinks about solving the problem(s) by applying the strategic ideas within the figure bubble. This demands intuitive, holistic, dynamic, and abstract thinking.

Since the combinations of strategic ideas are inexhaustible, strategic thinking is a very powerful way to develop insight about problems and solve them in novel, unanticipated, and creative ways. It is from this kind of thinking that advantage is born and nourished.

DATA WAREHOUSING AND STRATEGIC THINKING

To understand data warehousing strategically, we should now appreciate that it is the consequence of strategic thinking, which means that it is the product (result) of some combination of strategic ideas. In this case, we must reverse-engineer strategic thinking. We know the result of the strategic thinking process (data warehousing), but what are the strategic ideas from which it emanated?

Data warehousing is an unusually rich strategic action. A strong case can be made that it is the product of numerous strategic ideas. If we argue, however, that data warehousing is the product of everything, we cloud our analysis. What are the key ideas that it realizes?

In Miyamoto Musashi's classical book on strategy, *The Five Rings*, he teaches that all weapons have a distinctive spirit. It is the challenge of a warrior to understand that spirit, master it, and become in harmony with it. In that way, there is perfect integration between the warrior and his weapon.

When I think about data warehousing's distinctive spirit, I think about *time.* I believe that more than any other strategic theme, what data warehousing does is permit one to compete across time. One competes across time:

- *Past:* One must learn from the past so that the best lessons can be learned and deployed, and mistakes avoided.

- *Present:* One must be able to analyze current events quickly so that one can maneuver in real time to adapt to them.

- *Future:* One must have prescience about the future so that opportunistic investments and actions can be taken now to position for an even better tomorrow. Foreknowledge is the source of extraordinary success.

So the strategic ideas from which data warehousing emanates are the time-oriented ones of learning, maneuverability, prescience, and foreknowledge.

These four strategic ideas are not just any set of strategic ideas; they are uniquely important. They are uniquely important because they overlay the time dimension of strategic thinking (Figure 13–1 and 13–2, lateral axis). Time is one of the three fundamental dimensions of strategic thought and data warehousing that enables one to think directly in that dimension. Data warehousing is, therefore, not just another good result of strategic thinking: it is a very special result because it provides the tools to permit an organization, through the action of building data warehouses, to compete in the primary strategic dimension of time. By giving your employees robust access to information about customers, markets, suppliers, financial results, and others, you enable them to *learn* strategically from the past, *adapt* in the present, and *position* for the future. To the non-strategist, the mundane thinker, data warehousing is about spending (wasting?) money to let employees play with data. To the strategist, data warehousing is about winning the endless battle against time.

Data Warehousing as a Raising-Tide Strategy

There is a special name given to certain strategic actions. This name is a *raising-tide strategy*. As the tide comes in, it raises all the ships in the harbor. The tide does not discriminate; it raises the dingy, the canoe, the yacht, the warship, and the ocean liner. The single action of the incoming tide raises all ships. All of them, by no action of their own, enjoy the effect of the raising tide.

A raising tide symbolizes the strategic notion of *leverage.* Leverage is what gives strategy muscle. Leverage means that you do one thing, but multiple benefits derive from it. Typical words used to describe leveraged events are *reuse, sharing, economies of scale, economies of scope, cascading, cloning, duplicating, layering, amplifying*, and *multiplying*. Mathematically, the value of leverage equals individual payoff times instances of payoff.

Data warehousing supports a raising-tide strategy. By the single action of making information readily available to employees, we can bring benefits to all the employees as they go about their daily work. Hundreds of times every day, employees solve problems, make decisions, control processes, develop insights, share information, relate to others, and attempt to influence others. All of these actions can be made more efficient and effective if better information is made available in a timely manner at the point of need. This is called *informating* your business. Data warehousing *informates* the business.

Raising-tide strategies are cherished strategies. They are cherished because of the *multiplier effect.* So while it is excellent that data warehousing permits you to compete in time, what is remarkable about data warehousing is that it can permit all of your employees to compete across time. The single act of making information available creates distinct strategic leverage for the business. You have the ability to further increase your leverage by increasing the amount of data available and the number of employees to whom it is made accessible. Data warehousing is an awesomely powerful raising tide strategy. A strategy that is most effective when the tide is kept as high as possible and raises as many ships as possible.

DATA WAREHOUSING AND STRATEGIC PARADOX

In conducting our daily lives, purposeful opposition to our routine efforts does not exist. No one has the goal to deliberately and continually thwart our actions. We use what is called *linear logic* to solve our problems. Linear logic consists of using common sense, deductive/inductive reasoning, and concern for economies of time, cost, and effort to problem-solve. One is commonly criticized for taking a circuitous route when a more direct one is available. Daily life applauds the logical, the economic, and the application of common sense.

Business strategy, to the contrary, is executed against a background of hyper-conflict and intelligent counter-measures. Able and motivated competitors purposely and energetically attempt to foil your ambition. Because of this excessive state of conflict, many strategic actions demonstrate a surprising paradoxical logic.

There are two types of strategic paradox:

- coming together of opposites: A linear logic action or state evolves into a reversal of itself ("A" becomes "not A") or "you can have too much of a good thing." An example of this is that an advantage, unrefreshed, becomes a disadvantage. This paradox occurs because conflict causes an inevitable reversal due to the complacency of the winner and the hunger of the loser. While the current winner gloats in his success, this same success lulls him into a false sense of permanent security while it paradoxically stimulates the current losers to tax their ingenuity to overcome it.

- reversal of opposites: To accomplish your objectives, do the reverse of what linear logic would dictate. So, "If you wish peace, prepare for war;" to accomplish "A", do the set of actions to accomplish "not A", or your primary competitor should be yourself. This occurs because the nature of conflict reverses normal linear logic. Although taking a long, dangerous, and circuitous route is bad logic under daily circumstances, in a state of conflict (i.e., war), this bad logic is good logic exactly because it is bad logic (it is less likely to be defended). The logic of conflict is often in total opposition to the logic of daily life.

Conflict causes strategic paradox to occur, bad logic becomes good logic exactly because it is bad logic, and the able strategist must learn to think and act paradoxically. Figure 13–3 updates our illustration of strategic thinking to extend the thought bubble to a fourth dimension of linear logic and paradoxical thinking. Paradoxically, strategists often have to recommend, to an unbelieving and astonished audience, that they should take actions that are directly contrary to routine business sense.

Figure 13–3 Advanced strategic thinking. More advanced strategic thinking adds the fourth dimension of paradox. (Source: Bernard H. Boar, *Practical Steps to Aligning Information Technology with Business Strategies*, John Wiley & Sons, 1995)

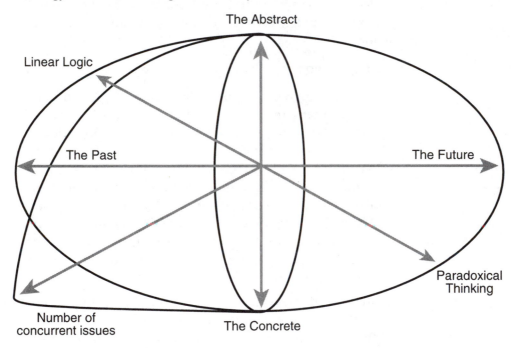

An example of reversal of opposites thinking is illustrated by the *Kano Methodology*: the Kano Methodology is an analytical method used to stimulate strategic thinking. As illustrated in Figure 13–4, the logic of Kano suggests that candidate strategic actions be divided into three types:

Figure 13–4 Kano Methodology. The Kano Methodology uses the notion of paradox by converting excitement attributes to threshold attributes. (Source: Bernard H. Boar, *The Art of Strategic Planning for Information Technology,* John Wiley & Sons, 1994)

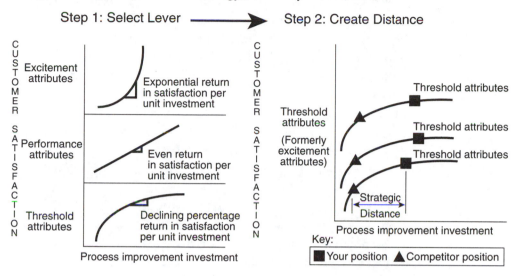

- threshold actions: For every dollar invested in this type of action, customer satisfaction increases but gradually reaches a point where less than a dollar of satisfaction is achieved for each dollar of investment. It therefore doesn't make sense to invest beyond the break-even point.

- performance actions: For every dollar invested in this type of action, there is a constant positive increase in customer satisfaction in excess of your investment. It pays to continue to invest in these actions.

- excitement actions: For every additional dollar invested in this type of action, there is an exponential increase in customer satisfaction. These are prized actions and are the best actions to invest in.

While this is solid linear thinking, the true brilliance of the methodology occurs next through using paradoxical thinking. What is suggested is that after one has developed the excitement capability, it be presented to the customer as a threshold attribute (that is, paradoxically, the truly exceptional is most exceptional when it is the ordinary). What this does is position your capability as minimum ante to play the game. A customer may be willing to forego the exceptional, but will minimally expect and demand the ordinary. Since you can do it and your competitors can't, you create strategic distance between yourself and your competitors. While they struggle to do the exceptional as the norm, you raise the tempo of the game and work on converting another excitement attribute to a threshold attribute and ad infinitum. So the great insight of the Kano Methodology is not the linear thinking of excitement attributes, where most people would have stopped, but the recognition that maximum value and market disruption occur when excitement capabilities are presented, paradoxically, as the ordinary (reversal of opposites).[2]

The strategic paradox of data warehousing is that the strategist concerned about cost does not seek to use just enough means, but an excess[3] of means to accomplish her end. Data warehousing achieves, paradoxically, its greatest value for the business when it is used in excess. It is typical to observe customer teams engage in extensive and exhaustive cost justifications exercises (net present value, return on investment, cost/benefit justification, payback period, and so on) to convince cost-conscious decision-makers to approve data warehousing expenditures for a predetermined fixed set of uses. Their actions are linear logic understandable, but inappropriate because of reversal of opposites. When the weaponry shifts to I/T fighting, data warehousing becomes subject to strategic paradox and must be managed as such to achieve optimum results.

Consider a military commander who needs to engage his enemy. If he uses linear logic and deploys *just enough* resources, he will win, but it will be an expensive (Pyrrhic) victory. If he applies a force far in excess of his opponent, he will achieve his ends with minor casualities. All the downstream costs of battle will be avoided (damaged weapons, confusion, wounded/killed soldiers, etc.). So at the point of conflict, the efficient commander does not seek to use *just enough*, but applies far in excess. He does not use accounting logic that holds in non-conflict situations, but applies paradoxical logic, which rules at the point of battle.

In the information age, data warehousing is a key strategic weapon. As we have discussed, not only does it let you compete across time, it is a raising-tide strategy that can elevate the strategic acumen of all employees. The attempt to cost-justify such powerful weaponry in terms of net present value misses the whole point. When one invests in a national highway infrastructure, one does not cost-justify or attempt to anticipate each event of commerce that will transverse the highway. Rather, one has the strategic vision to understand that the strategic action is putting in place the enabling infrastructure and then to permit the marketplace to take care of the rest.

I believe the same is true with data warehousing. Once the infrastructure is in place, you have raised the tide for all employees. Your initial justifications are constrained by the limits of your imagination. How the data warehouse will ultimately be beneficial will emerge as your employees use it to respond to the dynamics of the marketplace and it is exploited by their creativity. As they respond by using the *excessive* data warehouse, they will experience the same phenomena as the military commander. Though they will be spending in excess at the point of conflict, it will ultimately prove to be much cheaper because all the downstream business processes will be more efficient and effective. So while cost-consciousness is always in vogue and a specific set of business needs to be addressed is welcomed, the absence of a priori adequate tactical savings should not dissuade you from the deep and far-reaching strategic merits of an encompassing data warehousing initiative.

Unquestionably, it is easier to accept this paradox with regard to the military commander than data warehousing. This is because of the differences between cause and effect in the two situations. In the military situation, the cause and effect are tightly coupled in time and space. One can immediately see the results of the excess and correlate the success to that excess. In the data warehousing situation, the cause and effect are often dispersed across wide gaps of time and space. The use of excess data warehousing will have the desired effect, but it will occur, perhaps, months later at a remote branch office.

The strategist must take solace in that he or she is engaged in deep and far-reaching strategy, not tactical short-term decisions. Things that are readily cost-justifiable are things that are obvious and known to all. Strategic thinking is involved in seeing victory before it exists. How can anyone cost-justify the formless?[4] While cost-conscious accounting methods are appropriate for sustaining wealth, strategic vision has always been the required ingredient to create it.[5]

So while strategic paradox stretches and strains your business common sense, I believe that strategic paradox is an important dimension of the spirit of data warehousing. Ultimately, experience will prove that those who use it in excess, will achieve greater benefits than those who attempt to cost-justify rigorously and constrain its deployment. They will learn that their approach is mathematically correct, but strategically sterile. You do not want a raising tide, you want a permanent high tide of information with which you can win the battles for the past, the present, and the future.

Use data warehousing to position yourself so that you will surely win, prevailing over those who have already lost. Win through intelligence, not brute force. Cost-justification is supposed to be a tool of strategy, not the reverse. Strategic paradox alters the rules; understand and justify data warehousing strategically.

DATA WAREHOUSING AND MANEUVER

Businesses must always be prepared to respond creatively to marketplace dynamics. The normal marketplace state is constant upheaval. It is, therefore, obvious that those companies that can navigate with greater alacrity, speed, and dexterity have a distinct advantage. In fact, with speed, dexterity, and alacrity as your allies, you can further exaggerate your advantage by deliberately promoting marketplace mayhem to the benefit of your customers and the detriment of your competitors.

Companies take two basic roles in engaging the marketplace:

1. Attrition fighter: Marketplace supremacy is achieved by taking a strong but fixed position and "slugging it out" for marketplace dominance. Through confrontational marketplace battles and by concentrating superior assets against inferior foes, you win by exhausting the opponent's will and ability to compete. The optimum situation is to win in a few decisive battles and, by virtue of your proven superior power, deter prospective competitors from stepping into your marketplace and challenging you. An attrition fighter, like a classical heavy-weight boxer, wins by brute superiority of assets and the ability to deliver a crushing and decisive knockout blow.

2. Maneuver fighter: Marketplace superiority is achieved by staying in a state of perpetual motion. A maneuver fighter continually looks for opportunistic gaps in the marketplace and moves assets swiftly to maximize the opportunity. The maneuver fighter attempts to disrupt the marketplace by changing the rules of competition continually. It is through the actions of movement that advantage is gained. Advantage is best understood as a succession of overlapping temporary advantages rather than a set of sustainable competitive advantages. The maneuver fighter expects that the maneuver process will cause friction and that disruption will occur in the ability of opponents to respond. At best, this will eventually lead to a collapse in the opponents' business systems. A maneuver fighter uses speed, flexibility, opportunism, and dexterity to chip away at the edges of the marketplace until the entire marketplace has been taken. In doing so, unlike the attrition fighter, a deliberate attempt is made to avoid expensive, time consuming, and exhausting confrontations with competitors. You win by artfulness and indirection—not by brute force. The great heavy-weight fighter Muhammad Ali summed up the defining style of the maneuver fighter when he said, "Float like a butterfly, sting like a bee."

A global and fundamental marketplace transition is now occurring, from national wars of attrition to global wars of maneuver, and successful companies must adapt to this shift.

Sun Tzu described the eternal character of maneuver warfare when he said: "Go forth where they do not expect it; attack where they are unprepared."[6]

As advantageous as this is, it is not easy to do. It demands intelligence. Intelligence is both the sense of being smart and having knowledge about your competitors and customers. A maneuver fighter must continually zig and zag. The problem is to decide where and when to zig and zag. Done well, the maneuver fighter will delight customers and drive competitors crazy. Done poorly, the maneuver fighter will inadvertently zig or zag directly into the attrition fighter, who will crush him or her.

Data warehousing is a prerequisite to a maneuver strategy. An infrastructure of knowledge must be available to engage in maneuver fighting. With a solid infrastructure of accessible information that can be manipulated as demanded by swirling times and circumstances, the maneuver fighter can make calculated judgments as to where and when to move. Without such knowledge, a maneuver fighter will make one guess too many and be cornered by the behemoth attrition competitor.

An instructive example of maneuver is happening in the retail industry. Historically, retailers engaged in *push* marketing where they purchased large volumes of an item from a supplier and then attempted to convince their customers to buy it. Retailers are now moving to *pull* marketing wherein they attempt to understand exactly what customers want to buy and provide a desired product assortment at ideal value points. The former doesn't require much knowledge about one's customers, but the latter requires a great deal. The push retailer stands still and doesn't need much data, while the pull retailer needs precise information to support continuous moving (zigging) and maneuvering (zagging) slightly ahead of customers.

So the final way to understand data warehousing strategically is to understand it as the necessary foundation for changing your business from being a slow and ponderous attrition fighter to an agile and quick maneuver fighter. Attrition fighters stand still. If you're going to stand still, of what value is knowledge to you? To the contrary, and as illustrated in Figure 13–5, a maneuver fighter is a business in constant motion. Maneuver fighters win through intelligence, not brute force. In this way, by virtue of knowledge-enabled maneuvering, you act sooner rather than later, you learn rather than repeat, you anticipate rather than react, you know rather than guess, you change rather than atrophy, exceed rather than satisfy, and ultimately, through the accumulation of *rathers*, win rather than lose.

Figure 13–5 Maneuver fighter vs. attrition fighter. A maneuver fighter moves, stands, and moves, while an attrition fighter stands, moves, and stands.

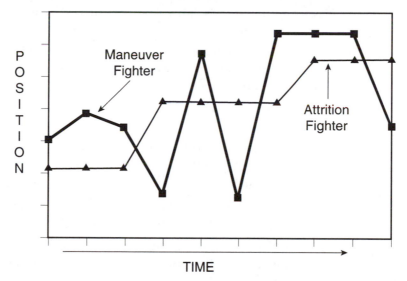

CONCLUSION

Our strategic analysis of data warehousing is as follows:

- Strategy is about, and only about, building advantage. The business need to build, compound, and sustain advantage is the most fundamental and dominant business need, and it is insatiable.

- Advantage is built through deep and far-reaching strategic thinking.

- The strategic ideas that support data warehousing as a strategic initiative are learning, maneuverability, prescience, and foreknowledge. Data warehousing meets the fundamental business needs to compete in a superior manner across the elementary strategic dimension of time.

- Data warehousing is a rare instance of a raising-tide strategy. A raising-tide strategy occurs when an action yields tremendous leverage. Data warehousing raises the ability of all employees to serve their customers and out-think their competitors.

- Data warehousing achieves optimal results when one understands strategic paradox. When used as a weapon of conflict in the information age, data warehousing, paradoxically, achieves the greatest economies when it is applied in excess. One always wants the tide to be at high tide.

- Data warehousing is a mandatory prerequisite to engage in a market-style maneuver that will be the dominant form of marketplace warfare as we begin the next millennium. To continually and abruptly change business direction requires both judgment and knowledge. Hard-won experience provides the former, and data warehousing provides the latter.

Companies enter markets to win profits, not to engage in expensive and endless pitched battles with competitors. Data warehousing is of strategic value because it enables us to achieve the former while deftly avoiding the latter. This is the strategic spirit in which we should understand, implement, and manage data warehousing.

A very powerful introduction to a data warehousing business case said the following:

The strategic intent of our data warehousing strategy is to enable the business to win in the marketplace every day, with every customer, and with every purchase. By repositioning our operational data and combining it with selected foreign data, we will empower our employees so that they can routinely delight and excite our customers. Through our unique appreciation of the value of our data assets, we will elevate our data warehouses to the point where they become a compelling and durable contributor to the sustainable competitive advantage of the business. In this way, data warehousing will enable the business to impress its attitude on the marketplace and prevail over its competitors who have already lost.

Have you implemented data warehousing with such a cogent strategic intent? Sun Tzu said:

> *Strategy is important to the nation—it is the ground of death and life, the path of survival and destruction, so it is imperative to examine it. There is a way of survival which helps and strengthens you; there is a way of destruction which pushes you into oblivion.*[7]

Data warehousing is a path to survival that *helps and strengthens you*. Our strategic understanding of data warehousing is complete.

NOTES

1. Sun Tzu, *The Art of War*, translated by Thomas Cleary, Shambhala Publications, 1988. *The Art of War* is generally recognized as the greatest treatise ever written on strategy. At least seven current English translations are available, all with variant translations of the original Chinese. My strategic thinking is strongly influenced by Sun Tzu's teachings, as should yours be.
2. The strategic paradox of client/server computing is "To concentrate computing power, you must disperse it." See Bernard H. Boar, *Cost Effective Strategies for Client/Server Systems* (John Wiley and Sons, 1996), for a complete analysis.
3. Excess means much more than analytically justified by circumstances; it does not, however, mean wasteful or prodigious.
4. Sun Tzu said, "Vision is seeing victory before it exists. This is the strategists path to strategic triumph."
5. In a recent magazine interview (*Industry Week*: 11/20/95), Bill Gates, CEO of Microsoft, described the qualities of leadership as "vision, innovation, long-term thinking, and risk-taking." Maximizing your return on data warehousing requires these qualities. Blind adherence to net present value or any other economic justification method was not mentioned by Mr. Gates in the article.
6. Sun Tzu, *The Art of War*.
7. Ibid.

Index